DOES GOD PLAY FAVORITES?

GOD'S UNIQUE RELATIONSHIP WITH ISRAEL

Does God Play Favorites?

God's Unique Relationship with Israel

Jim Gerrish

Minneapolis, Minnesota

DEDICATION

This book is dedicated to my wife, Betsy, who has given me her faithful love and support for the last forty-six years, and who has helped me immensely in all states of manuscript preparation.

CONTENTS

ACKNOWLEDGEMENTS

No book of this scope could be written without the help of many other people. I am indebted to Clarence H. Wagner, Jr. who assisted me with several sections of the book and made his personal library available to me. I am deeply indebted to my associates who patiently read the manuscript and offered their suggestions. These include Neal and Julie George, Earl Davis, Fran Grow and, of course, my wife who labored over the manuscript many months.

Also, I am indebted to Judy Stone, Anne Davis and others who looked over various sections of the manuscript and offered their good advice. Certainly I wish to express my gratitude to Edmund Lambeth, Professor of Journalism at the University of Missouri, for his patient assistance.

I am very grateful for the constant prayer support from my dear friends, Bill and Gloria Brereton, without which the book may never have come into existence.

I am especially grateful to Dr. Marvin Wilson, Professor of Biblical and Theological Studies at Gordon College, Wenham, Massachusetts, who took time from his busy year-end schedule to carefully read this manuscript and offer his valuable suggestions and insights.

Most of all, I am grateful to God who put Israel on my heart early in 1974. It is God who has sustained my wife and me in Israel for almost thirteen years. It is God who has allowed us to feed upon the heritage of our father Jacob and to walk upon the land of his promise.

Perhaps this book will be a partial release of this spiritual burden God has placed upon me.

INTRODUCTION

Several years ago I remember speaking about Israel at a certain church gathering. At the close of my sermon I was amazed to find that the pastor, who had previously acted friendly towards me, would no longer speak to me or even face me. As I remember, I left that church without receiving another word from him. I had spoken directly from the Bible but this man of God would have no part of the message. Over the years in my Israel ministry I have experienced other such perplexing episodes.

Perhaps I should not be so amazed at the action of this pastor. I remember in my early ministry that I also had little concern for Israel. It was not until God dealt with me miraculously in 1974, that my eyes were opened to his nation and people. My study of Israel since that time, and during my fourteen years in the land, have been further eye-openers. It is unfortunate that so many millions of otherwise good Christians remain indifferent to the incredibly important subject of Israel.

It is now apparent that during our lifetimes, God has done a miraculous work of restoring the nation of Israel. We modern Christians now have to deal with something that other generations have not had to deal with. We must deal with a partially restored Israel in our midst. Yes, Israel has arisen from dust and ashes, as was foretold long ago by her prophets.

The rise of Israel is greatly impacting the Church, and many Christians, realizing this, are hungering for a deeper knowledge and understanding of Israel. It is my purpose in this book to share a portion of the things the Lord has shared with me over the years.

As we seek understanding we must bear in mind that we will never comprehend Israel unless we first understand that she is incredibly unique. For instance, tiny Israel, with less than one-half of one percent of the earth's population, now commands the second largest press corps in the world. But Israel is not just unique naturally. She is unique spiritually. The Bible tells us that God's eyes are upon Israel continually.

The Jews are a special people, as is related to us in the Bible. Just as the Jews are unlike other people, their history is also unlike that of others. It may even be called "redemptive history" or "holy history." It is the most amazing history in the world. Other nations have come and gone but the Jews seem to remain immortal. From father Abraham; to Moses; to Jesus; to the Holocaust and now to the restoration of the nation, we have a four-thousand-year span of redemptive history.

However, because Israel is chosen by God, the enemy has been busy. In the last hundred years Islam has raised its head to challenge the existence of Israel and even the existence of the Jewish people. Until fairly recent times, Islam had been of slight concern to Christians, especially those living in the west. Yet, since the 1991 Gulf War and the September 11, 2001 attack on America, Christians have been forced to take notice of this religion. It now appears likely that Islam may be the biggest spiritual threat in our world today. It is a mortal threat not only to Israel and Judaism, but also to Christianity. The great Islamic battle against Israel and the Bible seems to have its focus in the Middle East. However, in spite of the sworn hatred of millions of Muslims in this area, the nation of Israel was not only born against incredible odds, but has prospered for half a century.

Modern Israel is causing us to examine our Bibles more closely. When we look carefully in the scripture we find some shocking facts about our Christian family tree. We learn that our family tree is actually a Jewish one, as is made clear in Romans 11:17-18. Thus we are somehow spiritually connected to Israel. This fact has been carefully hidden from us almost since Apostolic Times. It is now evident that there was a subtle shift from a totally Jewish Christianity of the first century to an almost totally Gentile Christianity of the fourth century. Now after almost sixteen centuries the Church is left, cut off from its rich Hebrew roots, nurturing an animosity toward Israel and the Jews. Instead of the heritage of Israel, the church is left with the heritage of anti-Semitism. The recent, awful Holocaust was only a natural result of almost two thousand years of Christian anti-Semitic teaching.

As we look more closely at our Bibles we must ask if the ancient promise to Abraham in Genesis 12:2-3 is still effective? Are individuals and nations still blessed or cursed depending upon their treatment of Abraham and his seed, the Jewish people? We have only to travel quickly through history to see many evidences of this strange fact. When we do, we will see how Jewish genius particularly blessed Holland, America, and many other nations. We will see how nations like Spain, Portugal, England and especially the Palestinian people have all come under a curse because of their treatment of the Jews. Which will it be for us? Will we receive blessing or cursing?

Has the Church's shabby treatment of the Jews been noticed by God? Does it concern our Messiah? Could it be that the Messiah is involved in Israel and is even re-gathering the nation? There is a great deal of biblical evidence supporting this, especially in the so-called "Servant Songs" of Isaiah 41 and following. If Messiah is gathering and restoring Israel, it certainly places the Church in an embarrassing and awkward position. Not only has the Church failed to help with this messianic work – we have positively hindered it.

A few centuries ago, as the Bible became available to the common reader, the Church began to wake up. The beginning of the modern Christian Zionist movement (formerly known as Restorationism) can be traced back to the sixteenth century Puritans. Along the way, common people, presidents, prime ministers, and poets spoke out for the Jews and their homeland.

Today the rise of Israel is forcing Christians to take another look at the Old Testament. It is also forcing us to take a new look at the New Testament. New archaeological discoveries in the land are shedding light on the whole Bible and broadening our understanding. The rebirth of Israel is helping us better understand Bible prophecy, especially that prophecy related to the end days.

Although the ancient prophets spoke of the redeemed someday returning to Zion, the terminology has become politically loaded today. Where do God and the Bible stand in the present day conflicts? Disregarding the world's concepts of "political correctness," we must look at God's special connection with Jerusalem and the Jews. In no uncertain terms God calls himself a Zionist.

How is all this working out in our modern world? How will it all end? The scripture is very clear that God will deal with all nations. The time for this dealing seems to be close at hand. There will be a "storm before the calm" in world events according to the Bible. Nations will be drawn to Israel for one "final solution" of the world's Jewish problem. The Mighty God of Israel will then intervene to fight for little Israel in a dramatic manner. Strangely, the Messiah will stand on the Mount of Olives for the specific purpose of delivering Israel from the wrath of the nations.

After God has dealt with nations for their hatred and hypocrisy, a wonderful era of peace, real peace, Messianic peace, will rule in our world.

-1-

ISRAEL'S UNIQUENESS

How can a little country some fifty miles wide and a mere one-hundred-fifty miles long keep the world in an uproar all the time?

How can tiny Israel be the constant focus of world news reports, and why should such a small place have the second largest concentration of news bureaus in the world?[1] Why should the little mountain town of Jerusalem always get a lion's share of world publicity?

How can the Israeli people, numbering about six million, be considered such a mortal threat to the some 200 million heavily-armed Muslims in the Middle East? And why would such an august body as the United Nations spend a third of its time dealing with little Israel?[2]

These things all seem preposterous, but they certainly attest to Israel's amazing uniqueness as a nation.

For instance, just "down the road" from Jerusalem is the great city of Cairo and the country of Egypt. Cairo, the largest city in Africa, has over ten million people, yet it is rarely mentioned on the evening news. However, almost daily on world news reports we hear of Jerusalem, whose population is scarcely over a half million. The world's news bureaus do not jostle each other for space in Cairo or in Egypt. The city and country have been of little concern to the United Nations.

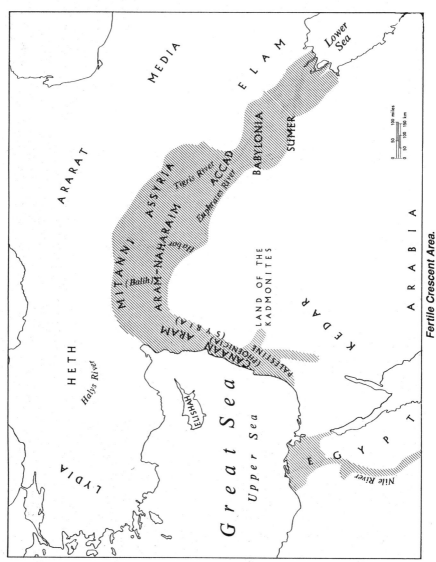

Fertile Crescent Area.

ISRAEL, A TINY PLACE

The nation of Israel is minuscule in comparison with other nations of the world. When compared to the US, Israel is about the size of the little state of New Jersey. The nation of France could hold twenty-six Israels.

Of course, Israel should rightly be compared with countries in her own neighborhood, the Middle East. It is shocking when we realize that the Middle East nations of the Arab League are spread over five million square miles, while Israel consists of less than 8,000 square miles.[3]

Israel is so small that one can easily drive from the biblical border cities of Dan in the north, to Beersheba in the south, in half a day. We have cause to pity the Israeli jet pilots, who in a few careless moments of maneuvers could find themselves flying over hostile Syria or Saudi Arabia.

Israel is tiny, but the nation possesses a geographic and political importance far out of proportion to its size.

CROSSROADS OF THE WORLD

Israel not only commands a disproportionate amount of media coverage, but the land is a veritable crossroads of the world's peoples and cultures even today.

In ancient times, people and armies traveled over the roads situated in what is known as the Fertile Crescent. This strip of fertile land ran from Egypt to the other great centers of Assyria and Babylonia. This ancient "super-highway" system ran directly through Israel, which was then called Canaan. Thus the great nations of the Middle East always struggled between themselves for this passageway.

One famous ancient route was the Way of the Sea (*Via Maris*) mentioned in Isaiah 9:1-2, and also in Matthew 4:15-16. This ancient road ran through Capernaum where Jesus established a base for his ministry. The prophet Isaiah, who lived in the eighth century BC, had prophesied that a bright light would shine along this highway.

Israel was not only a land bridge from north to south, but also from east to west. Many ancient caravans bearing spices and other items from the east, traveled through the general area. Also, from the time of Solomon, Israel had periodic access to the Far East via the Gulf of Aqaba and the Red Sea.

Even today, Israel is still a world crossroads. People from almost every nation live in the country and millions more visit it.The Jews themselves have returned home from more than one hundred nations. On a bus ride, or a stroll through the park, one may see people reading newspapers from virtually every corner of the world.

The Jerusalem taxi drivers have the very difficult task of communicating with people from every language background. It often seems that as soon as passengers open their mouths, the drivers are able to communicate in the necessary tongues.

Israel is not just a crossroads for people, but one for birds as well. For instance, twice each year, in spring and again in the fall, millions of birds pass over Israel, as they make their trips to and from Europe, Asia and Africa. In all, there are 121 species of migratory birds, plus another 94 species that come to spend the winter in Israel. There are honeybuzzards, storks, pelicans and many more winged visitors.[4] Some of these birds love Israel so much that they decide to stay, much to the chagrin of fish farmers.

LAND OF AMAZING BEAUTY AND DIVERSITY

The Bible assures us that Israel is the most beautiful land in all the earth. In Ezekiel 20:6 we read:

On that day I swore to them that I would bring them out of Egypt into a land I had searched out for them, a land flowing with milk and honey, the most beautiful of all lands.

The physical setting of Israel is not just beautiful, but it is also extremely interesting and diversified, as we read in Deuteronomy 8:7-9:

For the LORD your God is bringing you into a good land — a land with streams and pools of water, with springs flowing in the valleys and hills; a land with

Mt. Hermon

wheat and barley, vines and fig trees, pomegranates, olive oil and honey; a land where bread will not be scarce and you will lack nothing; a land where the rocks are iron and you can dig copper out of the hills.

Israel has a vast diversity in its terrain. There is cool, snow-capped Mount Hermon in the north, reaching to an altitude of 9,232 ft. (2,841 m.), and there are the blistering semi-deserts of the Negev in the south. Also, in contrast with the heights of Hermon are the depths of the Jordan Rift and the Dead Sea. This body of water marks the lowest habitable spot on earth, at 1,312 ft. (404 m.) below sea level.

Israel also enjoys a great variety in climate. When Jerusalemites are shivering in the winter cold, they can take comfort in the fact that they are a mere thirty-minute drive from semi-tropical Jericho, and the warm resorts at the Dead Sea.

Since Israel borders on three deserts, much of the area to the east of its central chain of mountains is desert of some type. This desert runs from the areas around Jericho to the Dead Sea, on to The Wilderness of Zin and then to Eilat.

The amount of rainfall in the country ranges from about 60 inches per year on Mt. Hermon in the north, to less than an inch for Eilat in the south.[5] The central mountains of Israel may be blasted with snow and cold in the winter months, and yet may swelter with an early spring heat wave. The heat wave, or *sharav,* blowing in from the desert can quickly drive temperatures into the 90 degree F. range (32 C.).

In Deuteronomy 6:18, Israel is referred to as *ha-eretz ha-tovah*, or *"the good land."* Then again in Psalm 106:24, the Psalmist refers to Israel as *"the pleasant land."* Even in the hot summer, there are cool, pleasant breezes that come up from the Mediterranean in the afternoon. In the winter, even cities with the highest elevations like Jerusalem and Zefat, seldom see temperatures drop below freezing. Roses usually bloom all winter in Jerusalem. There are no tornadoes or hurricanes.

DIVERSITY OF FLORA AND FAUNA

The uniqueness of Israel really becomes apparent when we look at the country's flora and fauna. Because of Israel's geographic position, linking three continents, there is an amazing variety of plant and animal life. For instance, within the tiny land of Israel there are five distinct vegetation zones. This great variety of life has perplexed naturalists as they have labored to make the proper classifications.

Lambert states, "The rich variety of vegetation zones, make it the meeting ground of plants native to widely differing parts of the earth, plants with such differing origins as Siberia, Western Europe, Inner Asia, North Africa and East Africa."[6]

Israel at present has some 2500 plant types. For the sake of comparison, Egypt with its rich Nile Delta has only 1500. Britain has 1700, and Norway has 1335. "No other place in the world has such floral wealth concentrated within such a comparatively small area."[7]

For instance, in the Hula swampland one might find the tropical papyrus plant flourishing. Papyrus is an African plant and Israel is as far north as it grows.[8] At Ein Gedi on

the Dead Sea one might see the Moringa tree, which is a
native of Sudan. In the Jordan Valley alone there are some
forty varieties of tropical flora.

In the southernmost tip of Israel at Eilat, the visitor is
treated to a magnificent desert climate with its special vegetation. For instance, the Doum Palm *(Dome Mitzri - Hyphaene
thebaica)*, normally found in Sudan, grows around Eilat.[9] The
Doum Palm has a distinguished look with a trunk that forks
out about mid-way up giving it the appearance of having two
horns.

Numerous animals have ventured in from Africa in the
south, or from Syria and points further in the north and have
made Israel their home. For instance, the land of Israel
marks the southernmost limit in the range of the Siberian
wolf. The little coney has come up to Israel from Africa, and
Israel and Syria mark its northernmost limits. Israel also has
about twenty-five species of bat, from the three continents of
Europe, Asia and Africa.[10]

At Eilat, the visitor will see what has been called "one of the
three richest coral reefs in the world."[11] From Eilat's under-
water observatory one can see a vast array of colorful tropical
fish in their natural habitat. A trip to Eilat is a thrilling and
unforgettable experience.

SPIRITUAL UNIQUENESS

Israel is certainly unique in the natural sense, because of
its size, location and diversity of climate and wild life.
However, its greatest uniqueness is in the spiritual realm. We
see this clearly reflected in the pages of the Bible. The Bible,
after all, is the Church's guide and authority, not only in
matters of theology, but in matters of our everyday lives.

For centuries, preachers and biblical expositors have
realized that the frequency of words found in the scripture
gives us some indication as to the importance of the subjects.
As an example, Christianity rests upon three pillars, as Paul
tells us in 1 Corinthians 13:13. The pillars are faith, hope and
love. When the frequency of these words is checked in the

Authorized Version of the Bible, we find that faith appears 257 times, and hope appears 129 times. Love, being the most important of the three, appears 310 times. This is a respectable amount of appearances.

However when the occurrence of "Jerusalem" is checked in scripture it might surprise us to learn that it appears 811 times – more than faith, hope and love combined. Jerusalem is just one of the many names the city is called in scripture. Also, when a search is done under the subject of "Israel," it is amazing to find that it appears 2566 times. We should realize by this that "Jerusalem" and "Israel" are subjects very close to the heart of God.

In the scripture, the expression "God of Israel" appears over 200 times. This is only one of several expressions like "God of Jacob," and "God of Abraham," which connect the God of the universe closely with the Jewish people and the land of Israel. These are names by which God wishes to be known. However, these names are deemed "not politically correct" by many in our day.

The Bible, tells us about God's great attachment to the land of Israel. In Deuteronomy 11:12, we learn that *"It is a land the LORD your God cares for; the eyes of the LORD your God are continually on it from the beginning of the year to its end."*

The Bible makes it clear that Israel is central in God's plan for the earth. In Ezekiel 38:12, it is mentioned that the land of Israel is at the very center of the earth. The Hebrew word used here is *tabbuwr,* and in modern Hebrew it means "navel" or "bellybutton." The earth does have a navel, a place where the umbilical cord between heaven and earth was once attached. In Revelation 21:1-4, the Bible indicates that it will someday be re-attached as this world undergoes a re-creation.

In Psalm 76:1 we read, *"...In Judah God is known; his name is great in Israel."* For thousands of years, God has been busy building a salvation infrastructure in the land of Israel. He has done this so that peoples and nations the world over may fully know him.

In a real sense, *"...He has set his foundation on the holy mountain..."* (Psa. 87:1). God had to establish the patterns, types, and pictures that would help us understand his great salvation. For instance, the Tabernacle and Temple with all their rites help us understand the sacrifice of Jesus. Without these pictures we would be at a total loss to understand.

Jerusalem, being the very center or hub of God's redemptive activity, is extremely important to him. We read in Isaiah 49:16, *"See, I have engraved you [Jerusalem] on the palms of my hands; your walls are ever before me."*

Israel, and its capital city of Jerusalem, are certain to be the focus of last-day activity. This will transpire as sinful man and his systems collide head-on with God and his coming kingdom. We are assured in scripture that God will gather all nations to Jerusalem for battle (Zech. 14:2). At that time the Lord will fight for Israel and afterward the nations of the earth will know that the Lord is God.

CLAIMED BY THE WORLD'S LARGEST RELIGIONS

To illustrate her great spiritual importance, Jerusalem is claimed jointly by the religions of Judaism, Christianity and Islam. These claims apply not only to Jerusalem but also to most other parts of the land. Since these religions include almost three billion people, we can see that Jerusalem and Israel are extremely important to more than half the world's population.

Jerusalem has long been the focal point of Jewish aspirations. Over the centuries the Passover *seder* has ended with the longing and hopeful words, "Next year in Jerusalem!"

The Jewish National Anthem, *Ha Tikva,* by Naphtali Herz Imber, also expresses that eternal hope within the Jewish heart in these words translated into English:

> *As long as in depth of the heart a Jewish soul is yearning, and towards the east an eye is still looking to Zion, our hope is not lost yet, the 2000-year-old hope to be a free nation in our land, the land of Zion and Jerusalem.*

Church of Holy Sepulchre. *(Courtesy Ron Cantrell)*

In addition to being at the very heart of the Jewish faith, Jerusalem is the cradle of Christianity. The dramas of the birth, death and resurrection of Jesus all took place in the general area of Jerusalem. The Church of the Nativity in the city of Bethlehem marks the traditional location of Messiah's birth. This city, which is now a part of the Palestinian Authority, is still practically a suburb of Jerusalem. The twin sites, the Church of the Holy Sepulchre in Jerusalem's Old City, and the Garden Tomb just outside the north city wall, both mark possible places of the death, burial and resurrection of Jesus.

In modern times, the dark clouds of political turmoil have increased over Israel and Jerusalem. This has been especially true as the Jews have returned home from the nations. Because of Muslim political aspirations concerning the land, Jerusalem and Israel have taken on an increased importance to Islam.

Although Jerusalem's Temple Mount has been the location of the Dome of the Rock and El Aksa Mosque since the early eighth century, Jerusalem was a "backwater" so far as its importance to Muslims until the twentieth century. For instance, in the thirteen hundred years that Islam exercised general domination over Israel, Jerusalem was never a Muslim capital city or even an administrative center. The administrative center was at Ramle near the coast.

Today, because of the increasing political struggle over Jerusalem, Muslims are flocking in greater numbers to the Temple Mount for prayer and pilgrimage, although prior to the twentieth century the Temple Mount had not been a place of Muslim pilgrimage.[12] Thousands of Muslims now gather to the area on Fridays for weekly prayers. The religious struggle over the Temple Mount has greatly intensified in recent years, with occasional flare-ups of violence as Jews and Muslims worship in close proximity.

SITE OF PILGRIMAGE SINCE ANCIENT TIMES

The Jewish people have made pilgrimage to Jerusalem since ancient times. According to Jewish law, each male was required to come to Jerusalem every year for the three major festivals of Passover *(Pe-sach)*, Pentecost *(Sha-vu-ot)* and Tabernacles *(Suk-kot)* (Ex. 23:17). Since Jerusalem sits astride the mountain ridge running through the country, it was necessary to climb up to Jerusalem. The trip was dangerous, difficult, and often had to be done on foot, in the heat of the sun.

In our Bibles we still have recorded many poems and songs that were undoubtedly sung by pilgrims as they ascended to the city and to the Temple Mount. These "Psalms of ascents," or of "going up," are very descriptive of the journey. They begin with Psalm 120 and continue through Psalm 134.

It is interesting today that the process by which one becomes a citizen of modern Israel is called "making *aliya*." In Hebrew it simply means "going up."

A Psalm of "going up." Psalm 121:1-8

1 *I lift up my eyes to the hills —*
where does my help come from?
2 *My help comes from the LORD,*
the Maker of heaven and earth.
3 *He will not let your foot slip—*
he who watches over you will not slumber;
4 *indeed, he who watches over Israel*
will neither slumber nor sleep.
5 *The LORD watches over you—*
the LORD is your shade at your right hand;
6 *the sun will not harm you by day,*
nor the moon by night.
7 *The LORD will keep you from all harm—*
he will watch over your life;
8 *the LORD will watch over your coming and going*
both now and forevermore.

In the Book of Acts we learn that great numbers of Jewish pilgrims had come to the Feast of Pentecost from many different parts of the world. After witnessing the outpouring of the Holy Spirit these pilgrims replied:

Then how is it that each of us hears them in his own native language? Parthians, Medes and Elamites; residents of Mesopotamia, Judea and Cappadocia, Pontus and Asia, Phrygia and Pamphylia, Egypt and the parts of Libya near Cyrene; visitors from Rome (both Jews and converts to Judaism); Cretans and Arabs — we hear them declaring the wonders of God in our own tongues! (Acts 2:8-11).

Modern tourists stroll through the Old City in Jerusalem.

In the fourth century, after Christianity was finally established as the *religio licita* (legal religion) in the Roman Empire, Christian pilgrims began to make their appearance in Jerusalem. Even Emperor Constantine's mother, Helena, became a pilgrim in the fourth century AD. It was due to her influence that some of the great churches were built, such as the Church of the Holy Sepulchre and the Church of the Nativity.

Another pilgrim in the latter part of the fourth century was named Egeria. Archaeologists and Bible scholars still use her written accounts to try and piece together the locations of authentic biblical sites. What a shame it is that many other pilgrims did not visit the land and heed the command of Psalm 48:12-13:

> *Walk about Zion, go around her, count her towers, consider well her ramparts, view her citadels, that you may tell of them to the next generation.*

Today, millions of modern pilgrims journey by airliner to Israel and then travel by luxurious air-conditioned buses throughout the land. They know few of the hardships of pilgrims in earlier times. However, they are pilgrims nonetheless, with their notepads, recorders, cameras and videos. It is interesting that the bulk of these pilgrims are Christians.

A visit to the land is important for Christians. The land of Israel has often been called "the fifth gospel." There are four gospels we can read anywhere in the world, but one we can only experience by a visit to Israel. This "gospel" quickly brings the other four gospels into perspective. It does the same for the rest of the Bible. As one enlightened visitor remarked: "I used to see the Bible only in black and white – now I see in living color."

When one travels about the land, the stories of the Bible come to life. Almost everywhere one looks or walks in Israel, there is a contact made with the Bible and history. One may drive past Rachel's Tomb near Bethlehem and be reminded that there she died while giving birth to her son Benjamin (Gen 35:16-20; Matt. 2:18). One may see the Temple complex and suddenly realize the accuracy of Jesus' prophecy that one of those original stones would not be left upon another on top of this Temple platform (Matt. 24:2).

The land of Israel is no doubt the world's biggest "show-and-tell." God designed it that way so that we can picture the mysteries of his kingdom.

As millions of pilgrims arrive in Israel, and as Israel and Jerusalem come more and more into the spotlight of the world media, we need to reflect much upon Israel's great significance. Today, many Bible believers will have to admit that Israel, with its heart in Jerusalem, is God's project. It is an age-old project.

In all the ages God has had only one plan, and that plan is that his glory and his salvation should go forth from Israel to all nations. As one old preacher said, "God plans his work and works his plan." God has never had to change his plan, because he knew the end from the beginning. All this gives

Israel and Jerusalem a uniqueness not possessed by other nations or cities. Israel and Jerusalem are truly unique in that they are central in God's great plan for the earth. God himself says:

> Remember the former things, those of long ago; I am God, and there is no other;
>
> I am God, and there is none like me. I make known the end from the beginning, from ancient times, what is still to come.
>
> I say: My purpose will stand, and I will do all that I please. (Isa. 46:9-10)

STUDY QUESTIONS:

Give some reasons why God chose the physical land of Israel as a base for his redemptive work.

Is it still important for Christians to visit Israel and Jerusalem in this modern day? If so, why?

Give two reasons why it might be beneficial to pray for Jerusalem (Psalm 122:6-9).

Why might Israel and Jerusalem become a "bone of contention" to nations and peoples in the future?

NOTES

1. Ramon Bennett, *The Great Deception Philistine* (Jerusalem: Arm of Salvation, 1995) p. 181.
2. See Editorial, "The UN Impediment," *The Jerusalem Post,* 9 June, 1991.
3. Leonard Davis, *Myths and Facts, A Concise Record of the Arab-Israeli Conflict* (Washington, DC: Near East Report, 1984) pp. 248-49.

4. See "Birds of Passage Pass Over," *Dispatch From Jerusalem,* September/October 1995, p. 9.
5. *Facts About Israel* (Jerusalem: Ministry of Foreign Affairs, Information Division, 1985), p. 5.
6. Lance Lambert, *The Uniqueness of Israel* (Eastbourne: Kingsway Publications Ltd., 1980) p. 20.
7. Goeffrey Wigoder, *Israel Pocket Library, Geography* (Jerusalem: Keter Publishing House Jerusalem Ltd, 1973) p. 137.
8. Azzaria Alon, *Flowers and Trees of the Holy Land* (Printed in the Holy Land: Palpot Ltd.,) p. 31.
9. Uzi Plitman, Clara Heyn, Avinoam Danin and Avishai Shmidah, *Plants in Israel,* trans. from Hebrew (Masada, Israel 1983) p. 260.
10. Lambert, *The Uniqueness of Israel,* p. 24.
11. Lambert, *The Uniqueness of Israel,* p. 25.
12. Eliyahu Tal, *Whose Jerusalem* (Jerusalem: International Forum for a United Jerusalem, 1994) p. 74.

-2-

ARE THE JEWS
REALLY SPECIAL?

For ages, the Jews have been called "the chosen people." How did they get such a title? Did they make it up themselves? The Bible has much to say about this. In Deuteronomy 7:6, we read this about the Jews:

For you are a people holy to the LORD your God. The LORD your God has chosen you out of all the peoples on the face of the earth to be his people, his treasured possession.

So it was God who chose the Jewish people. We might ask the question, "Why the Jews?" They are certainly not a plentiful people on earth, since they number somewhat over 13 million today, or less than one half of one percent of world population. Nor were they the largest or greatest people of antiquity. When we look at the Bible in Deuteronomy 7:7, we read that quite the opposite was the case:

The LORD did not set his affection on you and choose you because you were more numerous than other peoples, for you were the fewest of all peoples.

THEIR CHOICE – A SOVEREIGN ACT OF GOD

The Bible makes it plain that the choice of the Jewish people was a sovereign act of God. God as the Creator of the universe has the right to choose whom he wills. In Romans 9:21, we see that he can choose the vessels he has made, whether men or nations, for honor or for dishonor.

God does not play favorites however. The sovereign choice of Israel was for God's own redemptive purposes on earth. In his wisdom he chose a family to influence families and a nation to influence nations. God chose Israel to introduce his word to the world.

Then in the fullness of time, God allowed Israel to bring forth his Messiah, in order that all nations could be blessed through him. God's choice bore with it a great amount of responsibility, and it has resulted in an incredible degree of suffering for the Jewish people.

Because of this responsibility and suffering, there are many Jews today who would just as soon not be the chosen people. They echo the words of Tevye in the famous play, *Fiddler on the Roof.* After Tevye heard news about an impending pogrom (persecution) he had another one of his little talks with God, complaining to him: "I know, I know we are the chosen people, but once in a while can't you choose someone else!"

We see from the scripture that the sovereign choice of the Jewish people goes back to Abram, in Genesis 12:1-3:

> *The LORD had said to Abram, "Leave your country, your people and your father's household and go to the land I will show you. I will make you into a great nation and I will bless you; I will make your name great, and you will be a blessing. I will bless those who bless you, and whoever curses you I will curse; and all peoples on earth will be blessed through you."*

This divine choice of Abram and his heirs as a redemptive family in the earth, and later as a redemptive nation, is documented in numerous places in scripture. In Genesis 17:3-9, it is repeated to Abram, whose name is then changed to

Abraham. In Genesis 26:2-5, it is repeated to Isaac. Then in Genesis 28:13-15, it is repeated to Jacob. References are made to this covenant in many other places, such as Leviticus 20:26, Psalm 105:8-11 and Amos 3:2.

A UNIQUE AND SPECIAL PEOPLE

It is clear from scripture that the Jewish people are chosen in a unique and special sense. In the passage we quoted earlier in Deuteronomy 7:6, the Hebrew expression used for "treasured possession" is *am se-gu-lah*. It also has the meaning of "peculiar or extraordinary people."

Balaam, who has been referred to by the Jews as the first Gentile prophet, has this to say about the Jews in Numbers 23:9:

> *From the rocky peaks I see them, from the heights I view them. I see a people who live apart and do not consider themselves one of the nations.*

Israel is not considered a part of all the other nations, but a unique entity all by itself. In addition, we see an amazing fact about Israel in Deuteronomy 32:8:

> *When the Most High gave the nations their inheritance, when he divided all mankind, he set up boundaries for the peoples according to the number of the sons of Israel.*

This is a puzzling and astonishing verse. It seems to mean that when the Almighty marked out the nations of the world, he did so in reference to the number of Jewish people. Possibly he did this in reference to the Jews who would live in these very nations.

We learn more in Psalm 148:14 about the special nature of the Children of Israel. The Psalm reads:

> *He has raised up for his people a horn, the praise of all his saints, of Israel, the people close to his heart. Praise the LORD.*

An old man praying at the Western Wall. (Courtesy Ron Cantrell)

Of all the people on the face of the earth, only the people of Israel and those grafted into them are described as being close to God's very heart. What a special place and privilege!

Because of God's redemptive choice, he did not choose other people in the same way he chose Israel. In Psalm 147:19-20, we are surprised to read:

He has revealed his word to Jacob, his laws and decrees to Israel. He has done this for no other nation; they do not know his laws. Praise the LORD.

Why does the Psalmist say, "Praise the Lord" after making a statement like this? It is probably because he realized that the Jewish people would keep God's word intact and deliver it safely to coming peoples throughout history. God once said of Abraham in Genesis 18:19:

For I have chosen him, so that he will direct his children and his household after him to keep the way of the LORD by doing what is right and just, so that the LORD will bring about for Abraham what he has promised him.

The idea here may well be better expressed in the King James Version. It is the thought that God knew Abraham and thus chose him. God knew that Abraham would command his children after him regarding the ways of the Almighty.

The idea is still prevalent in Israel that one must guard the commands of God and keep them *(shomer mitzvot)*. Many Israelis believe strongly that they must carefully instruct their children to also guard the things of the Lord.

In Deuteronomy 11:19-20, the Jewish people are commanded to teach the word of God when they rise up, when they sit down, and when they walk. They are also taught to write the word of God upon their doorposts and gates. The fulfillment of this command can be seen today in the many *mezuzot* on doorposts of Jewish homes in Israel.

We might wonder what would have happened if God had given his precious word to the nations at large. How would they have handled the word over the last 3500 years? The answer seems to be apparent. We Gentiles have had the word for approximately half that amount of time and many are already busily corrupting it.

These tiny wood, ceramic, or metal containers (mezuzot) have within them a parchment with the words of Deuteronomy 6:4-9 and 11:13-21.
(Courtesy Israel Information Office)

Consider some of the ideas floating around about the scriptures today.   Some people are trying to make God feminine.   Others are trying to remove every reference to Zion and Israel in order to make the Bible "politically correct."   Thank God that he gave the word to the Jewish people. They have faithfully delivered it intact to us.

CAN GOD CAST AWAY HIS PEOPLE?

Since the early centuries of Christianity there have been voices proclaiming in the Church that God is finished with the Jews.   Can such a thing be?   According to this theology the Jews failed God, so the Lord has washed his hands of them forever.   Can God cast away his people? The scripture is clear on this.   God knew beforehand that Israel would not be faithful.   He also knows the same thing about us Christians.   In Leviticus 26:14-43, Moses speaks in detail about all of Israel's failures.   Yet, in verse 44, God still says of them:

Yet in spite of this, when they are in the land of their enemies, I will not reject them or abhor them so as to destroy them completely, breaking my covenant with them. I am the LORD their God.

This is a rather shocking passage.   It simply means that God has never changed his mind about the Jews.   Still today, almost 2700 years after the beginning of their exiles in 722 BC, they are still his people.   Those Jewish people whom we have known, associated with, and often persecuted are still a special people to God. Whenever we touch them, we touch *"...the apple of his eye"* (Zech. 2:8).

God speaks to us of their continuing special relationship to him in yet another passage. God, who is the Creator of the vast universe above us and the earth below us declares in Jeremiah 31:35-37:

> *This is what the LORD says, he who appoints the sun to shine by day, who decrees the moon and stars to shine by night, who stirs up the sea so that its waves roar – the LORD Almighty is his name: "Only if these decrees vanish from my sight," declares the LORD, "will the descendants of Israel ever cease to be a nation before me." This is what the LORD says: "Only if the heavens above can be measured and the foundations of the earth below be searched out will I reject all the descendants of Israel because of all they have done," declares the LORD.*

When the sun stops shining; when the stars stop twinkling in the heavens; and when the waves of the sea stop roaring, then there might be a possibility that God can reject his chosen people Israel. Until that time they remain chosen and we Christians need to come to understand this. The New Testament verifies this truth to us in Romans 11:29 as Paul assures us, *"...God's gifts and his call are irrevocable."*

"All things are mortal but the Jew; all other forces pass, but he remains. What is the secret of his immortality?" (American author, Mark Twain)[1]

Paul asks and answers his own question about the Jews in Romans 11:1-2. He is almost aghast at the thought that God could forsake them: *"...Did God reject his people? By no means! ...God did not reject his people, whom he foreknew..."*

CHOSEN PEOPLE – CHOSEN LAND

God chose a special people, the people of Israel, and a special land, the land of Israel. Once more after two thousand years we see the chosen people inhabiting the chosen land.

It may surprise many today in our modern world that God gave this special land to his special people. It was given to them as an eternal inheritance. Let us look at this eternal promise in Genesis 17:8, as made to Abraham:

Also I give to you and your descendants after you the land in which you are a stranger, all the land of Canaan, as an everlasting possession; and I will be their God.

Some have objected saying that all God's promises are conditional. Certain of God's promises do have a conditional nature about them. Each generation may or may not receive the benefits of these promises and covenants, depending upon its faithfulness or lack of it. However, the promises themselves are eternal and this fact is stated plainly in the above passage and in numerous other places.

In Genesis 15:9-21, God made the covenant with Abram to give him all the land of Canaan, from the River of Egypt to the Euphrates. As was the custom in ancient times, animals were slaughtered in the traditional fashion of a blood covenant. The bloody parts were then laid out so that the makers of the covenant could pass between them. Interestingly, Abram fell into a deep sleep and God alone passed between the parts, signifying that it is God alone who maintains the covenant.

God is very emphatic about giving the land of Israel to his chosen people forever. Not only does Israel have the "title deed" fully written out in Genesis 17:8, but in a real sense, the title has been legally recorded and published in the Bible so that all the world can know of its existence.

God does not stop here. God even goes to the extreme of swearing an oath about this. We have reference to this oath in Genesis 24:7:

The LORD, the God of heaven, who brought me out of my father's household and my native land and who spoke to me and promised me on oath, saying, 'To your offspring I will give this land...'.

This must be something very important for the God of the whole universe, that he would swear an oath about it. Let us pause and try to get this incredible picture.

Imagine the Almighty standing before all the angels, heavenly beings, principalities, powers and saying something like this: "I God Almighty do solemnly swear that the land of Israel shall be the possession of the children of Israel forever!"

Now the Bible tells us that there was no one greater by whom God could swear, so he swore by his own great name (Heb. 6:13-14). Perhaps as in the movie "O God," he just put his hand on his own shoulder and said, "So help me – me!"

BUT WHAT ABOUT THE ARABS?

It is important for us to notice that God specifically did not give his land to Ishmael or to his descendants, the Arabs (Gen 17:21). This is the core of the problem in the Middle East today. Does it mean that God discriminated against Ishmael and the Arabs? Absolutely not!

God greatly loved Ishmael and he loves the Arabs today. God promised to surely bless Ishmael and multiply him into twelve princes and to make him great (Gen. 17:18-20). In fact, God loved Ishmael so much that he gave him twenty-two sovereign nations that make up the Arab League. He gave the Arab League almost five million square miles as compared with only eight thousand square miles of land in Israel.[2]

God loved Ishmael so much that he has made him incredibly rich. Today, 67 percent of the world's oil reserves are located in the Arab Middle Eastern countries of Saudi Arabia, Kuwait, Iran, Iraq, and United Arab Emirates.[3] God blessed Ishmael with abundant land and fantastic wealth, but he has not given him Israel, and he will not do so for all time and eternity.

Does this mean that the Arabs cannot live in Israel? Of course not! Some Arabs have been living in the land since the Muslim conquest of the seventh century. They have every right to live in the land. However, the issue is not one of living in the land but of sovereignty.

Certainly Gentiles may come and live in the land and even be protected by Israel's laws. However, as Gentiles we must realize that we have a responsibility to Israel to respect and act according to the laws and customs of the land (Exo. 12:49).

If we believe the Bible, we must believe that God is a bit upset by what is happening today. The land of Israel has become a political "hot potato." There is much agitation throughout the Middle East for Palestinian sovereignty in the territory of Israel. This agitation is seen and heard constantly in the media and it resounds in many foreign capitals.

Many of the nations of the earth and their leaders are now working feverishly to separate the people of Israel from the land of Israel. Through this effort known as the "peace process" Israel has already lost control of Shechem, Hebron, Bethlehem and several other important cities in its mountainous area. The Israeli government is now surrendering vast amounts of territory in this area, and much of the ancient land has been lost. This mountainous area is to be the very area of Israel's return and resettlement according to the prophet Ezekiel (36:1-15).

What will God eventually do about this problem? In Joel 3:2, we read these sobering verses:

> *I will gather all nations and bring them down to the Valley of Jehoshaphat. There I will enter into judgment against them concerning my inheritance, my people Israel, for they scattered my people among the nations and divided up my land.*

It is clear that judgment is coming for people and nations who do not respect the word of God.

TODAY, GOD IS VERIFYING HIS COVENANT

Had we lived a hundred years ago we might have wondered if God would be true to the Jewish people. At that time they were hopelessly scattered over the world. The idea of a Jewish homeland was just the dream of a few visionaries.

However, today God has moved with a mighty hand to re-establish his chosen people in his chosen land. He has restored their cities, their farmlands, their language, their military power, their government, etc. He has done this in spite of much interference and outright opposition of men and nations. In our day God has fulfilled dozens of prophecies such as Isaiah 11:11; Isaiah 43:5-6; Jeremiah 32:15, etc. It is now possible to come to Israel and see for oneself what God has done for his people.

How ironic it is, that at a time like this, a time of restoration, that there are those who teach that God has broken his covenant with Israel! These voices come from the adherents of Replacement Theology.

God's dealing with the Jewish people should be a cause for great confidence among Christians. Quite simply, if God remains faithful to his Old Covenant people, then he will also remain faithful to his New Covenant people. If God is capricious with Israel, then he could certainly act the same way with the Church couldn't he?

Thank God that he is a covenant making and covenant keeping God. In Psalm 94:14 we read: *"For the LORD will not reject his people; he will never forsake his inheritance."*

In fact, God's dealing with Israel after all these thousands of years is really a great proof of his existence. "There is a story of Friedrich the Great of Prussia. He was an atheist but had a very pious medical doctor. Once, he demanded of his doctor: 'Give me proof that there is a God! But hurry up, I have no time!' The doctor replied immediately: 'The Jews, Your Majesty!' "[4]

STUDY QUESTIONS:

Why did God choose the Jewish people above all other people?

How does this fit with the scripture in Acts 10:34-35, that God is no respecter of persons?

Are God's promises to Israel unconditional or are they conditional and based upon Israel's obedience? Read Hosea 1-3 before formulating your answer.

Some Arabs have lived in the land of Israel for centuries, even before Israel became a nation in 1948. Some areas are predominately Arab. Should these Arab people now have a right to declare their own sovereignty?   Give a reason for your answer.

NOTES

1. Lance Lambert, *The Uniqueness of Israel* (Eastbourne: Kingsway Publications Ltd., 1980) p. 57.
2. Leonard J. Davis, *Myths and Facts 1985, A Concise Record of the Arab-Israeli Conflict* (Washington, DC: Near East Report, 1984) pp. 248-49.
3. *Comptons Interactive Encyclopedia,* CD-ROM, 1992, 1993, 1994.
4. Goran Larsson, *"The Jews! Your Majesty"* (San Diego, CA., Jerusalem, Israel: Jerusalem Center for Biblical Studies and Research, second revised edition, 1989) p. 37.

-3-

SEVEN SCENES FROM HOLY HISTORY

The history of Israel is unlike the history of other nations. Since Israel is special to God, and since the nation figures prominently in God's worldwide redemptive program, the history of Israel may be more accurately called "redemptive history," "salvation history," or even "holy history."

Trying to summarize the history of Israel is like trying to summarize the history of the world. Because of God's great redemptive plan, the Jews have been dispersed to almost every place on this globe. They have also lived in virtually every time frame in recorded history.

Although the land of Israel was given to them as their dwelling place, they have lived outside the land much more than they have lived in it. This fact impacts the study of Israel's history to a considerable degree.

Let us take a quick look at the redemptive history of Israel as we attempt to picture it in seven critical events. These events are:

1) The call of Abram
2) Birth of the nation (deliverance from Egypt and giving of the law)
3) Conquest and settlement of Canaan
4) Rise of the Davidic kingship and its messianic implications

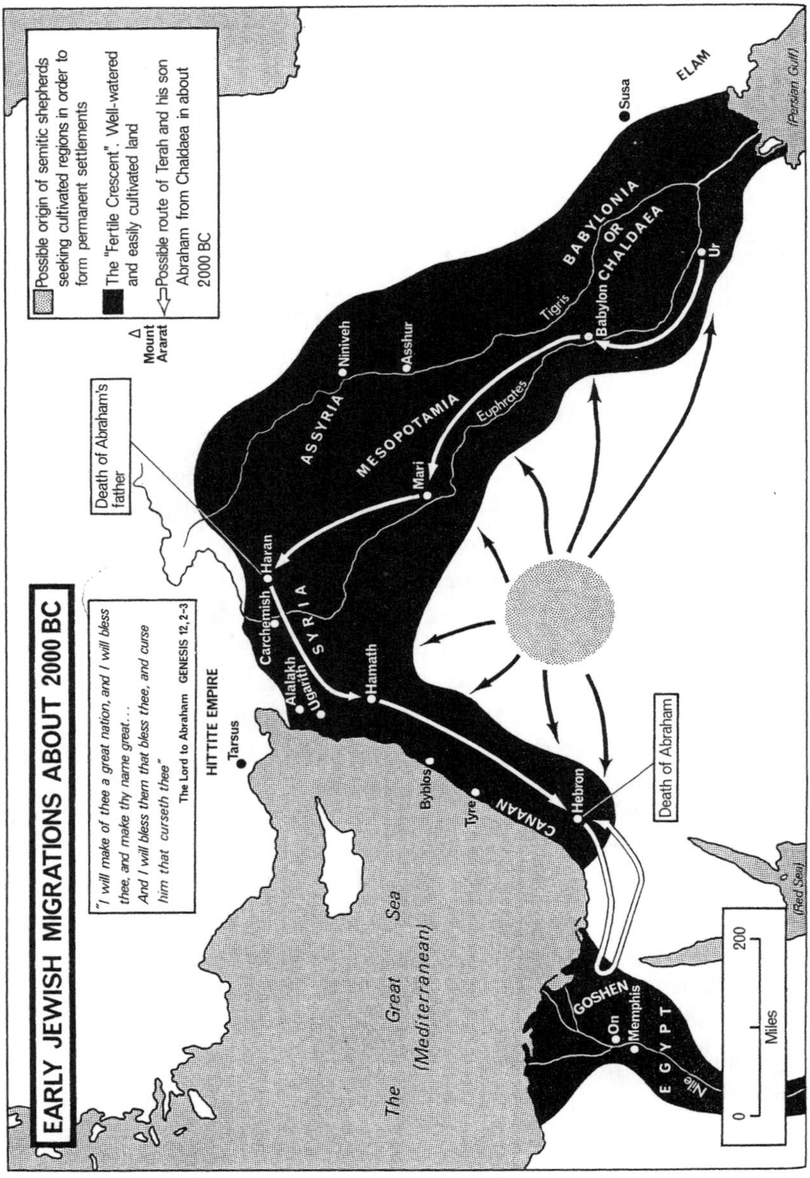
EARLY JEWISH MIGRATIONS ABOUT 2000 BC
"I will make of thee a great nation, and I will bless thee, and make thy name great . . .
And I will bless them that bless thee, and curse him that curseth thee"
The Lord to Abraham GENESIS 12, 2-3
Possible origin of semitic shepherds seeking cultivated regions in order to form permanent settlements
The "Fertile Crescent". Well-watered and easily cultivated land
Possible route of Terah and his son Abraham from Chaldaea in about 2000 BC
Death of Abraham's father
Death of Abraham
Mount Ararat
HITTITE EMPIRE
Tarsus
Carchemish
Haran
Alalakh
Ugarith
Hamath
SYRIA
Mari
MESOPOTAMIA
ASSYRIA
Niniveh
Asshur
Euphrates
Tigris
Babylon
BABYLONIA OR CHALDAEA
Ur
Susa
ELAM
(Persian Gulf)
Byblos
Tyre
CANAAN
Hebron
The Great Sea (Mediterranean)
GOSHEN
On
Memphis
EGYPT
Nile
(Red Sea)
0
200
Miles

Early Jewish Migrations. ***(Courtesy Martin Gilbert)***

5) First dispersion and restoration, including Daniel's
    view of history
6) Coming of the Messiah
7) Second dispersion and restoration, including the
    Holocaust

SCENE ONE: THE CALL OF ABRAM

Abram was one of the most remarkable men this world has
ever known. He was remarkable in that he introduced the
whole pagan world to the unique and incredible concept of the
one true God.

We can imagine that in the pagan land where Abram lived,
he often heard the screams of babies as they were burned
alive in the fires at pagan altars. He must have often passed
the pagan temples, which were the churches and synagogues
of his day. As he passed them, he probably saw the open and
flagrant adultery and homosexuality, because this was the
way people worshipped their gods in Abram's time.

People worshipped many gods. In fact, every nation had its
own panoply of pagan gods. Ancient Babylon, in the area
where Abram lived, is said to have had 300 gods of heaven
and another 600 of earth. This did not count the many spirits,
who were also worshipped.[1] The gods of the past were
capricious and demonic. Many times the gods were more
unrighteous than men.

God desired to redeem mankind from this dismal environ-
ment of idolatry. For God to redeem a whole world it was
necessary for him first to redeem a man, then a family, and
finally a whole nation.

Let us look back to the days of Abram. In his day, what was
to be the land of Israel was a part of "the Fertile Crescent."
On one end of the crescent was the future land of Israel, God's
proposed redemptive base in the world. On the other end of
the crescent was Abram, the man who would bring the nation
of Israel into being, and who would become the redemptive
"father" of all believers everywhere. His name, Abram
(exalted father), was thus changed to Abraham (father of a
multitude).

We read in the Bible that Abraham was from Ur of the Chaldees in Babylonia. He hailed from the land of the two rivers, the Tigris and Euphrates. Abraham first lived in Ur, then later his family moved to Haran. While in Haran, God called him to leave his father's house and his country and to go to Canaan (Gen. 12:1-3). The time of his journey was probably around 2000 BC, and Abraham was seventy-five years old, a time when most people retire to their rocking chairs.

Abraham crossed the Euphrates, and its tributaries, and set out for the land to which God had called him. In so doing, he inadvertently supplied the name to his future people, the Hebrews. The root for their name in the Hebrew language is *abar*, and it means "to cross over."

Abraham crossed over from his idolatrous and depraved world to become a man of God and to bring forth a people of God. The followers of Abraham today, who number into the multiplied millions, are likewise people who "cross over." They cross over the sea from Egypt (flesh) into the realm of the Spirit. They cross over the Jordan to possess the heavenly country God has given (Heb.11:14-16).

Father Abraham arrived in Canaan with Sarah his wife, his nephew Lot, and all their possessions, including their servants (Gen. 12:4-5). His first recorded visit in the land was at Shechem (today's Nablus). There, by the great tree of Moreh, among strangers, God appeared to him and promised to give the land to his offspring (Gen. 12:7). The everlasting drama of the land and the man had begun.

Although Abraham was a remarkable man, he was still very much a human being like all the rest of us. There were times when his faith wavered. There were other times when he stood as a giant in the earth. His faith must have wavered when God told him to leave Haran and his father's house. Somehow, Abraham took his nephew Lot along with him (Gen. 12:4). Lot caused Abraham much heartache. The descendants of Lot, Ammon and Moab (present day Jordan), have continued to vex Israel to this time.

Abraham was promised a son by faith, although he was very old and his wife Sarah was far past the age of child-bearing. Apparently Abraham had some slight doubts about this promise. At Sarah's urging he finally took her handmaid Hagar and from her was born Ishmael. Today almost a billion Muslims in the world look to Ishmael as their founder and father.

On other occasions Abraham stood as a mighty tower of faith. One of these occasions particularly stands out. After Abraham and Lot were separated, the latter was taken captive by a Mesopotamian raid into the area. If Abraham had been like most of us he would have probably said, "Thank God, my troubles are over. Lot has finally gotten what he deserves!"

Abraham didn't react that way. He called his little group of 318 servants together. We can imagine that Abraham had to give some quick instruction to those of his men who were not trained as warriors. He might have said something like this: "Now guys, this is a bow, and this is an arrow. Please remember to keep the feathers next to you when you try to shoot the thing!"

It was no doubt a motley crew that Abraham had as an army. Who would think of taking such an army to fight one of the greatest powers of the ancient world? But Abraham was a man of faith in the Mighty God.

As he led his tiny army through the brush that night in northern Galilee, something incredible happened. Abraham with his very small band somehow defeated the armies of Mesopotamia. These armies apparently fled in disarray. Abraham and his men collected the vast booty, including Lot and all that belonged to him, and returned home victorious.

This was to be the first of many such strange victories that Abraham's people would fight through future centuries. Little would pagan enemies understand that they were not just fighting against Abraham or his seed, but against the mighty God of Israel and his eternal redemptive program.

Abraham became the father of Israel and of all those who believe (Rom. 4:11). His son Isaac carried on the redemptive history to the next generation. After him, Jacob carried on the tradition and brought forth the twelve tribes of Israel.

Tombs of Abraham and the Patriarchs in Hebron. (Courtesy Israel Information Office)

Through the envy of his brothers, one of Jacob's sons, Joseph, was sold into Egypt as a slave. In time, through God's providence, he rose to great heights of power, becoming second only to Pharaoh. Joseph, through prophecy, had foretold a seven-year famine in the whole land. He had also predicted seven years of plenty before the famine. As a result, Joseph was placed in charge of grain storage and abundant provisions were laid up in Egypt.

At last, to stave off famine, the whole house of Israel, some seventy souls, came to sojourn in Egypt. The people were treated kindly at first, but after four hundred years, the people were made slaves and they cried out to the God of Abraham.

SCENE TWO: BIRTH OF THE NATION
(DELIVERANCE FROM EGYPT AND GIVING OF THE LAW)

It seemed that Moses had missed his calling in life. He had a great beginning, being adopted into the family of Pharaoh, king of Egypt. Afterward he had fallen from grace in the Egyptian court, and quite frankly had also fallen on bad times. Because of this, he came to spend his days herding sheep and goats on the back side of the desert of Sinai.

Moses once thought that he would deliver his oppressed people from Egypt, but that idea seemed remote. Moses' life was now well spent, seeing that he was already about 80 years old.

However, God had not forgotten Moses, nor had he forgotten his people suffering in Egypt. God knew that the sojourn in Egypt was necessary for the Children of Israel. It had also been necessary for Moses. It seems that the faithful of every age have had to endure the "Egypt experience." On one occasion even Abraham had to go down into Egypt and sojourn there for a time. Now the whole nation of Israel was stuck in Egypt.

The Living God, who had heard the cries of his captive people, now paid a visit to lonely Moses in the desert of Sinai. There Moses saw the Living God, the "I AM" of scripture. He is the only man who ever did so and lived to tell about it.

God sent stammering Moses along with his brother Aaron down to Egypt to pay a call on perhaps the most powerful monarch of the ancient world. Moses went with the message "Let my people go!"

Again we need to use our imaginations just a little as we picture this shepherd from the back side of the desert coming before mighty Pharaoh. What happened when Moses delivered this message? Pharaoh and his whole court probably had some good belly laughter. After this, Pharaoh said something equivalent to "No way *Mo-shea!*"

Pharaoh's refusal was the beginning of one of the most unusual periods in the history of the world. God with a mighty hand began to plague Egypt.

The story of the deliverance from Egypt is one of the classic dramas of all time. Never before in history had a nation been born in the midst of another nation (Deut. 4:34). Never before had the world seen such a miraculous visitation with astounding supernatural displays.

Awesome and fearful plagues fell on Egypt. There were plagues of blood and frogs. Mrs. Pharaoh couldn't go to the bathroom at night without stepping on the squishy, croaking things. There were gnats, insects, pestilence, and boils. We can imagine mighty Pharaoh waddling out gingerly to speak to Moses, having a boil on each foot, and perhaps another one on the very place where he would have sat down.

There were plagues of hail, locusts, and darkness devastating the land. Finally there was the death of the first-born in Egypt. That night the people of Israel were spared while Egypt's firstborn all died. Through Moses, God had instructed his people to slay the Passover lamb and place its blood on the lintels and doorposts of their houses. When this last plague came, the people of Israel were spared. At this last plague the whole house of Israel was freed from bondage.

The whole drama of salvation is pictured vividly in the plagues of Egypt, particularly the slaying of the firstborn. The slaying of an unblemished lamb, the blood upon the door-post, the passing over of the death angel and the following deliverance would always stand out as vivid types of God's salvation. For us as Christians, we see Passover in light of our deliverance from the bondage to sin and death by the sacrifice that God provided for us in his Son the Messiah.

Later, as Israel was leaving Egypt and as they were in the awkward position of trying to cross the Red Sea without boats, Pharaoh changed his mind and pursued them.

That night, as Moses held his staff over the sea and as the horses of Pharaoh pawed and neighed a short distance away, the east wind began to blow and the sea stood up in columns revealing the dry ground beneath. The people of Israel then began to pass through the sea on dry ground.

At this, one would think that Pharaoh would have dismounted his chariot, bowed his face to the ground and repented of his evil. Instead, in his insane rage, he dared send his army after the Israelites.

After Moses and all the people had passed through the sea, and as the whole army of Pharaoh was now in the midst of the sea, the waters closed upon them. That night there must have been something like twin tidal waves coming together with such velocity that Egyptian horses and their riders were hurled through the air and into the sea.

Too often we read the accounts of scripture without truly getting the picture of the awesome works of God. We need again to stop and meditate until we can smell the sea water and hear the cries of the drowning.

That morning as the bodies of Egyptians washed up on the shores, all the women sang with tambourines. Miriam led them in this chorus: *"Sing to the LORD, for he is highly exalted. The horse and its rider he has hurled into the sea"* (Exo. 15:21).

Moses then led the people which God himself describes as *"stiff necked"* (Exo. 32:9) into the wilderness of Sinai. It was there that the nation, or at least the remnant of the nation, was molded into the people God desired. There in the desert God fed them daily with manna from heaven. In the desert they were given commandments from the mouth of God. In all the history of the world, no people had ever heard God's voice out of the fire and smoke (Deut. 5:26). This experience made a lasting impression upon the Jewish people.

The generation that came out of Egypt was not able to enter the land of Canaan due to their lack of faith and vision. However, the following generation began to enter the land that God had long before promised forever to Abraham and to his sons.

SCENE THREE: CONQUEST AND SETTLEMENT OF CANAAN

Moses led the people forty years in the wilderness and, finally he led them to the Jordan River. However, God did not permit him to lead them any further. He did help them to

View from the ancient tell (hill) of Jericho.

experience their first great victories in battle, as they fought against Sihon, king of Heshbon (today's Jordan) and Og, the king of Bashan (today's Golan Heights). As a result of these two battles the people began to inherit the land on the east side of the Jordan River. The tribes of Reuben, Gad and the half-tribe of Manasseh settled in this area.

After the death of Moses, his able assistant Joshua took command. Joshua led the people miraculously over the

Ruins of ancient Hazor.

Jordan River. Again, they walked through on dry ground, even though the river was at flood stage.

Joshua then led the people in victory over the city of Jericho. Many scholars today believe that Jericho is actually the oldest known walled city in the world. There is presently even a sign to that effect on the outskirts of the city. Even by Joshua's time, Jericho was heavily fortified and virtually impossible to conquer. Through a great miracle the mighty walls of Jericho fell down. There is no trace of city walls from Joshua's time on the ancient mound of Jericho today.

After the miraculous victory at Jericho, Joshua proceeded to cut the land of Canaan in two just a few kilometers north of Jerusalem. In swift succession he defeated the principal cities of influence in the land of Canaan. These cities included Ai, Makkedah, Libnah, Lachish, Gezer, Eglon, Hebron, and Debir. Joshua accomplished this in one campaign, because the Lord God fought for Israel (Josh. 10:42).

Later, Joshua fought a confederation of northern kings led by Jabin, king of Hazor. Their warriors were as numerous as sand on the seashore (Josh. 11:4). Hazor was one of the mightiest cities in Canaan and was actually the gateway city into the land from the north. This confederation of kings was also defeated, and Hazor was then burned by Joshua. The burn line from Joshua's time can still be seen in this ancient city.

The land was then divided among the remaining tribes and settlement was begun. The battles for the land, however, would continue on for many generations. Sometime after Israel's settlement in the land, the Philistines, a sea people from the area of Crete, began to settle along the seacoast in the Gaza area. They were destined to become one of Israel's greatest antagonists.

In appraising the conquest of Canaan by the Israelites we must stop and marvel. Canaan was a well-developed area with greatly fortified cities that had been built over many centuries. The Israelites were a band of desert wanderers with little skill in the type warfare required to conquer fortified cities.

The conquest was a series of miracles. God had promised this land to Abraham's seed long before. As he had promised, God came to fight for Israel. Even nature was incorporated on several occasions to fight against the Canaanites. We see that hornets went on the offensive against them (Josh. 24:12). Hailstones fell from heaven (Josh. 10:11). Even *"...the stars fought, from their courses..."* against the northern commander, Sisera (Jud. 5:20).

The entry of Israel into the land of Canaan has been variously set by scholars, with dates ranging from 1550 to 1200 BC. It is clear that the actual settlement was not without its problems. After the death of the great leader Joshua, the people began to turn away from the true God to serve the idols of the Canaanites. Swift punishment came from God, and he allowed them to be harassed by various enemies. When the people cried out to God he sent judges to deliver them from their foes.

Some of the most famous of these judges were Deborah and her military assistant Barak (Judges chs. 4-5), who delivered Israel from another league of Canaanite kings in the north; Gideon (Judges chs. 6-8), who delivered the people from the Midianites; and Samson (Judges chs. 13-16), who began to deliver the people from the Philistines.

In time, the people of Israel began to long for a king like the other nations. Again, God heard their requests and gave them their first king, Saul. Saul began to make a serious attempt to war against the Philistines, who were at this time imposing their rule upon Israel. At last, through his own disobedience, Saul was killed in battle by the Philistines on Mount Gilboa.

SCENE FOUR: RISE OF THE DAVIDIC KINGDOM (AND ITS MESSIANIC IMPLICATIONS)

Even before Saul's death, God had chosen the next king of Israel. This time it was a man after God's own heart (1 Sam. 13:14). Of all the kings who have ever ruled on this earth, David was unique. Even as a child he was able to play on his harp and soothe the deranged King Saul. As a mere child he went forth to fight mighty Goliath, the Philistine giant. This giant was over nine feet tall and was heavily armed. David came against him with a sling and stone, and with the mighty power of God. The giant was slain and Israel won another of her miraculous victories.

David was gifted as a mighty warrior and leader of men. Saul soon began to envy David, and for many years thereafter, David and his men hid out as fugitives in the various wilderness areas of the country.

After the death of Saul on Mount Gilboa, and the humiliating defeat of Israel by the Philistines, David became king. He first ruled at Hebron in the south, but he later moved to consolidate his kingdom in Jerusalem about 998-995 BC. For the most part, David ruled very wisely over the people of Israel.

During his reign the kingdom was greatly expanded to include most of the land God had promised Israel. With the

A view of the ancient city of Bet Shean. The bodies of Saul and Jonathan were hung here after the defeat on Mt. Gilboa.

direct help of God he scored numerous victories over Israel's persistent foes. For the first time, even the Philistines began to wilt away before the onslaught of David.

David was not only a mighty warrior; he was an extremely sensitive spiritual person. While other kings of the earth, no doubt, immersed themselves in politics, David immersed himself in God. His many Psalms bear witness to this. In Psalm 63:1, David cries out:

> *O God, you are my God, earnestly I seek you; my soul thirsts for you, my body longs for you, in a dry and weary land where there is no water.*

Of all men on earth, David may have been the most urgent seeker after God. He worshipped God with a whole-hearted devotion. He longed to dwell in God's house (Psa. 23:6). He danced unashamedly before the Lord (2 Sam. 6:14). David began a revolution in worship that has had a tremendous affect upon Jews and Christians alike. His Psalms have comforted Israel for three thousand years and the Church for two thousand years.

It is interesting that as the end-days come upon us, the style of David's worship is returning to the Church. We may assume that it will also return to Israel. This is in full accordance with the words of the prophet:

> *In that day I will restore David's fallen tent. I will repair its broken places, restore its ruins, and build it as it used to be* (Amos 9:11).

Once he was settled in his kingdom, David greatly desired to build God a house. Since the days of the wilderness wanderings the "house" of God had been a tabernacle or tent. David spoke to the prophet Nathan about his desire. However, God did not permit David to build his house or Temple. Instead, Nathan informed him that God instead desired to build a house for David.

The divine promises to King David are unique. There has never been a king in history who has received such promises. God said to David in 2 Samuel 7:16:

> *Your house and your kingdom will endure forever before me; your throne will be established forever.*

Hence, we have in David the beginnings of an eternal Messianic kingdom. It was not just a natural kingdom, but also one with deep spiritual implications. In time, David the king died. Later, his son Solomon reigned and died. Finally in our day the natural line of David has all but disappeared from among men. Yet, the kingdom of David continues through his heir, the Messiah.

The kingdom was split in 928 BC upon the death of Solomon. The northern section was called Israel, and the southern section became known as Judah. The kingdom generally disintegrated in both these areas as the people were prone to mix their unique faith with that of their pagan Canaanite neighbors.

It was in this turbulent period that the mighty voices of Israel's prophets began to thunder out, starting with those of Elijah and Elisha.

By the eighth century BC the voice of Israel's prophets reached a high water mark in Isaiah, Micah and others. Later in 627 BC, Jeremiah began his prophetic work in the southern kingdom of Judah.

The prophets of Israel have had far-reaching influence and have, over the centuries, touched people in many nations of the earth.

SCENE FIVE: ISRAEL'S FIRST DISPERSIONS AND HER RESTORATION (Including Daniel's unique view of history)

It was becoming more and more apparent that Israel was called to live in the middle of a super highway. The only way she could live there was by faith and absolute obedience to God. Unfortunately, both of these qualities were waning in the land. By 722 BC, the northern kingdom of Israel was so weakened by idolatry that it fell to the Assyrian king, Shalmanezer V, and the people were carried into captivity.

The Assyrians, who had a policy of displacing rebellious kingdoms with people from other conquered provinces, brought in alien people to settle the land. Hence, we have the beginnings of the Samaritans. The ten northern tribes of Israel who were dispersed in the land of Assyria became known in history and legend as the "Ten Lost Tribes." Although these tribes have disappeared from history, the prophets speak of their resurrection in the end-days (Hos. 1:10-11).

The southern kingdom of Judah continued until it was finally conquered by Nebuchadnezzar of Babylonia in 586 BC. The beautiful Temple built by Solomon, David's son, was destroyed and the people were also carried away captive. However, this time they were carried to Babylon. Unlike the dispersion of Israel, the people of Judah soon had an opportunity to return and experience a restoration in the land, just as the prophets had foretold.

In Mesopotamia the suzerainty soon passed from Babylon to the Media-Persian empire. The policy of the Persians was opposite to that of the Assyrians and Babylonians, in that they sought to restore captive peoples to their native lands. In addition, God had specifically spoken to King Cyrus that he might let the people of Judah return home. God had even called Cyrus "his anointed" (Isa. 45:1).

We can be certain that Daniel, who rose to great power both in the Babylonian and Persian empires, had some influence on these events. Daniel prayed earnestly for restoration and he also had opportunities to speak with these kings.

As a result, the decree of Cyrus allowing the exiles to return was issued in 536 BC (Ezra 1:1-4). Shortly thereafter the first wave of Jewish exiles began the journey home under Zerubbabel.

We can sense the divine favor riding upon the small company of some forty-two thousand who returned. Although we do not know the names of those who preferred to remain in Babylon, we certainly know the names of many who came home. We even know how many donkeys returned. There were 6,720 of them and they are recorded in God's book (Ezra 2:67). At this, we might assume that it is better to be a donkey and return home to Israel, than to remain and be a prince in Babylon.

When we look at this whole period, we have to marvel at how God has worked in history. This sets him apart from the pagan gods, who all failed to work in history. In fact, history worked on them. History consigned their images to its dustbins and their names are long since forgotten. However, the name of the God of Israel is an everlasting memorial (Ex. 3:15). His mighty acts have been repeated by the lips of millions through the ages.

Upon arrival home, the exiles rebuilt the altar and began also to rebuild the Temple. Their work was greatly hindered by the surrounding peoples in the land, and it was finally stopped altogether by decree of the new Persian king. It was not until the prophetic work of Haggai and Zechariah in 520 BC that the work began again. The Temple was finally completed in 516 BC.

Daniel's unusual view of history (Daniel 2:1-49)

Daniel shares with us what must be described as a most unusual view of history. Daniel was close to God and was especially gifted to see things otherwise hidden. He was often called upon to interpret dreams and spiritual phenomenon to the kings of Babylon and Persia.

Once Daniel interpreted a dream for King Nebuchadnezzar of Babylon. The king had dreamed about an enormous, dazzling statue. The statue had a head of gold. Its chest and arms were of silver, and its belly and thighs of bronze. The legs were of iron, with its feet and toes of iron mixed with baked clay. The king then saw in his dream that a rock hewn out of the mountain without human hands crashed into the image with great force, turning it into dust. The rock then grew into a great mountain, filling the whole earth.

Daniel interpreted the vision as a picture of the Gentile age. That age would apparently begin as the sovereign kingdom of Israel was ended by the Babylonians in 586 BC. There would then be four world empires in the long and painful Gentile era, and all would continue spiritually intact until the present. Daniel realized that the image represented the four empires of Babylon, Media-Persia, Greece, and Rome. Daniel correctly observed that the Roman Empire would divide into eastern and western portions like the two legs of a man. He saw that it would later divide into ten sections like a man's toes.

Later in the book (7:8), he saw that from these ten toes a king of fierce countenance would arise and bring a brief age of terror and persecution the likes of which the world has never seen before. This man is generally conceded to be the Beast or Antichrist.

Daniel saw that the kingdoms represented by the image would all fall at the same time (2:35). Thus their insidious influence continues to the present day. At the time of their fall, they will be demolished by a rock hewn out of the mountain without hands. When we look at Daniel and also compare the book with Revelation 11:15 & 14:1, there is little doubt left that the mountain is Mt. Zion, and the rock is the Messiah and his supernatural government from Jerusalem. After that, the kingdom would return to Israel and to the triumphant saints of the Most High God (Dan. 7:18).

The prophet Daniel saw that the fall of Israel began the Gentile age, and it appears that the final restoration of Israel will bring that age to an abrupt end.

What an unusual view of history! Probably such a view would not be taught in most schools today, yet it seems to be the biblical view. Someday everyone will most likely understand history in just the way Daniel interpreted it. Someday the history of the whole world may be taught and interpreted, from the standpoint of Israel.

In the latter days of the Persian Empire, God intervened once more in history to elevate a young Jewess to the heights of imperial majesty by making her Queen of Persia. Queen Esther later found it necessary to go before her husband, the all-powerful monarch, in a bid to rescue her own Jewish people from the plots of evil Haman.

The historian Josephus sheds some interesting light on her visit to the king. After fasting three days, Esther approached the king without his bidding. In ancient Persia this usually resulted in the death sentence. Josephus says that as Esther saw the king sitting on the throne and looking sternly at her, she fainted, whereupon the king sprang from his throne and lifted her up, placing his scepter in her hand and reassuring her.[2] Esther saved her people and her great influence may well have helped later in re-establishing the people of Israel in the land.

Perhaps it was somehow a result of her influence that two Jewish luminaries from the Persian Empire came to give much needed assistance to the returned exiles. The first was Ezra the Scribe. Ezra did much to mold Israel into the "people of the Book," a title by which they are known even to this day.

Later, Nehemiah, who was cupbearer of the Persian king Artaxerxes I, came to Israel with the specific commission from God to rebuild the wall of defense around Jerusalem. He faced immense persecution from the people of the land, the Samaritans and Arabs. Nevertheless, about 444 BC, the wall was completed. Judah was at last firmly established, awaiting the crucial period of history leading up to the coming of her Messiah.

SCENE SIX: COMING OF THE MESSIAH

Israel's most famous son was born during the turbulent period at the turn of the millennium. At this time, due to the oppression of the Romans, messianic expectations were at an extremely high pitch. This unique period in history had been chosen by God long before and was known as "the fullness of

time" (Gal. 4:4-5). During this special time frame God gave
his son Yeshua (Jesus) to the world.

He was not born in the royal Jerusalem palaces of Herod,
but according to the prophecy of Micah 5:2, he was born in the
nearby town of Bethlehem. He was born in a lowly stable. His
birth and life as the Savior of Israel and of the world are without parallel.

The coming of this long-awaited Messiah was God's utmost
intervention into human history. The Messiah was not just
man, but he was the unique combination of God and man, or
the God-man. At last, God had come to live in his world. Jesus
fulfilled the word of Isaiah spoken many centuries before in
Isaiah 7:14, "...The virgin will be with child and will give
birth to a son, and will call him Immanuel* [God with us].

Yeshua fulfilled numerous other prophecies in the
scriptures. He was born of the tribe of Judah (Gen. 49:10). He
was of the house of David and heir to that house forever
(Luke 1:32-33 & Isa. 9:7).

His eternal nature is set forth in Psalm 45:6-7:

> Your throne, O God, will last for ever and ever; a
> scepter of justice will be the scepter of your kingdom.
> You love righteousness and hate wickedness;
> therefore God, your God, has set you above your
> companions by anointing you with the oil of joy.

Also, in Psalm 110:1 we read:

> The LORD says to my Lord: "Sit at my right hand
> until I make your enemies a footstool for your feet."

We do not believe that God was talking to himself. In these
passages God was talking to his Son, the Messiah.

The historical events surrounding Jesus' birth also
correspond to the Hebrew scriptures. He was preceded by a
forerunner (Luke 3:2-6; cf. Isa. 40:3-5). According to Daniel's
prophecy he was born prior to the destruction of the Second
Temple (Dan. 9:25-26). Even the slaughter of infants in the
Bethlehem area was foretold (Matt. 2:16-18; cf. Jer. 31:15).

After his birth he was taken to Egypt because of the wrath of Herod (Matt. 2:14-15; cf. Hos. 11:1).

Years later when Jesus began in his ministry, he was declared to be God's son (Matt. 3:17; cf. Psa. 2:7). He was not another god, but the physical manifestation of the one true God. Jesus conducted his ministry very much in the pattern of Moses: he fed the people miraculously, he brought healing, he gave a new law, etc. Thus he fulfilled the word of God in Deuteronomy 18:15:

> *The LORD your God will raise up for you a prophet like me from among your own brothers. You must listen to him.*

Yeshua spoke in parables (Matt 13:34-35; cf. Psa. 78:2-3), bound up the brokenhearted (Luke 4:18; cf. Isa. 61:1), he healed the blind, deaf, dumb and lame (Luke 4:18-19; cf. Isa. 35:5-6). He was adored by small children (Matt. 21:15; cf. Psa. 8:2). Although the religious leaders of his day could remember nothing in scripture spoken about a Messiah from Galilee (John 7:52), he fulfilled Isaiah 9:1-2 which says:

> *Nevertheless, there will be no more gloom for those who were in distress. In the past he humbled the land of Zebulun and the land of Naphtali, but in the future he will honor Galilee of the Gentiles, by the way of the sea, along the Jordan – The people walking in darkness have seen a great light; on those living in the land of the shadow of death a light has dawned.*

Jesus spent a great deal of his ministry on the northern and northwestern shores of the Sea of Galilee. He even made his base at nearby Capernaum along the Way of the Sea *(Via Maris)*. At Capernaum, along that famous road, the Light of the World was manifested.

Unfortunately for Israel, Yeshua was not accepted, but was in fact rejected and despised by the leaders (John 1:11; cf. Isa. 53:3). His good news of salvation was not believed by the majority (John 12:37; cf. Isa. 53:1), although the common

An ancient tomb with a rolling stone in Jerusalem. (Courtesy Ron Cantrell)

people seem to have heard him gladly. The Jewish leaders did not know the time of their visitation, and now it would be hidden from their eyes (Luke 19:42-44).

Jesus was betrayed by his close friend (Lk. 22:47; cf. Psa. 41:9) for thirty pieces of silver (Matt. 26:14-15; cf. Zech. 11:12).

During his trial before the religious court he was abused and spat upon (Matt. 26:67; cf. Isa. 50:6). He was tried and accused by false witnesses (Mark 14:57; cf. Psa. 35:11). To these accusations he opened not his mouth (Mark 15:4-5; cf. Isa. 53:7).

Later he was crucified with criminals as the scripture foretold (Mark 15:27; cf. Isa. 53:12). He was pierced through his hands and his feet (John 20:27; cf. Psa. 22:16). He was mocked and reproached (Luke 23:35; cf. Psa. 22:7-8). But no bone of his was broken (John 19:32-33; cf. Psa. 34:20).

In that dark hour on the cross, even God the Father found it necessary to turn his face away from him (Matt. 27:46; cf. Psa. 22:1). Yet, while he hung there on the cross he prayed for his enemies (Luke 23:34; Psa. 109:4).

After his agonizing death, the Roman soldiers cast lots for his clothing just as the Psalmist had spoken long before (Matt. 27:35-36; cf. Psa. 22:17-18). He was then taken from the cross and buried with the rich as Isaiah had prophesied (Matt. 27:57-60; cf. Isa. 53:9). He did not die as a malefactor, but as a redeemer. Isaiah 53:5 speaks of his death in this way:

> *But he was pierced for our transgressions, he was crushed for our iniquities; the punishment that brought us peace was upon him, and by his wounds we are healed.*

His death was not the end. God would not leave his Messiah in Sheol, but he was raised from the dead (Mark 16:6; cf. Psa. 16:10). After appearing on many occasions to his disciples, he ascended to the Father and took his seat at the Father's right hand (Heb. 1:3; cf. Psa. 68:18).

It is the fervent belief of the Church that he will come again according to scripture. His feet will stand again upon the Mount of Olives at Jerusalem (Zech. 14:4). He will come when his people can at last speak in sincerity the words of Matthew 23:39:

> *For I tell you, you will not see me again until you say, "Blessed is he who comes in the name of the Lord."*

Today, as we look back on the history of two thousand years, we realize that a truly momentous event took place. We are living on a visited planet. The Almighty God, the King of the Universe, came to live on earth as a man. The shock waves of that visit continue to reverberate through the world and through history.

SCENE SEVEN: ISRAEL'S SECOND DISPERSION AND RESTORATION

Within a generation of Jesus' death, a disaster of immense magnitude befell Israel. This disaster had been spoken of by Jesus as he was being led to his death in Luke 23:28-29:

> ...Daughters of Jerusalem, do not weep for me; weep for yourselves and for your children. For the time will come when you will say, "Blessed are the barren women, the wombs that never bore and the breasts that never nursed!"

He had also spoken of this event as his disciples were admiring the beauty of the Temple. Jesus warned them sternly by saying in Luke 19:43-44:

> The days will come upon you when your enemies will build an embankment against you and encircle you and hem you in on every side. They will dash you to the ground, you and the children within your walls. They will not leave one stone on another, because you did not recognize the time of God's coming to you.

During the years from AD 66-73, Israel became embroiled in a futile revolt to throw off the Roman yoke. As the revolt continued, Jerusalem was at last surrounded and shut up by the enemy. The situation became very grave for its inhabitants. The historian Josephus tells of the deaths of countless thousands from hunger. He even relates how a mother roasted her own child and dined upon it.[3]

At last the city walls were breached. Then the unthinkable happened: the beautiful Temple was set on fire and destroyed. Later the Romans proceeded to burn and sack the city.

*The Arch of Titus in Rome, showing captured Temple items
brought from Jerusalem. (Courtesy Israel Information Office)*

Josephus again describes the awful slaughter as one in which streams of blood ran down the streets in such volume as to actually put out the flames.[4] After the fall of Jerusalem the war lingered on until Masada, the last stronghold, fell in AD 73.

Israel's agony was not ended. Some years later, Simon Bar Kokhba was proclaimed by many to be the messiah. In the years AD 132-135, he led a second revolt against Rome. Once more the Romans cruelly ended this rebellion, but not before multiplied thousands were killed and the slave markets glutted once more with Jews.

At this time, Rome was determined to put an end to Jewish rebellions. In derision, the land was renamed Syria Palestina. They rebuilt the city of Jerusalem as a pagan city and renamed it Aelia Capitolina. Hadrian, the Roman Emperor, then prohibited the practice of Judaism and Jews were even forbidden to come near the city.

After the earlier defeat of Jerusalem in AD 70, the Jews had made a valiant attempt to continue on in the land. The Sanhederin was established near the Mediterranean coast in Yavne. From there the sages of the Torah continued their work. After the second revolt, however, the center of Judaism moved to the Galilee. Rome was determined to punish the leaders of the revolt so it was necessary for many of them to hide out in the Galilee for many years.

By the year 210, the work on the *Mishna,* the compilation of Jewish oral tradition, was completed and soon thereafter the first generations of Talmudic scholars were being produced in Israel. Nevertheless, Jewish life in the Holy Land was a flickering candle. In a few generations the center of Judaism would shift from Israel to Babylon once again. It would for the most part remain in Gentile lands for the next fifteen centuries.

In the early fourth century, the Roman ruler Constantine declared himself to be a Christian and Christianity began to hold sway in the Middle East. This further encouraged the Jews to disperse to other nations.

In the seventh century, Islam arose and one of its first acts was the conquest of Palestine including Jerusalem. With the exception of the brief interlude of the Crusades at the turn of the eleventh century, the Muslims would control Palestine until modern times.

After their unsuccessful revolts against the Romans, the Jews began their dispersion to the farthest reaches of the Roman Empire. They now began to make their homes in places like Alexandria, Tarsus, Ephesus, Byzantium, and Rome. By the year 300, they had settled in all parts of the empire except Britain.[5]

After the fall of the Roman Empire in 476, the Jews began to play a leading part in world trade. They traveled to the farthest reaches of the empire and even as far as India and China through their involvement in the spice trade.[6]

As the vast areas of Europe became civilized, the Jews settled in these areas also. In early years a thriving Jewish civilization flourished in Spain. The Jews settled in France and Germany.   Unfortunately, the lot of the Jews in "Christian" Europe would never be secure. Although they made great and lasting contributions to these societies, time and time again they were expelled from different cities and nations.

When the new world was discovered, a Jew (who was an interpreter for Columbus) was one of the first two people to set foot upon it. The Jews followed the wave of discovery and colonization to the ends of the earth and to the islands of the sea. This in itself was a fulfillment of prophecy. It is said in Isaiah 11:11:

> In that day the Lord will reach out his hand a second time to reclaim the remnant that is left of his people from Assyria, from Lower Egypt, from Upper Egypt, from Cush, from Elam, from Babylonia, from Hamath and from the islands of the sea.

During all their long centuries in gentile lands the Jews suffered persecution in many forms and were driven from one land to another. They suffered under Crusades, Inquisitions, blood libels, forced conversions and baptisms, pogroms, and slanders of many types. Under Islam their lot was only slightly improved.

In time, the virulent anti-Semitism, which had flourished in the Church since the fourth century, blossomed into severe persecution under the Nazis, beginning in 1933. During the Holocaust that followed, six million Jews lost their lives. From the ashes of that greatest of all disasters, the modern nation of Israel began to rise once more.

After World War II, the survivors made their way to Palestine to join with the many others who had come earlier from the persecutions of Russia and other places on the globe. The word of the Lord was fulfilled once again:

> This is what the LORD says: "The people who survive the sword will find favor in the desert; I will come to give rest to Israel." (Jer. 31:2)

On November 29, 1947, the United Nations approved the partition plan allowing Israel to become a nation once more after almost two thousand years.

Israel was declared a state in May 1948 and following this act she was forced into an agonizing War of Independence with her many Arab neighbors. At the close of this war the nation of Israel was once again firmly established among the family of nations.

STUDY QUESTIONS:

How does holy history, or redemptive history differ from regular history?

Was it unfair for God to almost destroy Egypt in order to bring Israel out of bondage? Why?

What kind of things often happened to pagan forces when they fought Israel in the Bible? Do you suppose such things still happen in Israel's wars today?

What are some qualities David had that enabled him to become a type of God's coming Messiah?

How does Daniel's view of history differ from most non-biblical views today?

In what ways were Jesus' claims different from all other great teachers?

NOTES

1. E.A. Wallis Budge, *Babylonian Life and History* (New York: Dorset Press, 1992) p. 110.
2. William Whiston, *The Works of Josephus, Complete and Unabridged* (Peabody, MA: Hendrickson Publishers, Peabody, MA, 1987) p. 301.

3. Whiston, *The Works of Josephus, Complete and Unabridged,* p. 737.
4. Whiston, *The Works of Josephus, Complete and Unabridged,* p.748.
5. Martin Gilbert, *Jewish History Atlas* (Jerusalem, Tel Aviv, Haifa: Steimatzky, Ltd, 1969, fourth edition 1992) p. 17.
6. Martin Gilbert, *Jewish History Atlas*, p. 22.

-4-

THE RISE OF ISLAM –
ITS IMPACT UPON ISRAEL
AND THE CHURCH

Only a few years ago Islam was of little concern to many living in the western world. It was thought to be a wholly Middle Eastern problem far removed from any effect upon westerners. However, in the last few years, particularly since the 1991 Gulf War, there has been a quickening of interest in this religion.

North Americans suddenly realized that there were over four million Muslims living in their midst. Muslims were now on the verge of outnumbering Jews in North America, making Islam the second largest religion.

Americans awoke to the fact that mosques were rising in many of their cities, and over 500 Islamic centers were already built in their country. Episcopalians in the US were no doubt shocked to find themselves outnumbered by the Muslims. Incredibly, the shrill cry of the *muezzin* was now competing with the ringing of church bells in many communities.

Europe also began experiencing the reality of Islam on the move. Citizens of England became aware that there were more Muslims living there than Methodists, or even evangelical Christians.[1] The French realized that Islam was now their second largest religion, with more Muslims living in their country than Protestants.[2]

People the world over have been forced to "come to grips" with this fast-rising phenomenon. They have had to contemplate the sobering fact that there are now almost one billion Muslims in the world. Roughly one in every five persons in the world is a Muslim. With Islam's rapid birthrate and its vigorous missionary efforts, it has now become the fastest growing religion in the world.

How could a religion develop so rapidly on the modern scene? What are the roots and the history of this religion? Does its rise have spiritual implications for Jews and Christians? Let us look across the centuries in an attempt to answer these questions and many more. Let us trace the roots of Islam to ancient and even biblical times.

RELIGION OF THE 'OTHER BROTHER'

The roots of Islam can be traced directly to the Bible. This is illustrated by the fact that the nearly one billion Muslims in the world today claim Ishmael as their father. In Muslim theology, it was Ishmael who was almost sacrificed to God by father Abraham, and not Isaac. It is also Ishmael who has received the covenants and promises.

It may surprise us to realize that the present struggle between Islam, Christianity and Judaism began almost four thousand years ago as a family problem. It is an ancient struggle between brothers, between the chosen and the not chosen. We might therefore appropriately call Islam the religion of the other brother.[3]

Let us further examine these ancient biblical roots. Our first glimpse of the family problem is found in Genesis, chapter 16. We are told here that God had promised father Abraham an heir. However, the patriarch was already 85 years old and no heir was born, due to the barrenness of Sarah. In what might have been a weak moment in Abraham's faith, he accepted his wife's offer of her Egyptian slave, Hagar. It was his hopes that perhaps she could bear them a son and an heir. As a result of this arrangement, Ishmael was born. Ishmael was described as a wild man:

He will be a wild donkey of a man; his hand will be against everyone and everyone's hand against him, and he will live in hostility toward all his brothers (Gen. 16:12; cf. Gen. 25:18).

It seems that much of the hostility of the Middle East today can be traced back through the ages to this man, especially since he is considered by Muslims everywhere to be the father of their religion.

This heir apparent to father Abraham was now on the scene. But God immediately intervened in the situation and assured Abraham a son of his wife, Sarah. When that son was finally born he was named Isaac (laughter), and God swore that he would establish an everlasting covenant with Isaac, giving him the land of Canaan as an eternal possession (Gen. 17:7, 19).

God still promised to bless Ishmael and to multiply him exceedingly, so that twelve princes would come from him (Gen. 17:20). But in Genesis 17:21, God was very careful to promise that Isaac, not Ishmael, would inherit the land of Israel.

Over the centuries God has been true to his promises to bless Ishmael. Today there are twenty-two sovereign Arab nations in the Middle East. The Arab League has well over one hundred thirty million people, compared to approximately six million in Israel. God has also blessed Ishmael with most of the world's oil. The Lord has kept his promise.

God also has kept his promise to Isaac. He has returned Isaac to his ancient possession, the land of Israel, much to the chagrin of Ishmael. The conflict between these two brothers has steadily increased in modern times. It has now become one of the greatest and most serious conflicts on the face of the earth. This conflict has made the Middle East one of the most volatile areas of our world today.

The story of brothers and half-brothers continued. Later after Sarah died, Abraham took another wife, Keturah, and another six children were born from this relationship. Among these children were other Arab sounding names like Midian, Sheba, Dedan. It is interesting in Genesis 25:6, that Abraham gave gifts to these sons and sent them off to the east country (the desert), away from his son Isaac.

The antagonisms and feuds between brothers continued with the children of Isaac. His wife bore him twins, Jacob and Esau. Again we have God intervening and making a sovereign choice for his own redemptive purposes. God chose Jacob to inherit the promise as well as all the land of Canaan, or the land of Israel as it is known today. Again, there was bitterness and resentment on the part of the one not chosen. Esau, like Ishmael, moved into the desert in the area of Mt. Seir, or Edom, a land to the southeast of the Dead Sea. There he became the progenitor of multitudes of other Arab peoples.

All these desert peoples were joined by the children of Abraham's nephew Lot. Their names were Ben Ammi, the father of the nation of Ammon, and Moab, the father of a people by that name. These two nations, along with Edom, are today combined to make up the modern Arab-Muslim state of Jordan. Jordan, of course, joined other Arab forces to attack Israel in 1948, 1967 and in 1973.

The bitter rivalry between all these desert peoples and Israel is a thread running through the remainder of the Old Testament. Time and time again these Arab nations came in fury and bitter hatred to destroy Israel. First there were the Amalekites, then the Moabites or the children of Lot. Later, at different times, most all these Arab descendants of Abraham sought to destroy the seed of Isaac and Jacob.

Bible history is replete with the attacks of Edomites, Ammonites, Ishmaelites, Moabites, and hordes of other Arabs. When Jerusalem fell to the Babylonians in 586 BC, the Edomites were present assisting in the destruction and bringing down God's eternal wrath upon themselves (Obad. 1:10-14). Later, as we see in Nehemiah 2:19, Arabs strongly resisted the re-building of Jerusalem under Ezra and Nehemiah.

When God's covenant people were finally exiled again after the wars of AD 70 and 135, Arab peoples soon began to filter into the land. With the rise of Islam in the seventh century they actually took possession of the land. With *"...glee and malice in their hearts..."* they claimed God's heritage as their own (Ezek. 36:5-6).

MUHAMMAD

What the Arab peoples could not attain in centuries of war against Israel, they at last achieved with the rise of the Muslim faith (Islam) and its prophet Muhammad. For most of the following 1300 years, Islam would dominate the Holy Land as well as the heart of what was the Byzantine Christian empire in the Middle East. Islam would also dominate Christians and Jews throughout the Middle East and even in North Africa, Spain and other areas. The Bible may speak of this Arab dominion over Israel in these words of Genesis 27:40: *"You [Ishmael] will live by the sword and you will serve your brother. But when you grow restless, you will throw his yoke from off your neck."*

The devil found his willing subject in Muhammad. Muhammad was born of the Quraysh tribe about AD 570 in the city of Mecca. He was born in poverty, and to make matters worse, his father died before his birth. His mother was of an excitable nature and often claimed she was visited by spirits *(jinns)*. She died before her son was two years old.[4] Muhammad was then raised by his grandfather, who died when the boy was six. From this point, his uncle took care of him.

Since Muhammad was a poor orphan, it was necessary for him to work some as a shepherd. He spent some time with the Bedouin, and from them he learned much about desert survival and self defense. By the time Muhammad was ten he was traveling with his uncle in caravans. They went on trips as far away as Syria. Payne says of his travels:

El Aqsa mosque and Dome of the Rock in Jerusalem.
(Courtesy Israel Information Office)

What is certain is that at an early impressionable age Muhammad showed a predilection for conversing with priests and rabbis when the caravans stopped at the trading posts, and he stored these conversations in his capacious memory.[5]

When he reached his twenties, he became employed by Khadija, a rich widow, fifteen years his senior. He assisted her with her caravan business and soon earned her approval. In time they were married and Khidija bore him six children, four girls and two boys. Unfortunately, the boys died in childhood. Much later, after Khidija's death, Muhammad took many wives and concubines, including the nine-year-old daughter of his devoted follower Abu Bakr.

While still in Mecca, Muhammad began to spend time meditating in nearby caves. About the year 610, he began receiving visions and visitations from the spirit world. Supposedly, the Angel Gabriel came to him and assured Muhammad that he was god's messenger. He continued to receive supernatural visitations for the rest of his life. When his visions and revelations came, he would often fall down, perspire profusely, and begin to jerk with his eyes rolling backwards. At the onset, he worried that he was demon possessed, and even attempted suicide. His wife Khadija reassured him that he was a real prophet and not demon possessed.[6]

It was during this period of the prophet's life that he reported a very unusual visitation of the Angel Gabriel and an ensuing trip on a winged horse to the farthest mosque *(El Aqsa,* later interpreted to refer to the Temple Mount in Jerusalem). From there he was taken into heaven where he was embraced by god. Those Muslims who believe this account, point today to what they say is Muhammad's footprint under the Dome of the Rock on the Temple Mount.

Before Muhammad's coming, the people of Mecca and that part of Arabia had worshipped for centuries at the *Kaaba,* a pagan shrine in Mecca. This shrine contained 365 idols, including Hubal the moon god, statues of Abraham and Ishmael, painted angels and even pictures of Jesus and the Virgin Mary.[7] One of the high gods at the Meccan shrine was Allah, who was acknowledged as creator god. Allah had three daughters, Al-Lat, Manat, and 'Uzza, who were also worshipped.[8]

After his first visit by the Angel Gabriel, Muhammad began to proclaim that Allah was the true and only god and that he himself was the prophet of Allah. This was an obvious threat to the idolatrous religion of the Meccans, and to the revenues from the pilgrimages of the devout. Muhammad was therefore not accepted by his fellow citizens of Mecca. They ridiculed and persecuted both he and his few followers. In time the persecutions became so severe that they were life threatening.

At this dark period, Muhammad and his followers were welcomed in Yathrib, a city some two hundred miles north of Mecca. This city was founded by Jews and there was apparently a great deal of messianic expectation there. The men of Yathrib were initially disposed to accept Muhammad as their promised Messiah.[9]

The flight of Muhammad and his followers from Mecca to Yathrib occurred in AD 622, and is called the *Hijra* (emigration). It marks the beginning of the Muslim calendar. Once there, the city was renamed Medina *(Medinat al-Nabi)*, or city of the prophet.

Payne comments about this period: "In the *suras* written at Medina, perhaps under the influence of the Jewish rabbis... Suddenly Abraham appears as the founder of the *Kaaba*, led there by a heavenly light, building on the place chosen for him and hearing a voice from the clouds, saying: 'Surrender!' "[10]

From Medina, the true nature of Islam began to take shape with a shift in emphasis. Muhammad began to turn frequently to the sword as a means of advancing his religion. He began to send out raiding parties to prey on passing caravans. Muhammad's men were encouraged by their leader's revelations assuring them that "Martyrdom in battle was to be regarded as the highest prize, the quickest means of entering Paradise."[11]

Muhammad's relationship with the Jews seems to have soured as they realized that he was not their promised Messiah after all. Arguments broke out with them and Muhammad's attitude toward them hardened. During this period, Muhammad proclaimed that prayer should no longer be made facing Jerusalem, but that it should be made facing Mecca.

Muhammad heard that the Jewish tribe, the Bani Quraiza, southeast of Medina was in collusion with his enemies. He besieged their city and exacted a terrible vengeance upon them, beheading 700-1000 of its men and selling the women and children into slavery. He and his men then looted their possessions.[12] He attacked other Jewish tribes in the area and ultimately forced the Jews from his base, Medina. As Islam grew, the Jews were forced from Arabia.

Although Muhammad was now the uncontested ruler of Medina he longed to include Mecca in his fast growing religious empire. To this end he began to raid the rich caravans of the Quraysh tribe of Mecca. In the year 624,

Muhammad and his followers won an important battle over the Meccans at Badr, near Medina.

Although he lost some other skirmishes, his confidence in a possible victory over Mecca continued to grow.   In 628, Muhammad initiated a ten-year treaty with the Meccans. This is known as the Treaty of *Hudaibiyah.* Two years later when Muhammad felt strong enough, he broke the treaty and conquered Mecca.   He then destroyed the idols and rededicated the *Kaaba* as the shrine of Islam.

The Treaty of *Hudaibiyah* became a model for Muslim relations with non-Islamic nations. From that time on it was believed that treaties could be made for expediency, but when it was to Islam's advantage these treaties should be broken and the lands conquered.

THE DOCTRINES OF ISLAM

Muhammad died in the year 632, after his doctrine had been largely crystallized and his armies had been set firmly on the path of conquest. The ensuing religion of Islam was based upon Muhammad's many revelations that later made up the Quran. These revelations were originally scribbled on palm leaves, or on pieces of bone and parchment. They were also committed to memory by some of his devoted followers. After his death, they were collected into one authorized volume. The resulting Quran is considered by Muslims to be the infallible word of their god.

The Muslim faith stands on five pillars. They are *Shahada,* the simple confession that Allah is god and Muhammad is his messenger; *Salat,* the formal worship of Allah; *Zakat,* the giving of alms; *Sawm,* fasting during the holy month of Ramadan; and the *Hajj,* pilgrimage to Mecca once in a lifetime. Some feel that a sixth pillar should be added, that of *Jihad,* which is interpreted as service, exertion or holy war against infidels.[13]

As to a summation of the Islamic faith, Morey describes it well by saying, "...that it is a form of cultural imperialism in which the religion and culture of seventh-century Arabia have been raised to the status of divine law."[14]

"Muhammad took the Arab culture around him, with all its secular and sacred customs, and made it into the religion of Islam."[15] He literally gave the Arab people of his day all the things they desired. They had always worshipped at the Kaaba and had made pilgrimage to it, so Muhammad instituted this worship into his religion. Many parts of this ancient pagan worship are virtually unchanged in Islam even today. They had always worshipped Allah along with many other gods, so Muhammad instituted the worship of Allah. They had always believed in polygamy so Muhammad instituted it with some restrictions, however he himself had a total of 22 women as wives and concubines.[16]

The residents of pre-Islamic Arabia had always fought between clans. Muhammad therefore instituted warfare or *jihad* as a virtual pillar of his faith, and even made it acceptable to raid unsuspecting caravans, to kill and rape innocent victims. He made it acceptable to break sacred treaties, to loot, to lie and steal in Allah's name. On one occasion Muhammad even took his adopted son's wife Zainab, and later conveniently got a Quranic revelation to support his action.[17]

In the western world, a lie is generally considered as something evil. This is not necessarily the case in Muslim theology. Al-Ghazzali, the great Muslim theologian who wrote in the eleventh-century had this to say:

> Know that a lie is not *haram* [wrong] in itself, but only because of the evil conclusions to which it leads the hearer, making him believe something that is not really the case.... If a lie is the only way of obtaining a good result, it is permissible.... We must lie when truth leads to unpleasant results.[18]

The Arab sociologist Sania Hamady adds to this:

> Lying is a widespread habit among the Arabs and they have a low idea of truth.... The Arab has no scruples about lying if by it he obtains his objective.... He is more interested in feeling than facts, in conveying an impression than in giving a report...[19]

We may also note that while other religions such as Christianity and Judaism have a linear concept of time and progress, Islam has a cyclical concept. In Islam the ideal is always to return to the era of Muhammad. This can be witnessed particularly in the Islamic revolution in Iran where the clock was turned back in many ways toward the seventh century.

THE SWORD OF ISLAM TRIUMPHS

After the death of Muhammad, his trusted friend Abu Bakr became the first Caliph or successor. After him were Umar 634-644; Uthman 644-656; and Ali 656-661. As the Arabian Caliphate emerged, the emphasis upon conquest with the sword continued. It is interesting that the first major Muslim drive for conquest outside of Arabia was in the Holy Land. After some preliminary raids as far north as the Dead Sea, the Muslim armies in 634 finally routed Emperor Heraclius and the Byzantines. This battle just west of Jerusalem opened the door to the conquest of Palestine.

On August 20, 636, the Muslims won a decisive victory at the mouth of the Yarmuk River near the Sea of Galilee. As in many of Islam's battles, it seemed that their god was with them. On that occasion a great sandstorm frustrated and maddened the Byzantine Christian forces.[20] By the year 638, the Muslims had taken Jerusalem. Later in 692, the Umayyid Caliph, Abd-al-Malik, built the Dome of the Rock on the Temple Mount.

Bernard Lewis points out that "The Dome of the Rock, along with the adjoining Aqsa Mosque constituted the first great religious building complex in the history of Islam."[21] Lewis concludes that such impressive building on the Temple Mount was of a polemic nature:

> The polemical purpose of the shrine is reinforced by the choice of Quranic verses and other inscriptions that decorate the interior. One verse occurs again and again: 'God is one, without partner, without companion.'[22]

The rejection of the Christian doctrine of the Trinity is clear, and is made explicit in other inscriptions:

> Praise be to God, who begets no son, and has no partner in [his] dominion: nor [needs] he any to protect him from humiliation: yes, magnify him for his greatness and glory!

Another repeated inscription is the famous Sura 1121 in its entirety: 'He is God, one, eternal. He does not beget, nor is he begotten, and he has no peer.'[23]

After subjugating Israel, the Muslim armies swept over Syria, the Persian Empire and Egypt. With the last Arabian Caliph, the Caliphate was moved to Damascus, and came under the influence of the Umayyids (661-750). In 750 the Abbasid Caliphate began and became centered in Baghdad. During this period, Islamic civilization reached its zenith. The center of Islamic influence remained in Baghdad until the city was conquered by the Mongols in 1258.

In an incredibly brief period, the Muslims methodically swept over the remainder of the Middle East, North Africa and as far west as Spain. Finally in 732, they were stopped at the Battle of Tours just outside Paris by the Frankish leader Charles Martel. The Islamic invasion of Europe was temporarily arrested and even reversed. By 1492 the Christian king, Ferdinand, pushed the Muslims (Moors) out of Spain.

However, later during the rise of the Ottoman Empire, the Muslims renewed their conquest of Europe. They captured the Christian Byzantine capital of Constantinople in 1453, and then pushed on toward central Europe. The Muslims even began a siege of Vienna in 1529, but were finally driven from most of Europe.

LIFE UNDER ISLAM

As Islam and its holy war burst out of the confines of Arabia, many peoples were forcefully confronted with this new religion. Generally, polytheists were given the choice of conversion or death.[24] However, Jews and Christians were referred to by Muhammad as "the people of the Book." Accordingly, they came under special consideration.

In one particular case in Arabia, Muhammad had attacked the Jews at the oasis of Khaybar. Under the treaty made with them in 628, called the *dhimma,* they became subject peoples to Islam. Their existence was thereafter only for the benefit of Islam. They were doomed to remain second-class citizens. They lived, it seemed, for the sole purpose of demonstrating to all the superiority of Islam over conquered religions.

Jews and Christians were thereafter treated according to the *dhimma* and were given the name *dhimmi.*[25] From this point the *dhimmi* were always at the mercy of the Muslim rulers, and subject at all times to the whims of Muslim mobs. The *dhimmi* status seemed to always hang in peril. In fact, in 640, the status of the *dhimmi* was revoked throughout the whole Arabian peninsula and the remaining Jews and Christians were expelled.

Soon the *dhimmi* status, for what it was worth, was applied to Jews and Christians in many conquered lands of the Middle East. The *dhimmi* began to be more clearly defined by Muslim law and by common practice. There were several things that came to define the *dhimmi* status in Muslim lands. Bat Ye'or, an authority on the *dhimmi,* in her very informative book by this title, lists three areas where the *dhimmi* were abused:[26]

1. Oppressive taxation

In each conquered land, the Jews and Christians were allowed to remain and cultivate the land in exchange for the payment of a tax to the local Muslim ruler. This tax was called the *Kharaj.* This system was designed to remind the tenants that Islam owned the land. Their national identities and histories were blotted out and soon became virtually non-existent. They were forbidden to possess arms and thus became totally dependent upon the occupying Muslim power. In some areas, such as Morocco, this system became so oppressive that the Jews of that area were virtual serfs even as late as 1913, and were, literally, the property of their Muslim masters.

In addition to the *Kharaj* tax, the *dhimmi* were subjected to the poll tax or *Jizya*. This tax had to be paid in person by each subject, and it had to be paid in a public and humiliating manner. It was common for the *dhimmi* to be struck on the head or on the nape of the neck as he paid the tax to demonstrate the superiority of Islam.[27]

The *dhimmi* were also victimized by higher commercial and travel taxes. In addition they were often victims of extortion and blackmail at the hand of their own rulers. Often, greedy rulers required them to pay an *avania*, or protection money. This was simply a sum of money extorted from the Jewish or Christian communities, under the threat of persecution. This practice of having to pay for their own protection soon became the norm for *dhimmi* communities in Muslim lands.

2. Social and legal discrimination

Dhimmi peoples were generally excluded from holding public office, were kept from many professions and high positions, or from being elevated, in any way over Muslims. In virtually all Muslim lands however, some Jews became elevated despite this ban.

Generally, the most degrading jobs, such as cleaning the public latrines, fell to the *dhimmi*. Yemenite Jews, until they immigrated to Israel in 1950, were still required to clean the public latrines and remove dead animals from the city streets.

In the courtroom, the evidence of a *dhimmi* could never be accepted in testimony against a Muslim. Thus it was often necessary for the *dhimmi* to hire Muslim 'witnesses' for his court appearance. The *dhimmi* was not allowed to raise a hand against his Muslim masters, even if raised in self-defense. Such a thoughtless act would often result in the death penalty. In many Muslim lands, Jews were routinely beaten and abused in the streets. They could only beg for mercy and attempt to flee their persecutors. They did not dare defend themselves.

To further clarify their inferior status, the *dhimmi* were required to wear special clothing. The type of clothing varied from country to country, but always it seemed to be designed to make Jews and Christians appear inferior and foolish. In many countries the Jews were even required to go barefoot. They were also required to walk to the left of the Muslims. They were almost universally forbidden to ride horses, and even when riding donkeys, they were required to dismount upon meeting a Muslim.

Jews and Christians were often confined to special quarters, and these areas were usually shut up after dark. They were not allowed to enter certain streets of Muslim cities. This practice continued in Persia, Yemen, and North Africa until the nineteenth century. These *dhimmi* ghettos were frequently the scenes of awful pogroms and persecutions by infuriated Muslim mobs. At the whim of local rulers these pitiful quarters could be confiscated and emptied on short notice. Whether they lived inside or outside of these quarters, the houses of *dhimmi* could never be taller or more elaborate than the houses of their Muslim neighbors.

3. Religious discrimination

In Muslim lands, the construction of new churches and synagogues was generally forbidden. The restoration of certain pre-Islamic structures was permitted so long as they were not enlarged or transformed. *Dhimmi* places of worship were often ransacked, burned or demolished at the whim of the Muslims. This trend has continued right up through modern times. In Saudi Arabia, the government bulldozed the last Christian church in the kingdom in 1987. It was a unique 12th century structure found near the Yemen border.

Liturgical forms were strictly controlled. It was generally prohibited to ring church bells, sound shofars, publicly display crosses, icons, banners and other religious objects. Early photos taken during the middle of the nineteenth century confirm that even the Church of the Holy Sepulchre in Jerusalem had been stripped of both its cross and belfry.

In many Muslim lands, Jews and Christians had to bury their dead without mourning. *Dhimmi* graves had to be specially marked lest a Muslim should accidentally pray over the grave of an infidel. The cemeteries of *dhimmi* were not respected since they were considered as being from the realm of hell. Commonly they were desecrated or even destroyed completely, as occurred in Jerusalem during Jordanian rule (1948-1967). At that time the Jordanian army used Jewish gravestones from the Mount of Olives to line their latrines.

The *dhimmi* had to take great care showing respect to Muslim holy places. In North Africa, if Jews and Christians entered a mosque it was considered a capital offense. It was not even permitted for them to look into a mosque when passing by. Any such accusation, whether true or false, could cost the *dhimmi* his life. This was especially the case in all charges of blasphemy. The *dhimmi* communities were religiously harassed and sometimes forced to convert. For instance, in Yemen, it was required that every Jewish orphan child be converted to Islam.

Of course, marriage or sexual relations between *dhimmi* and Muslim women called for the death sentence, although Muslim men could marry a *dhimmi* woman. To the Muslim, there was something about the *dhimmi* that was unclean and impure. This concept affected all Muslim relations with *dhimmi* peoples.

Is the *dhimmi* concept still around, and does it show up in the modern-day concept of *jihad*? We may think these Muslim concepts are grossly discriminatory in this modern age, but they are still very much alive in Muslim thinking. They are particularly evident in current ideas of *jihad*. The Islamic idea of world dominion has changed very little since the days of Muhammad. Involved in the Islamic concept is the complete military, religious and political domination of conquered peoples (which should ultimately include the whole world); Arabization of these peoples and nations; the absolute claim to their lands; the suppression of their historical, religious, and political traditions; and the extinguishing of their cultural and social aspirations.

It is unthinkable for Muslims that conquered peoples should rise up and throw off the yoke of Islam. Such a response is an affront to the Muslim religion. For this very reason the Muslim *jihad* has raged against Israel. Israel is like a tiny island surrounded by a sea of Islam. Not only was Israel once within the domain of Islam, but until the current immigration wave, over 60 percent of her inhabitants were descendants of *dhimmi*, whether they were refugees from Arab countries or indigenous to the land.[28]

The Muslims have used *jihad*, which can be expressed in many ways, as a continuous weapon against Israel. It has been expressed through military, economic, political, and educational means. In spite of the current peace agreements, Israel is continually oppressed by active terrorism. In spite of the present peace agreements, the economic boycott of Israeli products continues.

The history and culture of Israel is regularly appropriated by the Muslims, denied and even eradicated whenever possible. Today because of vast Muslim influence in the world newscasts, newspapers, and magazines are often slanted against Israel. Even educational and reference materials are being slanted and twisted to the Muslim viewpoint.

Thus the *jihad* rages on and on, even in this modern day. But for Islam to succeed in its plan of total world domination, there must be a people who are willing to play the part of the *dhimmi*.

ISLAM'S GREATEST INSULT

In Islam there developed another unusual concept related to all other peoples and nations. This concept is critical for the understanding of events in the Middle East and elsewhere today. The god Allah, is to the Muslim, the true and only god. All other nations are to be in subjection to this god and to his prophet Muhammad. In fact the very word "Islam" means "subjection." In Islam there is the concept of *dar-al Islam*, that refers to the lands under subjugation by Islam. Then there is the concept of *dar al-Harb*, or the abode of war, referring to all lands under the infidels.[29]

In Islam there can be no permanent peace with such lands. In addition, all lands once subjected to Allah must remain in Allah's dominion. In Christianity, the belief is that God will avenge; that he is big enough to take care of himself. In Islam, it is incumbent upon the Muslim to avenge Allah. Thus *jihad* (holy war) becomes an urgent necessity in order to claim new lands, and especially to reclaim all lands that have been lost to Islam.

The latter, of course, is the very situation with modern Israel today. With the exception of the brief Crusader period, the Holy Land was in subjection to Islam from the seventh century until the end of World War I. It was bad enough for Islam's armies to be defeated by Christians in 732, and it was especially irritating for the Muslims to be pushed out of Spain by the Christians in 1492. It was an even further insult for them to become subjects of French and British "Christian" colonialism in the nineteenth and twentieth centuries. But the crowning insult to Islam and to Allah was having a hated Jewish state declare itself independent in their midst, and on land that was once claimed by Allah.

A further insult was having the Jews again lay claim to Jerusalem. By this time Jerusalem had become one of Islam's holy cities, along with Mecca and Medina. It had also become a focus of Islamic political aspirations. All this was clearly in reaction to the growing Jewish presence. We can begin to sense why a Jerusalem controlled by the Jews seems especially designed by God to send the surrounding Arab nations reeling (Zech. 12:2-3).

We can now glimpse why the Muslims have fought the establishment of Israel since the days of the earliest pioneers and why they have launched four unsuccessful wars and hundreds of terrorist operations to destroy Israel. Israel, who declared independence and gained crushing victories over confederated Islamic armies in 1948, 1967 and again in 1973, shook the Islamic world to the core. Egypt's President Nasser well expressed Islamic feeling when he said, "To the disaster of Palestine there is no parallel in human history."[30]

Abdel al-Rahman al-Bazzar, the former Prime Minister of Iraq and professor of law at the University of Baghdad, had this to add to Nasser's remarks:

> The great danger of Israel is due to its being an ideological threat to our nationalism which challenges our entire national existence in the entire region. The existence of Israel nullifies the unity of our homeland, the unity of our nation and the unity of our civilization, which embraces the whole of this one region. Moreover, the existence of Israel is a flagrant challenge to our philosophy of life and the ideals for which we live, and a total barrier against the values and aims to which we aspire in the world.[31]

How can such a problem, that has been seething for almost four thousand years, be solved by simply sitting down at the negotiating table? This seems very plausible and appropriate to the western mind, however, Islam can never truly agree to have an Israel in the Middle East. Israel is looked upon as a defilement, something unclean, in the midst of holy Arab nations. The very presence of Israel undermines the credibility of Islam. The Muslims are therefore obligated to declare an eternal *jihad* against Israel.

Many, even in Israel, think the nation can somehow appease this ancient hatred by giving up some of their hard won territory. Someone has remarked that if Israel gave up territory until she had only one square meter left on the sea coast, the holy war or *jihad* would continue until this square meter was brought back into the domain of the god Allah.

With this perspective we can understand how futile and senseless are all the so-called "peace talks," and the current "peace process." We can see how the more than 200 million Muslims in the Middle East see tiny Israel as a threat to Islam and why they are constantly building up their armaments. It explains how Islamic nations like Iraq and Libya, although they have no common borders with Israel, also feel threatened.

SCENARIO FOR AN ISLAMIC ARMAGEDDON

When we add to this situation the recent rise of Islamic Fundamentalism, we have an extremely explosive situation on our hands. This fundamentalism that has been largely nurtured by Iran, not only threatens Israel, but it threatens the more stable and complacent Arab states like Saudi Arabia, Jordan, and Egypt. What the oil crisis of the early seventies could not accomplish in bringing all nations to a showdown war with Israel, Islamic Fundamentalism may now begin to accomplish.

After all, theological motivation is a powerful tool. Just a thousand years ago it was theological motivation that brought hordes of Crusaders on horseback to Israel, all the way from their homes in farthest Europe. We might be wise to consider that the hordes of armies coming from the North and East, which are spoken of by many of the prophets, just might be fanatical Muslimarmies. These armies could come from the remote reaches of Azerbaijan, from Iraq, from Iran, from Pakistan, and even from China's Xinjiang region. Of course, these invaders would always be gleefully assisted by Israel's Muslim neighbors.

The horrors of the Book of Revelation seem closer when we realize that some of these radical nations are now equipped with the most sophisticated chemical and biological weapons.

FINAL CONCLUSIONS

For those who believe that the Bible is the word of God, Islam represents a significant threat to both Judaism and Christianity. For those who do not believe the Bible, Islam is probably no more important than any other religion.

It is a time for Bible believers to be vigilant. Today many Christians including some famous preachers, have become close friends and supporters of Yasser Arafat, the terrorist PLO leader. Apparently they have not stopped to consider that this man represents everything that is abhorrent to Christianity. He is a mass murderer, thief and unblinking liar. He is diametrically opposed to Israel and the biblical heritage. Although he may not be the antichrist spoken of in the Bible, he certainly is against Christ and is an antichrist type. For sure, he is a Muslim and stands for everything Islam has always stood for, including the complete subjugation of all Christians on the face of the earth.

The threat that Islam imposes should be clear to us by the fact that this religion is firmly planted on the Temple Mount with two of its shrines, The Dome of the Rock and El Aqsa Mosque. This should be a wake-up call for us. Bear in mind that this is the spot where God will establish his throne (Jer. 3:17). There is no other religion on the face of the earth that boldly makes such a challenge to God. Islam may therefore be called the most dangerous of the earth's religions. It is uniquely situated for an end-time confrontation with the living God, the God of Israel.

We can surmise that Islam is the devil's answer, and somehow a part of his final plan of attack to overcome both Judaism and Christianity. The Dome of the Rock, with its Quranic inscriptions against the Son of God, stands as a constant blasphemy against Christianity. For the Christians and Jews, Islam could well play some part in the "abomination of desolation" spoken of by Daniel long ago.

Wherever Islam has gained complete sway, as in Iran and in Saudi Arabia, what is called *sharia* law has been put into effect. This law includes many crude punishments that seem to have passed to modern times from the seventh century. These are punishments like chopping off hands for stealing, and chopping off heads for greater offenses. Perhaps we should pay closer attention to the interesting verse in Revelation 20:4, where it is said:

And I saw the souls of those who had been beheaded because of their testimony for Jesus and because of the word of God. They had not worshipped the beast or his image and had not received his mark on their foreheads or their hands. They came to life and reigned with Christ a thousand years.

STUDY QUESTIONS:

Why should Islam be considered a greater threat to the Judeo/Christian tradition than all other religions?

Allah, is a designation often used in the Middle East for the God of Judaism and Christianity. Why does this not seem appropriate?

With the Islamic understanding of treaties, based on the treaty of Hudaibiyah, of what value are the agreements western nations are currently making with the Muslims? What value are the agreements being made between Israel and the Palestinian Authority?

Why are Muslim nations compelled to push the Jews out of the Middle East?

NOTES

1. Robert Morey, *The Islamic Invasion, Confronting the World's Fastest Growing Religion* (Eugene, OR: Harvest House Publishers, 1992) pp. 5-6.
2. Frederick M. Denny, *Islam*, (San Francisco: Harper & Row, Publishers, 1987) p. 110.
3. See Jim Gerrish, "Islam, Religion of the Other Brother," *Dispatch From Jerusalem*, 2nd. Qtr. 1990 p. 1. I have drawn heavily on this earlier article for my content here.
4. Morey, *The Islamic Invasion*, p. 71.
5. Robert Payne, *The History of Islam*, (New York: Dorsett Press, c.1959 pub. 1990) p. 12.
6. Morey, *The Islamic Invasion*, p. 71-72.
7. Payne, *The History of Islam*, p. 55.
8. Denny, *Islam*, p. 21.
9. Payne, *The History of Islam*, p. 23
10. Payne, *The History of Islam*, pp. 71-72.
11. Payne, *The History of Islam*, p. 37.
12. Morey, *The Islamic Invasion*, p. 83.
13. Denny, *Islam*, pp. 56-57.

14. Morey, *The Islamic Invasion,* p. 19.
15. Morey, *The Islamic Invasion,* p. 22.
16. Morey, *The Islamic Invasion,* p. 86.
17. Thomas Lippman, *Understanding Islam, An Introduction to the Muslim World,* (Penguin Books USA Inc., revised edition c 1982, 1990) p. 54.
18. Quoted in Samuel Katz, *Battleground, Fact and Fancy in Palestine,* (New York: Bantam Books, 1973) p. 134.
19. Quoted in Samuel Katz, *Battleground, Fact and Fancy in Palestine,* p. 134.
20. Payne, *The History of Islam,* p. 96.
21. Bernard Lewis, *The Middle East, 2000 Years of History From the Rise of Christianity to the Present Day,* (London: Phoenix Books Ltd., a division of Orion Books, Ltd., 1995) p. 68.
22. Bernard Lewis, *The Middle East, 2000 Years of History From the Rise of Christianity to the Present Day,* p. 69.
23. Bernard Lewis, *The Middle East, 2000 Years of History From the Rise of Christianity to the Present Day,* p. 69.
24. Bat Ye'or, *The Dhimmi, Jews and Christians Under Islam,* (Cranbury, NJ: Associated University Presses, English edition, 1985) p. 45. This is an excellent work with massive reproduction of original documents. I have drawn heavily upon her information in this section.
25. See Jim Gerrish, "The *Dhimmi* People: Jews and Christians Under Islam," *Dispatch From Jerusalem,* 1st Quarter, 1993, pp. 8-9. I have reproduced much information from this earlier article here.
26. Bat Ye'or, *The Dhimmi, Jews and Christians Under Islam,* pp. 51-66
27. Bat Ye'or, *The Dhimmi, Jews and Christians Under Islam,* p. 201.
28. Bat Ye'or, *The Dhimmi, Jews and Christians Under Islam,* p. 137.
29. Bat Ye'or, *The Dhimmi, Jews and Christians Under Islam,* p. 45.
30. Quoted in Bat Ye'or, *The Dhimmi, Jews and Christians Under Islam,* p. 122.
31. Quoted in Bat Ye'or, *The Dhimmi, Jews and Christians Under Islam,* p. 123.

- 5 -

THE LIE OF THE LAND, OR HOW TO STEAL A HERITAGE

For centuries the devil, that unseen spiritual enemy, has lied about the people of Israel. It therefore shouldn't surprise us that he has lied about the land of Israel as well. It is probably the most lied about piece of real estate on the face of the earth today. In this regard, the scripture assures us that the devil is a liar and the father of lies (John 8:44).

Let us carefully look at the land and try to separate fact from fiction. We need to be prepared however, because peeling off the lies and fiction will be much like peeling an onion.

Today we hear much about Palestine, Palestinians, Palestinian rights, and even a Palestinian state. Often the world media shows Palestinian leadership making demands upon a supposed "recalcitrant" Israel.

It might surprise the reader to learn that far into the 20th century, Arabs vehemently denied being called Palestinians, while strangely, it was the Jews who were referred to by this title. In the early 20th century, the Jewish English newspaper, *The Jerusalem Post* was called *The Palestine Post,* and the Israel Philharmonic Orchestra was then called the Palestine Philharmonic Orchestra.[1] Even today, one of the largest Jewish philanthropic funds for Israel still carries its pre-Israel name, the Palestine Endowment Fund (PEF).

The esteemed Arab historian, Philip Hitti, stated before the Anglo-American Committee of Inquiry in 1946, "There is no such thing as Palestine in [Arab] history, absolutely not."[2] Another noted Arab leader, Auni Bey Abdul-Hadi told the Peel Commission a few years earlier, "There is no such country [as Palestine]! 'Palestine' is a term the Zionists invented! There is no Palestine in the Bible. 'Palestine' is alien to us; it is the Zionist who introduced it!"[3]

In 1939, the Arab historian George Antonius spoke of Palestine as being a province of greater Syria. Even as late as 1974, Syria's President Assad also claimed Palestine as a part of his country. According to researcher, Joan Peters, the one identity that was never considered prior to the war of 1967 was "Arab Palestinian."[4]

How could the "Palestinian" identity do such a "flip-flop" in the last part of the twentieth century? Where did the name "Palestine" originate anyway? Is it mentioned in the Bible? Let us attempt to answer these questions looking at the Bible and at the last two millennia of history.

PALESTINE, ITS BEGINNINGS

By thumbing through the atlas at the back of our Bible we may see maps that read, "Palestine in the time of the early monarchy" [time of David and Solomon]; Palestine in New Testament times, etc. It might surprise us to realize that these descriptions contain misnomers. There was no Palestine in the time of David, or in New Testament times. In the New Testament the land was referred to as Israel, not as Palestine (Matt. 2:20). Jesus was not a Palestinian, contrary to what the Palestinian Liberation Organization (PLO) has claimed.[5] In fact, no one had ever heard of Palestine in his day.

---

the amazing historical fact is that the Jews were the very first "Palestinian refugees"

Palestine was a name given to the land of Judea after the unsuccessful ending of the Second Jewish Revolt against Rome in AD 135. It was a name given in derision by the Romans, in an attempt to erase all Jewish connections to the land. The land was re-named after the ancient Philistines, those proverbial enemies of Israel, in an attempt to sever its Jewish connection. At the time, Rome killed or expelled many of the Jews. Because of this, the amazing historical fact is that the Jews were the very first "Palestinian refugees."[6]

Palestine is therefore not mentioned in the Bible. Those who are using a King James Version will find "Palestine" in Joel 3:4, but in this place the Hebrew clearly refers to the land of the Philistines. Modern translations clarify this by using the designation "Philistia" in this passage.

The New American Standard Bible does have some interesting title headings that read, "Joshua's conquest of Southern Palestine" (Josh. 10:29); and "Northern Palestine Taken" (Josh. 11:1), but again these are unfortunate anachronisms supplied by editors, and are certainly not found in the Bible text.

ANCIENT THIEVES

The Romans were not the first people in history to try and steal the heritage of Israel, they just did the most thorough job of it. The Romans destroyed the land, killed thousands of its inhabitants and sold many of the survivors into slavery. Afterwards, they tried to steal the land away by renaming it. They also tried to steal the city of Jerusalem by placing a pagan shrine on the Temple Mount. The city was renamed *Aeilia Capitolina,* and Jews were forbidden to enter it.

The name *Aeilia* was the family name of Hadrian, and *Capitolina* was another name for the god Jupiter. This renaming was an attempt to erase the connection between the God of the Bible and his chosen city, thus supplanting it with pagan domination.

We see many instances of ancient people trying to take the land of Israel in biblical times. Perhaps the earliest instance

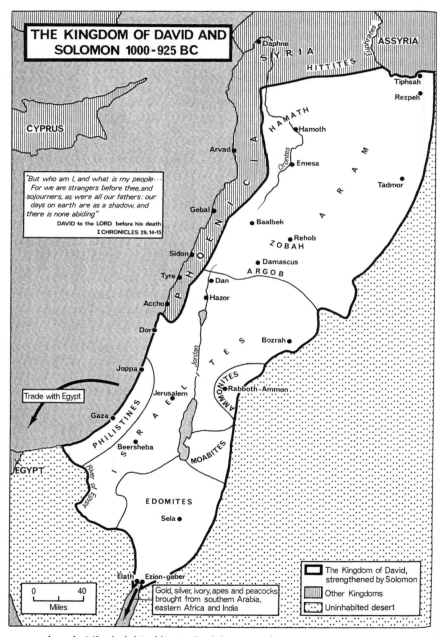

**THE KINGDOM OF DAVID AND
SOLOMON 1000-925 BC**

ASSYRIA

Daphne

SYRIA

HITTITES

Euphrates

Tiphsah

Rezpeh

CYPRUS

HAMATH

Hamoth

Arvad

Orontes

Emesa

Tadmor

"But who am I, and what is my people...
For we are strangers before thee, and
sojourners, as were all our fathers: our
days on earth are as a shadow, and
there is none abiding"
DAVID to the LORD before his death
I CHRONICLES 29, 14-15

Gebal

Baalbek

Rehob

ZOBAH

Sidon

Damascus

Tyre

Dan

ARGOB

Accho

Hazor

Dor

Jordan

Bozrah

Joppa

Trade with Egypt

Jerusalem

Rabboth-Ammon

Gaza

AMMONITES

Beersheba

MOABITES

EGYPT

River of Egypt

EDOMITES

Sela

Elath   Ezion-geber

0	40
Miles	

Gold, silver, ivory, apes and peacocks
brought from southern Arabia,
eastern Africa and India

☐ The Kingdom of David,
   strengthened by Solomon

▥ Other Kingdoms

⬚ Uninhabited desert

Israel at the height of its territorial possession. (Courtesy Martin Gilbert) is found in Judges 11:13. Here, when the judge Jephthah asked why the Ammonites were threatening invasion, the king answered:

> ...*Because Israel took away my land when they came up out of Egypt, from the Arnon as far as the Jabbok, and to the Jordan. Now therefore, restore those lands peaceably.*

It didn't seem to matter much to this ancient king that the Israelites had completely avoided Ammonite territory when they came out of Egypt. They avoided Ammon in order to follow God's specific command, since the Ammonites were their relatives (Deut. 2:19).

Many other ancient enemies of Israel also tried to take the land. Most of them tried by force and failed. Some of these were the Midianites, Ishmaelites, Edomites, and Moabites. During the time of the return from Babylon we see an interesting episode. Nehemiah was attempting to rebuild the wall around the devastated city of Jerusalem when he was confronted by the confederation of Geshem the Arab, Tobiah the Ammonite (area of today's Jordan) and Sanballat (from today's "West Bank"). They all claimed an interest in the city and demanded a part in its restoration. Nehemiah was certainly not a child of "political correctness." He boldly spoke the truth to these adversaries in words that would petrify today's political establishment:

> *I answered them by saying, "The God of heaven will give us success. We his servants will start rebuilding, but as for you, you have no share in Jerusalem or any claim or historic right to it."* (Neh. 2:20)

The attacks of surrounding enemies in biblical times are carefully recorded for us in Psalm 83. Also recorded is their clear sworn purpose against Israel. It is said of these enemies:

> *With cunning they conspire against your people; they plot against those you cherish. "Come," they say, "let us destroy them as a nation, that the name of Israel be remembered no more"* (Psa. 83:3-4).

These enemies, like the two Midianite princes Oreb and Zeeb, were saying: ..."*Let us take possession of the pasture-lands of God*" (vs. 11-12).

This Psalm was probably not completely fulfilled until the miraculous war of 1967. Charles DeLoach in his book, *Seeds of Conflict,* states that before 1967, the Arab nations had often come against Israel, but prior to that time they had never all conspired together to come against the nation. He adds that even Iraq (which includes ancient Assyria), mentioned in verse 8 of this Psalm, also sent a contingent of 5,000 troops in 1967. According to the prophetic words of this Psalm, they came to help the children of Lot (Modern Jordan).[7]

In later centuries the Byzantine Christians repeated what the ancient nations and what the Romans had done earlier. They claimed Jerusalem as their own and forbade Jews to enter the city. They built their shrines in Jerusalem and turned the Temple Mount into a garbage dump.

With the rise of Islam in the seventh century AD, we begin to see the truly diabolical dimensions to this ancient contest. The land of Israel was the first major target of the conquering Islamic armies. Somehow after their conquest, they were strangely compelled to build their Dome of the Rock and Al Aqsa mosque on the Temple Mount. By doing this, they drove their claim deep into the very heart of Judaism.

For the next 1300 years, with the exception of the brief Crusader episode, Islam would control the land of Israel. To some degree this was a fulfillment of Ezekiel 36:2, 5:

> ...*The enemy said of you, "Aha! The ancient heights have become our possession"... this is what the Sovereign LORD says: "In my burning zeal I have spoken against the rest of the nations, and against all Edom, for with glee and with malice in their hearts they made my land their own possession so that they might plunder its pastureland."*

They certainly did plunder the country. During the many centuries of Muslim possession, the land was neglected, ravaged by war, overtaxed, overgrazed by goats, and raided by

Bedouin tribes. In more modern times, the Muslim Turks even went to the extreme of taxing the trees.[8] Of course we can imagine what poverty stricken peasants did – they simply cut the trees down. The once beautiful Israel became a howling wasteland.

THE WILDERNESS AND SOLITARY PLACE

The PLO leader, Yasser Arafat, in one of his many attempts at revisionist history, would have us believe that Palestine was a virtual Arab paradise prior to the coming of the evil Jews. He says, "The Jewish invasion began in 1881 ...Palestine was then a verdant area, inhabited mainly by an Arab people in the course of building its life and dynamically enriching its indigenous culture."[9] Enough for revisionist history. Let us now take a look at the facts.

Numerous travelers to the Holy Land in the last three hundred years bear uniform witness to its almost total desolation. Among travelers in the 1700s, were British archaeologist, Thomas Shaw, and French author and historian Count Constantine Volney. Shaw commented that Palestine "was lacking people to till its fertile soil."[10] Volney speaks of the provinces as being laid waste. He gives an example of one province in these words:

> ...the traveler meets with nothing but houses in ruins, cisterns rendered useless, and fields abandoned. Those who cultivated them have fled...[11]

According to Volney's estimate, the whole population of Palestine in 1785 amounted to no more than 200,000 souls.[12]

Another traveler, Alphonse de Lamartine, describes the city of Jerusalem in 1835:

> Outside the gates of Jerusalem we saw indeed no living object, heard no living sound, we found the same void the same silence ... as we should have expected before the entombed gates of Pompeii or Herculaneam ... a complete eternal silence reigns in the town, on the highways, in the country ... the tomb of a whole people.[13]

In 1857, the British Consul in Palestine reported: "The country is in a considerable degree empty of inhabitants and therefore its greatest need is that of a body of population..."[14] By the middle of the nineteenth century one estimate is that the population of Palestine had actually shrunk to between 50,000 and 100,000 people.[15]

One of the most descriptive and informative accounts of the Holy Land was that given by American author Mark Twain. Twain departed on his tour in 1867, exactly one hundred years before Israel would gain much of the land in the miraculous Six-Day War. Twain commented about the now beautiful Galilee area:

> It is seven in the morning, and as we are in the country, the grass ought to be sparkling with dew, the flowers enriching the air with their fragrance, and the birds singing in the trees. But alas, there is no dew here, nor flowers, nor birds, nor trees. There is a plain and an unshaded lake, and beyond them some barren mountains.[16]

The off-handed remarks of Twain have shed much light on the condition of the whole area. He and his group traveled from the Sea of Galilee to Mount Tabor. He remarks, "We reached Tabor safely... We never saw a human being on the whole route..."[17] As his Palestinian pilgrimage ended at Jaffa, Twain summarized the whole tour by saying:

> Of all the lands there are for dismal scenery, I think Palestine must be the prince. The hills are barren, they are dull of color, they are unpicturesque in shape. The valleys are unsightly deserts fringed with a feeble vegetation that has an expression about it of being sorrowful and despondent... Palestine sits in sackcloth and ashes. Over it broods the spell of a curse that has withered its fields and fettered its energies... Renowned Jerusalem itself, the stateliest name in history, has lost all its ancient grandeur, and is become a pauper village... Palestine is desolate and unlovely.[18]

THE BRITISH, ISHMAEL AND OIL

The first *aliya* (Jewish immigration wave) arrived in Palestine in 1882. This wave primarily consisted of Russians who had just suffered greatly from the terrible pogroms. These new immigrants, like the many that would come after them, arrived as idealists desiring to rebuild their ancient nation with their own hands. They purchased land, drained mosquito infested swamps, planted trees and crops, and began to rebuild their cities. They had some success, in spite of the uncooperative Turkish government that exercised a corrupt and faltering jurisdiction over the land.

By the end of the First World War, Great Britain forced the Turks out of Palestine and took control in their stead. Also in 1917, the British originated the famous Balfour Declaration, which looked favorably upon the establishing of a Jewish national home in Palestine. The area involved included both sides of the Jordan River. In pursuit of this declaration the League of Nations at its San Remo Conference in 1920, granted to Great Britain what is known as the Palestine Mandate instructing Britain to establish a home for the Jewish people in Palestine.[19]

In God's great providence, the Jewish people of Palestine now had a legal guardian. We might say that Great Britain was in a unique position of all nations on earth, to work together with God in his age-old plan for the restoration of Israel. It was a great honor that had been accorded to just one other nation in history, to Persia in ancient times. Britain after the war was perhaps the most powerful nation on earth, with massive land holdings and colonies spanning the globe. What a bright future she had in store.

Unfortunately, Britain did not live up to these high expectations. She terribly bungled her divine assignment. The problem apparently began early with a group of British officials serving in Egypt and Sudan. They began to envision the vast Arab-speaking areas in the Middle East consolidated under British control.[20] This concept was in direct opposition and greatly detrimental to Zionists' dreams. Almost from its outset the British Mandate began to be twisted toward these ends.

A few years later, there was the additional enticement of the discovery of oil in the surrounding Arab lands. Soon the British spy Jack Philby was working hand in hand with Ibn Saud of Arabia. His purpose was not only to help Britain get an interest in the vast oil wealth, but to also spy on the Zionist. Loftus puts it simply, "The Jews were an obstacle to the smooth flow of Arab oil."[21]

One of the very first acts of Britain's new twisted policy was to lop off three-quarters of the Mandate area and present it to Abdullah ibn-Hussein.[22] This included all the area of Palestine east of the Jordan River, an area formerly parceled out to the Children of Israel by Moses (Num. 32:33). Also in Zechariah 10:10, God speaks of bringing his children home in the end days to Gilead which is a part of this eastern area. This vast area was called Tansjordan (today's Jordan), and was immediately closed to all Jewish settlement.

We constantly hear of the "West Bank" in the TV news, as if the Jordan River only had one bank. The "East Bank" that we never hear about was taken from the Jews by the British. It was given to form this first "Palestinian state" of Jordan in the twentieth century.

The British then began to pursue their new selfish policy by placing many restrictions upon the Jews. The British ruling group in Jerusalem saw the Balfour Declaration as an impediment to their plans and were determined to undermine it. To this end they helped mobilize the Arab resistance. Suddenly in 1919 the tiny militant Arab movement mushroomed with great explosive force. This movement arose with British backing.[23]

In pursuit of their shameful plan, the British began to patronize Haj Amin el Husseini, an Arab radical who later became a Nazi collaborator. In 1920, Col. Waters Taylor, Chief of Staff in Palestine, suggested to his Arab contacts that it would be advisable to organize anti-Jewish riots. The riots took place just before Easter in 1920, but only after the British had safely withdrawn their forces from the Old City.

The resulting Arab mobs swarmed over the city echoing the cry, "the government is with us."[24]

The Arab mobs, joined by Arab policemen rampaged, beat, killed, raped and looted for three days. When it was finished, six Jews were killed and 211 were wounded. In the end, the British arrested two Arabs for rape and twenty Jews for organizing their own self defense.[25]

After the riots, the British pursued their goals head-long by elevating Haj Amin el Husseini, to the position of *Mufti* of Jerusalem. He later became President of the Supreme Moslem Council, a body also established by the British. The mechanism was now in place for organized persecution of the Jews in their own God-given land.

Another weapon the British used quite effectively was an opening of the borders of the Mandate to Arabs from all the surrounding nations. The new Jewish industry in the land had created many jobs and made the land very attractive to those impoverished in nearby countries.

According to author and researcher, Joan Peters, the total population of Western Palestine when Jewish colonization began was between 300,000-400,000 people. This figure included Jews, Christians and wandering Bedouin tribes. Of this figure Peters calculates that about 200,000 Muslims were actually living in Western Palestine (west of the Jordan River) in 1882.[26]

Besides the 200,000 Muslim Arabs in Western Palestine other thousands were added by natural increase. Then Peters calculates that according to the most conservative figures, 170,000 Arab immigrants entered the land. They were purposely never recorded by the British.[27] Peters remarks of the Arab newcomers that they "...immediately acquired the status of 'indigenous native population since time immemorial...' "[28]

The British not only turned their backs upon illegal Arab immigration, they curtailed Jewish immigration and finally brought it to a standstill. They did this at the precise time when the Holocaust was looming in Europe and six million doomed Jews had no place on earth to flee.

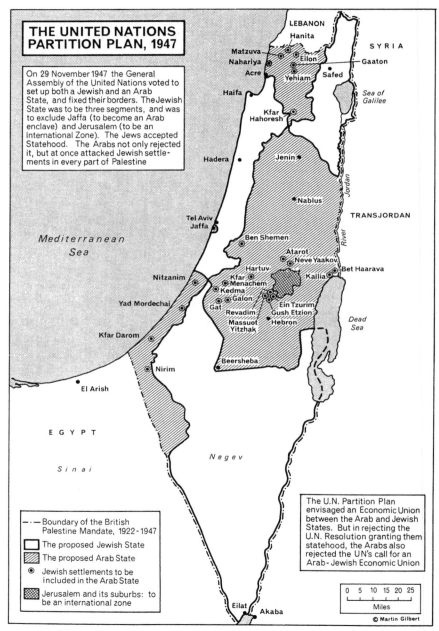

THE UNITED NATIONS PARTITION PLAN, 1947

On 29 November 1947 the General Assembly of the United Nations voted to set up both a Jewish and an Arab State, and fixed their borders. The Jewish State was to be three segments, and was to exclude Jaffa (to become an Arab enclave) and Jerusalem (to be an International Zone). The Jews accepted Statehood. The Arabs not only rejected it, but at once attacked Jewish settlements in every part of Palestine

LEBANON
Hanita
SYRIA
Matzuva
Nahariya
Eilon
Gaaton
Acre
Yehiam
Safed
Haifa
Sea of Galilee
Kfar Hahoresh
Hadera
Jenin
Mediterranean Sea
Nablus
TRANSJORDAN
Tel Aviv
Jaffa
Ben Shemen
Atarot
Neve Yaakov
Hartuv
Bet Haarava
Nitzanim
Kfar Menachem
Kallia
Yad Mordechai
Kedma
Galon
Gat
Ein Tzurim
Revadim
Gush Etzion
Massuot Yitzhak
Hebron
Dead Sea
Kfar Darom
Beersheba
Nirim
El Arish
Jordan River

EGYPT

Negev

Sinai

The U.N. Partition Plan envisaged an Economic Union between the Arab and Jewish States. But in rejecting the U.N. Resolution granting them statehood, the Arabs also rejected the UN's call for an Arab-Jewish Economic Union

— · — Boundary of the British Palestine Mandate, 1922-1947

☐ The proposed Jewish State

▨ The proposed Arab State

◉ Jewish settlements to be included in the Arab State

▩ Jerusalem and its suburbs: to be an international zone

Eilat
Akaba

0 5 10 15 20 25
Miles

© Martin Gilbert

The United Nations Partition Plan of 1947. *(Courtesy Martin Gilbert)*

In the twenty-six years of the British Mandate, only about 400,000 Jews were allowed into their very own country by their British guardians.[29]   This was the country assured to them by the British Balfour Declaration and the Palestine Mandate.

All through the period of the Mandate there were various riots and revolts, many of them at best tolerated or at worst instigated by the British. The so-called "Arab Revolt" of 1936-1939, was a cooperative action by the British and the Arabs.[30] After the infamous British "White Paper" of 1939, virtually closing the land to Jewish immigration, the Jewish resistance to British administration began to grow.

The Jews dropped their resistance during the Second World War and fought along with Britain and the Allies. However, at the close of the war their resistance was continued. In time, the British were forced to cast the now "hot potato" of Palestine back into the hands of the United Nations.

THE PARTITION PLAN AND INDEPENDENCE

Some three fourths of the proposed area of settlement outlined in the Balfour Declaration had already been given away by Britain in order to form the Arab/Muslim state of Transjordan.   The nations, not content with this, would attempt to steal away what remained in western Palestine.

In 1947 the UN proposed its partition plan for the area. The plan suggested that the Arabs receive most of the mountainous area. According to the Bible, the mountainous area was primarily where the ancient Israelites lived. It might be referred to as "biblical Israel" or Judea and Samaria. Most of the ancient biblical cities like Hebron and Shechem (Nablus) are in this area. The plan proposed that Israel would receive the desert of the Negev and precarious and indefensible strips of land along the Mediterranean coast and in the Galilee. In effect, the proposal called for Jewish and Palestinian states west of the Jordan River.

The Jews, betrayed, beleaguered, oppressed and almost annihilated by the Holocaust, agreed to the partition plan,

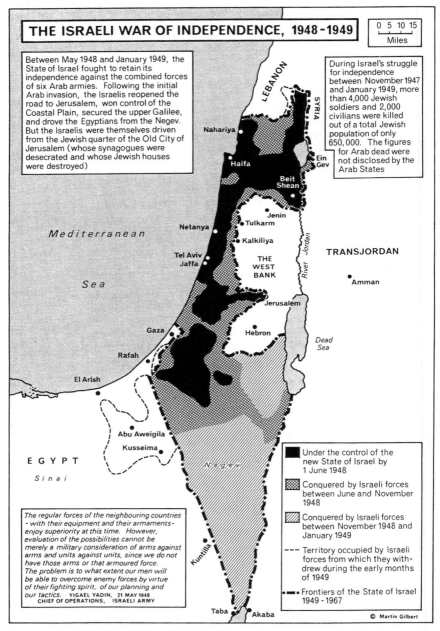

THE ISRAELI WAR OF INDEPENDENCE, 1948-1949

0 5 10 15
Miles

Between May 1948 and January 1949, the State of Israel fought to retain its independence against the combined forces of six Arab armies. Following the initial Arab invasion, the Israelis reopened the road to Jerusalem, won control of the Coastal Plain, secured the upper Galilee, and drove the Egyptians from the Negev. But the Israelis were themselves driven from the Jewish quarter of the Old City of Jerusalem (whose synagogues were desecrated and whose Jewish houses were destroyed)

During Israel's struggle for independence between November 1947 and January 1949, more than 4,000 Jewish soldiers and 2,000 civilians were killed out of a total Jewish population of only 650,000. The figures for Arab dead were not disclosed by the Arab States

LEBANON

SYRIA

Nahariya

Haifa

Ein Gev

Beit Shean

Jenin
Tulkarm

Netanya

Kalkiliya

Tel Aviv
Jaffa

THE WEST BANK

River Jordan

TRANSJORDAN

Amman

Jerusalem

Gaza

Hebron

Dead Sea

Rafah

El Arish

Abu Aweigila

Kusseima

EGYPT

Negev

Sinai

Mediterranean

Sea

The regular forces of the neighbouring countries - with their equipment and their armaments- enjoy superiority at this time. However, evaluation of the possibilities cannot be merely a military consideration of arms against arms and units against units, since we do not have those arms or that armoured force. The problem is to what extent our men will be able to overcome enemy forces by virtue of their fighting spirit, of our planning and our tactics. YIGAEL YADIN, 21 MAY 1948
CHIEF OF OPERATIONS, ISRAELI ARMY

■ Under the control of the new State of Israel by 1 June 1948

▨ Conquered by Israeli forces between June and November 1948

▧ Conquered by Israeli forces between November 1948 and January 1949

--- Territory occupied by Israeli forces from which they with-drew during the early months of 1949

■—• Frontiers of the State of Israel 1949 -1967

Kuntilla

Taba   Akaba

© Martin Gilbert

The Israeli War of Independence. *(Courtesy Martin Gilbert)*

however the Arabs vehemently opposed it, since they wanted the whole land. The plan was nevertheless approved by the UN on November 29, 1947, thus clearing the way for the establishment of the State of Israel.

In the days and weeks following the partition, there were riots and murders throughout the land. By the spring, the Arabs cut the road to Jerusalem, isolating and almost starving the city. The fighting continued between Arabs and Jewish defense groups resulting in an increasing toll of human life.

After the British finally evacuated the land, the Jews moved to declare their independence. On May 14, 1948 the nation of Israel was born. Immediately on May 15, the newborn nation was attacked by the six Arab armies of Egypt, Syria, Transjordan, Lebanon, Saudi Arabia and Iraq.

The Jews had few weapons, because weapons had been denied them by their British guardians. Even with their many limitations they defended themselves and then advanced to gain the coastal areas, the Upper Galilee, and the Negev. In the process, however, they suffered a tragic blow. The army of Transjordan, which had been trained and generously equipped by the British, occupied what is today's West Bank (biblical Israel) with its Old City of Jerusalem and Temple Mount.

The Jordanians, in their attempt to obliterate the ancient Jewish presence in Jerusalem, exiled the Jews and then destroyed the Jewish quarter, including 58 synagogues.[31] The ancient and hallowed Jewish cemetery on the Mount of Olives did not escape their wrath. Some 75 percent of its tombstones were removed in the building of a hotel and to pave the paths to army latrines.[32] From 1948 until 1967, no Jew could enter the Old City or pray at the Western Wall.

What an irony we see in the actions of the Jordanians. Their very existence had resulted from the outright misappropriation of three fourths of the original Jewish area of settlement. This area was originally given to the Jews, not only by God, but by the nations of the world in the San Remo Conference of 1920. Now it had been given by the British to found Transjordan. It was almost a first act of their administration. Now the Jordanians blatantly stole the area of the West Bank. We can safely say they stole it because not even the Arab nations recognized this occupation. The only nations recognizing it were Britain and Pakistan.[33]

At the same time, the Egyptians took control of the Gaza Strip. With the carving out of these two areas the stage was set for much of the political wrangling and military conflict that would ensue for the coming half century.

Although tiny Israel had defended itself against the combined might of six well-equipped Arab armies, there was more to come. In 1956 the Egyptians sealed off the Israeli port of Eilat by blockading the Strait of Tiran. In addition, numerous terrorist attacks were launched from the Egyptian territory of Gaza and the Sinai. Israel responded in what is known as the Sinai Campaign of October-November, 1956.

The British and French, who had been angered by Egypt's closing of the Suez Canal, were also involved in this campaign. In this action Israel took the whole Sinai, but due to UN and US pressure was forced to withdraw.

The problem with the Sinai and with Egypt was not solved. Although UN forces were stationed in the Sinai, they did not prevent Egypt from returning, setting the stage and repeating the blockade of the Strait of Tiran in 1967.

In addition to Egypt's belligerence, the nations of Syria, Iraq and Saudi Arabia moved their troops menacingly toward Israel's borders. There were united cries of *jihad* (holy war) from the surrounding Arab countries. Israel pre-empted the attack and the miraculous Six Day War of 1967 ensued. Israel again defeated combined Arab armies, gaining the whole Sinai, the Golan Heights, and the West Bank, including the Old City and Temple Mount.

Arab nations, slow to learn, would attack Israel again on her holiest day, Yom Kippur, 1973. Then followed endless terrorist attacks launched from all surrounding nations.

RISE OF THE PLO

With the terrible defeat in 1967 and the dreadful loss of Arab prestige, the Arab campaign to obliterate Israel took a new turn. After their humiliation, the Arab nations realized their chances of defeating Israel on the battlefield were slim. The new campaign would seek to wear Israel down with terror attacks while at the same time defeating her in the political realm.

A ready tool of this new campaign was the Palestine Liberation Organization (PLO). The organization, which was actually formed in Egypt in 1964, was ultimately headed by one who has become infamous to many Jews, Rahman Abdul Rauf Arafat al-Qudwa al-Husseini, alias Yasser Arafat.

Arafat's grandparents on his mother's side were Husseinis from Palestine and were thus connected by blood to the Mufti of Jerusalem, also a Husseini.[34] The Husseini family over the decades has produced several notable adversaries of Israel.

Arafat was most likely born in Cairo and not in Jerusalem.[35] As a youth he did spend some time in Jerusalem, as a member of an Arab gang. He attacked unarmed Jews, smashed and looted Jewish shops and was involved in other such activities.

One of his classmates described him as "a fat moody boy who managed to frighten everyone a little ... His eyes were hypnotic, and they could stop you cold."[36] One acquaintance of the youthful Arafat described him as "particularly brutal" and one who "grew crazed at the sight of our blood."[37] One of his Egyptian acquaintances described him in this way: "He had a certain charm which he could use to great advantage. But he also had a dark streak, a sort of permanent irrational anger that was always simmering below the surface."[38]

In 1949-50, Arafat became a member of the Mufti's youth gang in Gaza. In time he organized several other gangs and became their leader. Finally he became an engineering student at Cairo University. There he joined the extremist Muslim Brotherhood.

He had a lackluster stint in the Egyptian Army and finally was expelled from Egypt when the radical Muslim Brotherhood was outlawed. His name was actually carried on Egypt's official blacklist until 1968. After his expulsion he worked as an engineer in Kuwait, doing mostly plumbing jobs.

It was while in Kuwait that the concept of *Fatah* was born. The name was a reversed acronym for *Harakat at-Tahrir al-Filastin,* meaning the Movement for the Liberation of Palestine. It was not necessarily the idea of Arafat, but due to his financial genius and industry he soon rose to the top of the organization. Arafat also was the publisher of the newspaper *Our Palestine,* which promoted the viewpoint of *Fatah.* In time, *Fatah* became a major component of the PLO and ultimately Arafat became Chairman of the whole PLO organization.

Later, as leader of the PLO, Arafat became directly responsible for some of the bloodiest terror attacks in Israel's history. These included the murder of 11 members of the Israeli delegation at the Munich Olympics in 1972; the killing of 24 and wounding of 64 other Israelis at the Ma'alot school in 1974; and The Coastal Road Massacre, killing 21 Israelis in 1978.[39]

THE PLO PATH OF DESTRUCTION

The PLO became an umbrella organization for the many other terrorist groups that began in the 1960s and 1970s. Most of these groups arose due to splits and wrangling between various PLO officials. Arafat's Fatah would continue to form the backbone and dominant component of the whole structure.

An incomplete list of other organizations would include the Palestinian Liberation Army (PLA); Saika; The Popular Front for the Liberation of Palestine (PFLP) directed by George Habash; The Popular Democratic Front for the Liberation of Palestine (PDFLP) directed by Neyef Hawatmeh; the PFLP-General Command headed by Ahmed Jebril; The Palestine

Liberation Front (PFL); The Arab Liberation Front (AFL); and Black September.[40]

Although there has been deep rivalry between these groups there is one thing they always have in common – their hatred for Israel. They vow to root Israel out of every square foot of the Holy Land, and not just the "West Bank." This fact has been made abundantly clear by the symbols of all these groups. Their emblems picture the whole land of Israel as the object of Palestinian conquest.

The PLO and its affiliated groups have always relied upon terror to accomplish their end goal. Yasser Arafat is the first and only speaker to ever address the UN General Assembly while wearing a pistol. He held out an olive branch and gave the world the choice of the olive branch or his gun. Although this was a veiled threat, the whole assembly still broke into wild acclamation.[41]

Such violence has been expressed by the PLO, that few of their Arab brother nations are willing to give them assistance. In 1970, Jordan waged an all out war against the PLO following that organization's violent bid to take over the country. Afterward the PLO took up lodging in Lebanon, and quickly turned that beautiful country into a war zone. Bashir Jemayel Lebanon's president-elect stated in 1982:

> In eight years of fighting we have, out of a population of three million inhabitants, more than 100,000 killed, more than 300,000 wounded and almost half of the population uprooted from its homes...[42]

Jemayel himself was latter assassinated. Jemayel's remarks did not mention the rapes, even of young girls, thefts, and many other abuses the people suffered. They did not tell of the churches turned into ammunition dumps, of small children taken by force and trained by the PLO to be killers, of houses confiscated, etc. The PLO made Lebanon a giant training camp for terrorists. Groups like the Italian Red Brigade, the Irish Republican Army, and the Baader Meinhof gang all received training from the PLO in Lebanon.[43]

One can understand why the Israelis were greeted with joy when they responded to this PLO challenge and invaded southern Lebanon in 1982. The Israelis completely destroyed the PLO infrastructure in Lebanon and would have probably put an end to Arafat and his army. Unfortunately, the PLO was rescued because of world pressures and particularly by the intervention of the United States.

When they were pushed out of Lebanon, the PLO relocated in Tunisia. After their short-sighted backing of Saddam Hussein in the Gulf War, much of the support from rich Arab nations was lost and the whole organization fell on hard times. Yet, somehow the PLO and its related terror organizations seem to be needed by anti-Semitic and oil hungry nations. Beginning with the Madrid Conference of 1991 a rescue program was begun for Arafat. The rescue operation eventually resulted in the Oslo Peace Accords and what has come to be known as the "peace process."

THE "PEACE" PROCESS

Since the Madrid conference in 1991, and the Oslo Accords in 1993, the "peace process" is about the only thing Israelis hear on the radio and TV. The papers are saturated with it as if it were some special godsend. It seems that few people have stopped to consider the toll that this "peace" has exacted. By September, 1998, the fifth anniversary of the Oslo Accords, 279 Israelis had been killed in terrorist attacks. This figure exceeded the number of Israelis killed in the 15 years prior to the Oslo Peace Accords.[44]

Israel is now in the process of giving away to the Palestinians her precious and sacred heritage of land. Already, the cities of Jericho, Shechem (Nablus), Bethlehem, Hebron and several other urban areas have been surrendered to the PLO. Yasser Arafat is hoping to steal about 90 percent of what is known as the West Bank, but what Bible students know as ancient Israel. He is already in control of many of the ancient biblical cities.

Arafat, the PLO and other terrorist groups, including Hamas, have always maintained they will push Israel into the sea and take the whole land. This is clearly affirmed in the 1964 Palestine National Covenant, also known as the Palestine Charter. Since June, 1974, Arafat and the PLO have operated under what is called the Phased Plan. This plan has two points. First, the PLO will create a Palestinian state on whatever area they can get from Israel. Second, they will then mobilize an assault to destroy whatever remains of Israel.[45] The Peace Process fits nicely with these publicly stated PLO goals.

THE BIG LIE

The PLO has had considerable success in terrorizing Israel and the nations. However, their greatest success has been in the area of propaganda. The PLO has the "Goebbels touch." In fact, they were influenced by some famous Nazi propaganda experts, such as Von Lehrs, who escaped to Cairo after World War II.[46] Arafat is an expert not only at telling the big lie – that being that all of biblical heritage belongs to the Palestinians – but at telling it continually until the whole world believes it.

An example of this propaganda was seen in the 1982 Israel/ PLO war in Lebanon. As Israel was driving the PLO out of Lebanon the world was told that there were 10,000 Lebanese and Palestinians dead, 40,000 wounded, and 600,000 homeless because of Israel's bombardment. Apparently no one bothered to check the source of this information. Later it was revealed that it came from Arafat's brother who was head of the PLO-affiliated Red Crescent. The exaggerations were anywhere from 2000 to 3000 percent.[47]

Also, as the Israeli army was about to mop up the last stronghold of the PLO in Beirut, US President Ronald Reagan was shown the picture of an armless Palestinian girl who had reportedly lost her arms in an Israeli bombardment. The US president called Israel's Prime Minister and angrily demanded an end to the bombardment. Israel immediately complied.

It was not until later that the girl was located and the truth was revealed that she was in fact injured by an earlier Arab attack. It was too late. The damage was already done by the big lie, and Israel was once more the villain in international eyes.[48]

The big lie tactics are used most expertly in the PLOs many attempts to re-write history. In recent times Hanan Ashrawi, frequent spokeswoman for the Palestinians, has boldly stated for the worldwide TV audience that she is a true descendant of the first Christians, and that they were Palestinians.

Of course, this statement is inaccurate, since her Arab people did not inhabit the land of Israel until some six hundred years after the New Testament era. We seldom stop to evaluate the absurdity of these kind of statements. If Ashwari really was a descendant of the first Christians, then her ancestry would actually be Jewish.

There is a constant attempt by the PLO and by rich Arab nations to influence world-wide news reporting. Perhaps the most alarming attempt though is that of influencing publishers of reference materials. These materials have a very long shelf life and are read by millions of people, particularly by young, impressionable children.

A clear pattern has developed in the PLO, Hamas and other groups sworn to the destruction of Israel. They have killed and destroyed by terrorism and finally they have sought to steal Israel's heritage and history.

The researcher Bat Ye'or remarks about this:

> The masquerade of Arabs (or "Palestinians") posing as "Jews" transfers to them Israel's historical rights and the merits or sympathy earned after 4,000 years of existence and hardships. By robbing the Jews of their past (i.e., the stratagem of substitution), the PLO reduces them to a rootless shadowy group, worthy only of Arab toleration.[49]

Jacques Maritain also remarks:

It is a strange paradox to behold Israel being denied the only territory of which – considering the whole course of human history – it is absolutely, divinely certain that a people had a title to it.[50]

PALESTINE, A MODERN MYTH

Arab activist, Musa Alami, once summarized the situation so far as Arab nationalism is concerned. He said, "how can people struggle for their nation, when most of them do not know the meaning of the word?...The people are in great need of a 'myth' to fill their consciousness and imagination...."[51] The people got their myth. It is called "Palestine." Someday, "Palestine" might be known as the biggest myth of the twentieth century.

For decades people and nations, even impressive world bodies, have played their part in supporting and perpetuating this myth. In a sense, they have acted out Anderson's famous fable – *The Emperor's New Clothes*. In that fable, while everyone pretended and swooned over his new clothes, the stark truth was recognized and blurted out by a little child. The emperor was naked!

The truth today is that there never was a Palestinian state in all the annals of human history. There never was a distinct Arab-Palestinian people. The majority are an amalgamated mixture of Arab peoples who migrated into Israel to seek jobs. These jobs were provided by Jewish development in the area after 1881.

The Arab-Palestinian identity as is presented by the PLO and related groups thus far seems to be flawed and even fraudulent. We might ask, "Is it all a political ruse to steal away the heritage of Israel?"

STUDY QUESTIONS:

Why would the expression "Palestine in Jesus' time" be considered an anachronism?

Why would the name "Palestine" not be particularly appealing to the Jews from the standpoint of ancient history?

According to Nehemiah 2:20, should the restoration of Jerusalem be assigned to the Arab peoples?

What are some of the reasons that caused the British failure in their attempt to establish the Jewish homeland?

Why was the capture of the "West Bank" by Jordan in 1948 a double insult to Israel?

Does the PLO occupation in southern Lebanon give us any indication as to how life in the Palestinian Authority will eventually turn out? If so, what conclusions can be drawn?

NOTES

1. Eliyahu Tal, *Whose Jerusalem* (Jerusalem and Tel Aviv, Israel: The International Forum for a United Jerusalem, 1994) pp. 95-96.
2. Tal, *Whose Jerusalem,* p. 93.
3. Tal, *Whose Jerusalem,* p. 93.
4. Joan Peters, *From Time Immemorial, The Origins of the Arab-Jewish Conflict Over Palestine* (New York: Harper & Row, Publishers, 1984) pp. 139-140.
5. Bat Ye'or, *The Dhimmi, Jews and Christians Under Islam* (Cranbury, NJ: Associated University Press, English edition 1985) p. 145.
6. Peters, *From Time Immemorial,* p. 141.
7. Charles F. Deloach, *Seeds of Conflict* (Palinfield, N.J: Logos International, 1974) p. 38 -43.
8. Walter Clay Lowdermilk, *Palestine Land of Promise* (London: Victor Gollancz Ltd., 1944) p. 58.

9. Quoted in Benjamin Netanyahu, *A Place Among the Nations, Israel and the World* (New York: Bantam Books, 1993) p. 37.
10. Quoted in Peters, *From Time Immemorial*, p. 158.
11. Quoted in Peters, *From Time Immemorial*, p. 158.
12. Samuel Katz, *Battleground, Fact and Fantasy in Palestine* (New York: Bantam Books, 2nd printing, 1973) p. 108.
13. Quoted in Katz, *Battleground, Fact and Fantasy in Palestine*, p. 107.
14. Quoted in Peters, *From Time Immemorial*, p. 159.
15. Katz, *Battleground, Fact and Fantasy in Palestine*, p. 108.
16. Mark Twain, *The Innocents Abroad* (New York: Hippocrene Books Inc., originally published by American Publishing Co., Hartford, CT, 1869) pp. 486-487.
17. Twain, *The Innocents Abroad*, p. 520.
18. Twain, *The Innocents Abroad*, pp. 606-608.
19. Martin Gilbert, *The Arab-Israeli Conflict, Its History in Maps* (London: Widenfeld and Nicholson, 1974,76,79 Third Edition 1979) p. 10.
20. Katz, *Battleground, Fact and Fantasy in Palestine Battleground*, p. 46.
21. John Loftus and Mark Aarons, *The Secret War Against the Jews, How Western Espionage Betrayed the Jewish People* (New York: St. Martin Press, 1994) p. 40.
22. Katz, *Battleground, Fact and Fantasy in Palestine Battleground*, p. 56.
23. Katz, *Battleground, Fact and Fantasy in Palestine Battleground*, p. 59.
24. Katz, *Battleground, Fact and Fantasy in Palestine Battleground*, pp. 62-63.
25. Netanyahu, *A Place Among the Nations*, p. 57.
26. Peters, *From Time Immemorial*, p. 244.
27. Peters, *From Time Immemorial*, p. 246.
28. Peters, *From Time Immemorial*, p. 295.
29. Katz, *Battleground, Fact and Fantasy in Palestine Battleground*, p. 69.
30. Katz, *Battleground, Fact and Fantasy in Palestine Battleground*, p. 71.
31. Tal, *Whose Jerusalem*, p.160.

32. Tal, *Whose Jerusalem,* p. 157.
33. Gilbert, *The Arab-Israeli Conflict, Its History in Maps,* p. 52.
34. Thomas Kiernan, *Yasir Arafat* (London: Sphere Books, Ltd., London, 1975) p. 17.
35. Kiernan, *Yasir Arafat,* p. 25.
36. Kiernan, *Yasir Arafat,* p. 55.
37. Kiernan, *Yasir Arafat,* p. 134.
38. Kiernan, *Yasir Arafat,* p. 147.
39. Clarence H. Wagner, Jr., ed. *Dispatch From Jerusalem,* January/February 1994, p.2.
40. Eliyahu Tal, ed., *PLO* (Jerusalem: Department of Information, WZO, 1982) pp. 8-9.
41. Tal, *PLO* p. 3.
42. Quoted in Tal, *PLO,* p. 37.
43. Tal, *PLO,* pp. 38-56.
44. See *The Jerusalem Post,* 13 September, 1998.
45. Netanyahu, *A Place Among the Nations,* p. 220.
46. Tal, *PLO,* p. 76.
47. Tal, *PLO,* p. 77.
48. Netanyahu, *A Place Among the Nations,* pp. 355-356.
49. Bat Ye'or, *The Dhimmi, Jews and Christians Under Islam,* p. 145.
50. Quoted in Marvin R.Wilson, *Our Father Abraham, Jewish Roots of the Christian Faith* (Grand Rapids, MI: William B. Eerdmans Publishing Company, and Center for Judaic-Christian Studies, Dayton, OH, 1989) p. 265.
51. Quoted in Peters, *From Time Immemorial,* p. 13.

- 6 -

A NATION IS REBORN

It could be said that the Jewish people were literally "programmed" to return to Zion. The idea of Zion has always been attached to the Jewish heart. At the end of the Passover *seder*, these wistful words are usually spoken: "Next year in Jerusalem!" On Jewish walls there customarily hangs a small plaque with the word *mizrah* (east) inscribed. Three times every day the devout Jew faces toward the east and prays. He prays for Jerusalem at meals and also in the synagogue.

Indeed the scriptures themselves would not allow the Jews to forget God's holy city. In Psalm 137:5-6, there is an admonition and warning about forgetting Jerusalem.

EARLY ATTEMPTS AT RETURN

Through the long centuries of their dispersion, there were many attempts by the Jews to return to Jerusalem and to the land of Israel. Immigration attempts can be traced all the way back to the earliest days after the unsuccessful Bar Kochba Revolt in AD 135. In those days, a few Jewish scholars immigrated to Israel from Babylon. Much later in the eighth century, many Karaites, a sect of Judaism, immigrated to Israel.

In the twelfth century, the renowned Jewish poet, Judah Halevi penned these mournful words:

> My heart is in the east and I am in the far-away
> west ... How little would it mean to me to abandon
> all the bounty of Spain ... How precious it would be
> to behold even the dust of the Holy Temple that was
> destroyed.[1]

Halevi at last forsook his land and made the hazardous journey to Jerusalem. It is thought today that this beloved poet died in route.

Benjamin of Tudela, the noted traveler, who visited the country in 1167, reported that there were two hundred Jews living in Jerusalem, with 300 in Ramla, 300 in Ashkelon, and 200 both in Casearea and in Akko. Undoubtedly these decimated numbers reflected the ravages of the First Crusade. In 1211, three hundred Rabbis immigrated from France, settling in Acre and in Jerusalem.[2] Their *aliya* was followed in 1267 by the famous scholar Nahmanides.

The living conditions even in Jerusalem in these early times were difficult and discouraging. A Christian pilgrim visiting the land from 1491-92 made this report:

> Christians and Jews alike in Jerusalem lived in
> great poverty and in conditions of great deprivation,
> there are not many Christians but there are many
> Jews, and there the Moslems persecute in various
> ways. Christians and Jews go about in Jerusalem in
> clothes considered fit only for wandering beggars...[3]

Later, some Jews came from Germany, Spain and France. After the expulsion from Spain in 1492, and from Portugal in 1497, many more European Jews began to make their way to the Holy Land.

The seventeenth century saw a wave of immigration as a result of the false Messiah, Shabbetai Zevi. According to one observer, the Jewish community of Jerusalem had grown to 10,000 persons in 1741. In the eighteenth century the Hasidim, an ultra-orthodox group, began to make *aliya* to the country. Their immigration greatly benefited Jewish settlement.[4]

Many other groups trickled into the country in the early nineteenth century. These groups were primarily from Germany, Holland and Hungary.

THE BEGINNINGS OF MODERN *ALIYA*

It was not until the 1880s that the real movement toward settlement in Israel began. Before it could take place, a philosophical and even theological groundwork had to be laid. Initially there was fervent opposition to the idea.

Among the East European Jews, the restoration was considered only in messianic terms. Many believed that only the Messiah could restore Zion.[5] Two things began to have a bearing on this opinion. First, there were the almost prophetic voices that arose to proclaim the cause of Zion. Second, there were the waves of persecution that made the Jews consider a return to the land.

The earliest of these voices raised was Moses Hess (1812-1875). Hess wrote his book *Rome and Jerusalem* in 1862. His idea was that the Jews should be aided by mankind to re-establish their own nation. After Hess, was an Orthodox Rabbi, Zevi-Hirsch Kalischer. His book, *Derishat Zion* (Quest for Zion) was also published in 1862. In addition to publishing his book, Kalischer advocated the establishment of agricultural colonies in Palestine.

Due to Kalischer's influence, the first agricultural colony was founded in Palestine in 1869, by *Alliance Israelite Universelle*. The colony was given the name, *Mikveh Yisrael* (Hope of Israel). Kalischer traveled widely to promote Palestinian colonization. In doing so, he laid the foundations for what became a popular movement called *Houeve Zion* (Lovers of Zion).[6]

Another prophetic voice to arise among the Jews was Leo Pinsker, an Odessa physician. After the Russian pogroms of 1881-82, Pinsker wrote his pamphlet, *Auto-Emancipation* (freeing oneself). His thesis was that the Jews were obligated to free themselves, and not wait on others to do it for them. His cries, "Now or Never," electrified many Jews and particularly the societies of *Houeve Zion*.[7]

It seemed that these prophetic voices were a last and desperate attempt to save Israel's dispersed from the horrors that would soon engulf them in Europe.

RUSSIAN POGROMS

In the early 1880s a growing oppression of the Jews began in several European countries. This oppression was particularly strong in Russia. In that country, after the assassination of Alexander II, severe pogroms broke out against the Jews. In the next twenty years over a million Jews fled to the United States. Others however, felt it was time not just to flee, but to find a resolution of the Jewish problem. That resolution focused on the land of Israel.[8]

What it means to "make *aliya*."

Aliya is a Hebrew word meaning "ascent." It is used to describe the coming of the Jews to the land of Israel. The land of Israel ascends from the seashore upwards to Jerusalem, which is situated on one of its highest points. *Olim* is the collective term for those who have made citizenship. *Yoredim* (going down) is the term used for those who have left the land.

The First *Aliya* (1882-1903) - Some 25,000, mostly from Eastern Europe, came at this time.

The Second *Aliya* (1904-1914) - Consisted of about 40,000 and was inter- rupted by the outbreak of World War I

The Third *Aliya* (1919-1923) - Contained many young pioneers. About 35,000 arrived in this period.

The Fourth *Aliya* (1924-1928) - Totaled some 67,000 with many middle- class immigrants. The bulk of this group was from Poland.

The Fifth *Aliya* (1929-1939) - There was a total in this group of about 250,000, with many from Nazi Germany.

The Sixth and Seventh *Aliyot* (1940-1948) - About 100,000 entered the country during this period. Immigration was greatly hindered due to British restrictions.

The mass *aliya* or ingathering of exiles (1948 and following) – When Israel became a state, all immigration restrictions were removed. For instance, in the years 1948-1951, 684,000 immigrants returned home to Israel.[9]

Early Jewish settlers work the land. *(Courtesy Israel Information Office)*

From out of the *Houeve Zion* movement sprang the first wave of settlement in the land of Israel. These settlers gave themselves the acronym BILU, which taken from the Hebrew scripture in Isaiah 2:5 means, *"House of Jacob, come let us go!"* As expressed by another verse in Isaiah, those who were ready to perish, began to return to the holy mountain at Jerusalem (Isa. 27:13).

This group marked the beginning of what has come to be known as the First *Aliya*. The very first group of settlers in 1882 included only 14 people. Life in the desolate land of Israel was very difficult for this small group but they persisted. More new immigrants followed, and by 1884, six settlements had been established. These settlements included Gedera and the revival of the previously established settlement at Petah Tikvah (door of hope).[10]

In these early days settlement was greatly assisted by the philanthropist, Baron Edmond de Rothchild, who started four colonies, including Rishon le-Zion (First to Zion). At Rishon, Rothchild began a redevelopment of the ancient wine industry.

Most of these early settlers suffered severe hardships including a difficult climate and malaria from the surrounding swamps. They also endured attacks from hostile Arabs and harassment from corrupt Turkish officials.[11] Although unfamiliar with the rigors of farming, these settlers learned its rudiments and did their best. With these early arrivals and with many more who came after them, the words of the prophet Isaiah began to be fulfilled: *"As a young man marries a maiden, so will your sons marry you; as a bridegroom rejoices over his bride, so will your God rejoice over you [the land]"* (Isa. 62:5). The land that had been forsaken so many centuries would now be loved and married.

HERZL, THE PROPHET OF ZIONISM

As early settlement progressed in the land, the Zionist movement began to be greatly accelerated in Europe. The efforts of the Zionist pioneers soon began to focus on one man, Theodore Herzl.

Herzl, born in Budapest in 1860, exhibited a great deal of literary skill and personal charm. At first he had success by writing light, entertaining plays. Later he submitted regular features to the *Neue Freie Press,* the most important paper in Vienna, his hometown.[12]

In time the newspaper appointed the promising Herzl as its correspondent in Paris. It was in Paris, the cultural capital of Europe, that Herzl received the shock of his life. He witnessed there the trial of Captain Alfred Dreyfus. Dreyfus, a Jew, was tried on trumped up charges, stripped of his rank and exiled to Devil's Island. What amazed Herzl was not so much the trial, but the cries of the people that rang out, "Death to the Jews!"[13] These barbaric cries were coming from people who lived in what was considered at the time the most civilized part of the world. Herzl left Paris a shaken and changed man.

In a fever of inspiration, Herzl wrote his soon to be famous book, *Der Judenstaat* (The Jewish State). The book drew

Theodore Herzl
(Courtesy Israel Information Office)

immediate attention. Some Jews criticized the book while others rallied to Herzl's cause. Among the stalwarts who helped Herzl were Israel Zangwill, Max Nordeau and David Wolffson.

THE FIRST ZIONIST CONGRESS

By 1897 the tireless efforts of Herzl plus the rising momentum of Zionism brought about the First Zionist Congress in Basle. The congress was a great success and almost instantly the age-old idea of a restored Jewish state had a political and economic basis. It was no longer just a dream.

In his diary, Herzl recorded after the congress:

> At Basle, I founded the Jewish State! If I had said this out loud today I would be greeted by universal laughter. In five years perhaps, and certainly in fifty years, everyone will perceive it."[14]

In exactly fifty years, the UN voted to clear the way for the establishment of the State of Israel.

A LANGUAGE RESTORED

One problem that immediately surfaced as scattered Israel returned to the land was the need for a common language. The Jews came home speaking scores of languages, but they could not speak their own. The ancient Hebrew tongue had simply become a "dead" language. Its usage was limited to prayer, to study, to family or communal observances and to ritual purposes. Some even thought the language was too sacred to be used for everyday affairs. There was an additional problem, Hebrew was now missing thousands of modern words like ice cream, sidewalk, airplane, telephone, etc.

Today when one rides a bus in Israel and hears little children speaking Hebrew at lightning speed, or when one looks out of the bus window and sees multitudes of Hebrew signs on the streets, he must admit that a miracle has taken place. This miracle focused primarily on one man, Eliezer Ben-Yehuda. Although desperately sick with tuberculosis, Ben-Yehuda was driven to accomplish one great goal in life. His burning desire was to resurrect the Hebrew language. It was almost like a divine call and obsession with him.

In order to accomplish this goal, Ben-Yehuda and his wife moved to Jerusalem in 1881. Ben-Yehuda, although sick, worked 18 hours a day for the next 41 years to accomplish his goal. Eliezer published a Hebrew paper in Israel and he traveled abroad visiting libraries in search of ancient Hebrew roots. Eliezer was determined to raise the first Hebrew-speaking children in Israel. To this end he forbade anyone to speak with his children except in Hebrew.

Ben-Yehuda and his wife, Deborah, spoke Hebrew at home and in the street. The biographer, St. John, relates this story of one of their strolls through town:

> One day when Deborah and Eliezer were walking down one of Jerusalem's narrow streets, talking in Hebrew, a man stopped them. Tugging at the young journalist's sleeve, he asked in Yiddish: "Excuse me, sir. That language you two talk. What is it?" "Hebrew," Eliezer replied. "Hebrew! But people don't speak Hebrew. It's a dead language!" "You are wrong, my friend," Eliezer replied with a fervor. "I am alive. My wife is alive. We speak Hebrew. Therefore, Hebrew is alive."[15]

Eliezer Ben-Yehuda lived to gather the necessary material for his 16-volume dictionary of the revived Hebrew language. He lived to hear Hebrew become a spoken language once again, and he saw it gain the status as one of the three official languages of the re-born country.

FURTHER SETTLEMENT AND DEVELOPMENT

Following on the heels of the First *Aliya,* was the Second *Aliya,* beginning as a result of Kishinev pogroms of 1903. After that there was a Third *Aliya* beginning in 1919. These waves of immigration were followed by several more as the new century progressed.

With the Second *Aliya* the first *kibbutz* was founded (1909). These collective farms enabled the settlers to pool their resources for better and more efficient farming and for defense against Arab marauders.

At this time, the first organized attempt at Jewish self-defense was made with the *Ha-Shomer,* the mounted guards of the Jewish settlements. Also in this period the Jewish National Fund was established as a tool for acquiring and improving the land.

At the beginning of *aliya* in 1880, there had been approximately 470,000 Arabs and 24,000 Jews in the land. By the beginning of World War I, the Arabs numbered 500,000 and the Jewish settlers *(yishuv)* numbered approximately 85,000. During this same period over fifty Jewish settlements had been formed.[16]

WORLD WAR I AND THE MANDATE

Even before the close of World War I, the British and French had made the Sykes-Picot agreement to divide the area of Palestine between themselves.

At the close of the war, Turkey, the "sick man of Europe," collapsed, and the agreement became a reality. On November 2, 1917, in the famous Balfour Declaration, the British government declared themselves in favor of a Jewish national home in Palestine. Soon after the war ended, the League of Nations granted a mandate to Great Britain to establish the national home.

It quickly became apparent that the newly-assigned guardian was not seeking the Jews' best interests. This was made especially clear when Britain in 1921 gave away 75 percent of the mandate lands in order to found Transjordan (today's Jordan).

The Balfour Declaration of 2 November, 1917

His Majesty's Government view with favour the establishment in Palestine of a national home for the Jewish people, and will use their best endeavors to facilitate the achievement of this object, it being clearly understood that nothing shall be done which may prejudice the civil and religious rights of non-Jewish communities in Palestine or the rights and political status enjoyed by Jews in any other country.

As early as 1920, Britain also began to restrict Jewish immigration. Finally, with the British White Paper of 1939, the door of immigration was virtually closed to Jews. Millions of trapped Jews had no place to escape from the Nazis.

Britain was vigilant to guard against Jewish immigration, even to the point of firing upon "illegal" ships as they tried to deliver their human cargoes to the land. Some of the ships were turned back to face a certain Holocaust. Three ships sank, with two of them losing all aboard. Other "illegal" immigrants were captured and exiled to British colonies.[17]

While Britain sternly resisted Jewish immigration, she at the same time opened the doors wide to Arab immigration from the surrounding countries.

In order to protect their interest, the Jews were finally forced to organize an underground opposition to Britain.

WORLD WAR II AND THE HOLOCAUST

In Europe a dreadful thing was taking place. Millions of Jews were trapped by the rapidly moving Nazi armies. The Jews were immediately assigned to ghettoes where they were slowly starved. Soon the Nazis devised the plan of total extermination of the Jewish populations. Camps like Auschwitz, Chelmno, Treblinka and Sobibor, were established to bring about this extermination.

With all doors of escape closed, six million unarmed Jews were slaughtered. They were starved, worked to death, shot, and finally gassed in unbelievable numbers. Among the Jews murdered between 1939 and 1945, were two million children.

Could Israel arise from these ashes? The Lord had promised such a thing through his prophet Ezekiel centuries before:

> *Therefore prophesy and say to them: 'This is what the Sovereign LORD says: O my people, I am going to open your graves and bring you up from them; I will bring you back to the land of Israel.* (Ezek. 37:12)

The historian Paul Johnson remarks about the connection of the Holocaust with the rise of Zion in these words:

> The Holocaust and the new Zion were organically connected. The murder of six million Jews was a prime causative factor in the creation of the state of Israel. This was in accordance with an ancient and powerful dynamic of Jewish history: redemption through suffering.[18]

A NATION BORN IN A DAY

Israel as a political entity would be resurrected and brought forth. That too would happen as the prophets had spoken centuries before:

> *Who has ever heard of such a thing? Who has ever seen such things? Can a country be born in a day or a nation be brought forth in a moment? Yet no sooner is Zion in labor than she gives birth to her children* (Isa. 66:8).

Although it seemed impossible that a nation dispersed since AD 70, and even as far back as 586 BC and 722 BC could rise again, it indeed happened.

On November 29, 1947, against all odds, the United Nations voted for the partition plan. The acceptance of this plan by the nations cleared the way for the nation of Israel to be legally established the next year. Neither the American State Department nor the British Foreign Office wanted a Jewish state. For the most part the Russians did not want it, but still found themselves voting for it. Israel thus became a reality. Johnson remarks, "Israel slipped into existence through a fortuitous window in history which briefly opened for a few months in 1947-8."[19]

Arab opposition to this plan was intense and Arab violence continued until the British withdrew their forces the

Tomb of David Ben Gurion.

following year on May 14. On that date Israel declared its independence, with David Ben-Gurion heading the provisional government. The Arabs immediately declared war on the newly-born state.

Hannah Hurnard, a Christian witness of these momentous days states:

> As Israel again became a nation in the land of Israel, the thirty-seventh chapter of Ezekiel was read in Hebrew over the radio – the glorious prophecy of the scattered, dry bones that were suddenly joined together with flesh and sinews and then received the life of God. We who remained in the country while the astonishing miracle happened will never forget with what a noise and shaking those bones came together and were formed into one body and nation.[20]

Modern Israel celebrates her independence.

THE WAR OF INDEPENDENCE

Even prior to Israel's independence the Arabs had launched repeated and vicious attacks upon the Jews. The Jews had scored many impressive victories in response to these attacks. In April, the "Arab Army of Liberation" was routed by the *Haganah.* This marked the first military victory by the Jews since the days of Bar Kochba in the second century.[21] As the British departed, there were fierce battles for their deserted positions. The Jews took the cities of Tiberias, Haifa and Safed in the north.

It was at this time that many of the panic-stricken Arab residents fled their homes, causing the ticklish refugee problem. This problem would plague Israel for many decades to come. The Arabs were encouraged to leave by their own Arab leaders, while the Jews begged them to stay. As many as 65,000 Arabs fled Haifa and 50,000 fled Jaffa.[22]

On May 15, 1948, six Arab armies from Egypt, Syria, Transjordan, Lebanon, Saudi Arabia and Iraq attacked Israel.

The Arab armies were well equipped and trained. The armies of Transjordan were actually trained and staffed by British officers. The Jews were ill trained and poorly equipped. Yet the Jews fought fiercely, realizing that defeat meant annihilation. After only ten days the Jews were able to launch a counterattack.

Soon large areas fell into Jewish hands. The Arab cities of Ramleh, Lydda and Beersheba were captured. The blockade of Jerusalem was broken. The Israelis gained control of the coastal plain and much of the Galilee. Unfortunately they lost the Old City of Jerusalem, as the Jordanians occupied it along with the remainder of the area that came to be known as the "West Bank."

By the time of the conclusion of the War of Independence in 1949, the Israelis had won control of most of the land that presently makes up the state of Israel.

THE FLOOD OF IMMIGRATION

With the end of the war, the Israelis were able to do something they were never permitted to do under prior Turkish or British domination. They were able to bring the sons and daughters home from the nations without any limitation. The very declaration of Independence of the new nation stated: "The State of Israel shall be open to Jewish immigration and the ingathering of the exiles."[23]

In the short period between May 15, 1948 and the end of 1951, 684,201 new immigrants came home. This was more than the entire Jewish population on the day independence was proclaimed.[24] Possessed with an almost Messianic fervor, some 47,000 Jews of Yemen came home. They were flown out in an airlift known as "Operation Magic Carpet." The Jews of Iraq, over 124,000 strong, were also flown home in an airlift named "Operation Ezra-Nehemiah." Many of the Jews of Iraq (ancient Babylon) had been officially in captivity since 586 BC, and now they were home. The remarkable event prompted the President of Israel to declare that the Babylonian captivity had ended.

A ship loaded with Jewish immigrants arrives in Haifa. (Courtesy Yad Vashem)

The Jews of Yemen come home. (Courtesy Israel Information Office)

The defeated and embittered Arab nations immediately began to expel their Jewish populations. While an estimated 650,000 Palestinian Arabs were made refugees between 1947-49, an estimated 820,000 Jewish refugees were expelled or fled from Arab lands, in most cases leaving their property behind.[25] Only a few Arab refugees were absorbed by the surrounding Arab states. Instead, these Arab states have kept the refugee problem smoldering since 1949 and have used it for political reasons. In contrast, hundreds of thousands of Jews were immediately absorbed by the new state of Israel.

The Jews began to build their land, to establish new cities and farms. In the brief space between 1948-1951, the Israelis established 345 new villages of all types.[26] New industries sprang up as Israel was on the way to building a successful economy and a modern progressive democracy.

NEW STORM CLOUDS GATHER

Soon after Israel was securely established as a state, Arab belligerence began to flare up once more. The Arab League established a boycott against all Israeli products. That boycott has persisted until the present day. Passage through the Suez Canal and the Straits of Tiran was blocked to all shipping and cargoes bound to or from Israel. To make matters worse, Israel was regularly attacked by Arab *fedayeen* crossing her borders and launching terror attacks. In the years 1951-1955, there were 967 Israelis killed through such attacks.[27]

The situation soon became intolerable for Israel. On October 29, 1956, Israel launched a full scale successful attack into the Sinai. This became known as the Sinai Campaign. The attack was launched in cooperation with Britain and France, who were angered at Egypt's nationalization of the Suez Canal that same year.[28] However, because of US and UN pressure, Israel was forced to withdraw from the Sinai in 1957. The area was put under the supervision of the UN.

THE MIRACULOUS SIX-DAY WAR

The tiny nation of Israel was forced to develop her infrastructure, commerce, industry, agriculture, education and government while the threat of war hung over her at all times. Hostile Arab nations could have no rest with Israel in their midst.

By 1964, at the Arab summit in Cairo and Alexandria, the decision was made to intensify the struggle against Israel. The Palestine Liberation Organization (PLO) was founded. The Syrians also decided to divert the headwaters of the Jordan river and frustrate Israel's water development plans.[29]

The Syrians, had already been guilty of repeated sniping and bombarding of Israeli settlements after the War of Independence. The Syrian bombardments increased in 1966-67, until they could no longer be tolerated.

Egypt's President Nasser began to broadcast and publish anti-Israel rhetoric. He soon gathered support from the other Arab nations for an invasion of Israel. Beginning on May 16, 1967 Egyptian forces moved threateningly across the Sinai. Nasser demanded that the UN forces there be removed and the UN complied. By May 25, the armies of Syria, Iraq, Jordan, Saudi Arabia and Egypt all moved to the very borders of Israel. The armies of Israel were then outnumbered three to one by the Arabs.[30] Once more the Straits of Tiran were blocked by the Egyptians, denying Israel access to her markets in the Far East.

Assessing the grave situation, Israel decided to pre-empt the attack. On the morning of June 5, the Israeli air force struck the airfields of Egypt, Jordan, Iraq and Syria. In all, 452 enemy planes were destroyed, 391 of them on the ground.[31] In less than three hours Israel had gained complete air superiority.

The armies of Israel went on the attack, and in one of the largest armor battles in history, the Egyptian armored power was shattered. Israeli troops raced on and soon reached the Suez Canal. The Egyptian losses were: over 400 tanks destroyed, with another 200 captured; 10,000 men dead, with another 12,000 taken prisoner.[32]   Israel captured the Gaza Strip from Egypt and once again Israel took control of the whole Sinai Peninsula.

The war progressed on all fronts. Judea and Samaria (West Bank), which had been under Jordanian control since 1948, fell into Israeli hands. At last the Old City of Jerusalem came under Israeli control.

The 1967 war was so miraculous that even Israelis were stunned.   Tough, battle hardened soldiers wept like babies when the Western Wall was captured.   Gen. Shlomo Goren, the Chief Rabbi of the Israel Armed Forces arrived at the wall, with the Torah clutched in his hands.   Goren cried, "We have taken the city of God, we are entering the Messianic era for the Jewish People..."[33]

The Golan Heights, from which Syria had terrorized the Galilee for years, was captured by Israel.   In a mere six days the war was over and once again the vastly superior Arab armies were defeated.

ARAB TERRORISM AND THE YOM KIPPUR WAR

Unfortunately even miraculous wars do not have happy endings for Israel.   Arab terrorism continued to plague the land.   In the short period between June 1967 and December 1968, there were 159 terrorist raids deep inside Israel.   In addition, more than a thousand raids took place along Israel's borders.[34]   From 1968 onward, Palestinian terrorists began to operate against Israel from Jordan.   Egypt then began a war of attrition against the Israeli Bar Lev line, a defensive line established on the Suez Canal.

Soon, Arab armies were again at the door of Israel. In the afternoon of October 6, 1973, Egypt and Syria launched a coordinated attack.   They were soon joined by Jordan, Saudi Arabia, Iraq and a contingent from Kuwait.   It was Israel's holiest day, Yom Kippur.   On this day, many Israelis were fasting from both food and water.   All commerce, transportation and communication had ground to a halt.   In the midst of this holy day of prayer and fasting Israel was forced to mobilize.

New immigrants from the former USSR are welcomed in Israel
by members of the International Christian Embassy.
(Courtesy International Christian Embassy)

It was soon apparent that Israel could lose this war. The Arab armies were lavishly re-supplied from the USSR, but Israel soon began to run out of arms and equipment. Finally Israel was replenished by an emergency US airlift. The war waged on from October 6 until October 24. By that time Israel was the clear victor. The nation was once again saved but at the dreadful cost of 2,378 of its soldiers.[35]

THE MIRACLE CONTINUES

Israel would know more terrorist attacks and war. She would see eleven of her Olympic athletes slaughtered in Munich in 1972. She would see the miraculous rescue of her citizens hijacked to the Entebbe airport in 1976. Finally in 1982, it would be necessary to invade Lebanon to destroy the massive terrorist infrastructure built there by the PLO.

In spite of all her adversities the miracle of Israel would continue. In 1989 the Communist world started to crumble.

Ethiopian immigrants being airlifted. *(Courtesy Israel Information Office)*

The USSR had resisted Israel almost since her formation. The Communists had lavishly supplied Arab armies with weapons of all kinds that enabled them to attack Israel over and over. In addition, millions of Jews were being held captive in the USSR.

Finally, the finger of God touched these Communist nations and beginning in 1989, one Iron Curtain nation after another fell. In the words of Isaiah 43:5-6, God said to the north, *"Give them up!"* Suddenly Israel was almost overwhelmed with a massive new *aliya* from the north. In the years between the autumn of 1989 and the end of the century, almost a million new immigrants came home.

God not only brought them from the north, but in the words of Isaiah 43:6, he also said to the south, *"Do not hold them back!"* Ethiopia in the south had been detaining Ethiopian Jews at the airport for a year. Suddenly in one 33-hour period starting May 24, 1991, almost 15,000 Ethiopians were flown to Israel in one giant airlift.

According to the prophet Jeremiah this was a greater miracle than when Moses brought the children of Israel out of Egypt. Jeremiah says:

> *"However, the days are coming," declares the LORD, "when men   will no longer say, 'As surely as the LORD lives, who brought the Israelites up out of Egypt,' but they will say, 'As surely as the LORD lives, who brought the Israelites up out of the land of the north and out of all the countries where he had banished them.' For I will restore them to the land I gave their forefathers* (Jer.16:14-15).

In what seemingly was a demonic plan to stop the return of God's people, Saddam Hussein rained down missiles on the cities of Israel in the Gulf War of 1991. Israel was bombarded although she was not involved in this war in any way. It was not difficult to see the fury of Satan in these attacks. Nevertheless, the new immigrant flow continued.

Against all odds the people of Israel had come home from all the nations of earth to their own heritage. They had returned to the land promised to them forever by God. While the nations of the earth cursed them, those who believed the Lord could only say in the words of Deuteronomy 33:29:

> *Blessed are you, O Israel! Who is like you, a people saved by the LORD? He is your shield and helper and your glorious sword. Your enemies will cower before you, and you will trample down their high places.*

STUDY QUESTIONS:

Why did many Eastern European Jews resist the idea of returning to Israel under Zionist leadership?

What shocking truth did Herzl, the father of the Jewish state, realize while covering the Dreyfus trial in Paris?

What part did Great Britain play in hindering the Jewish escape from the Nazi Holocaust?

What parallel fact helps offset the fate of 650,000 Palestinian refugees after the war of Independence?

NOTES

1. Quoted in Eliyahu Tal, *Whose Jerusalem* (Jerusalem: International Forum for a United Jerusalem 1994) pp. 76-77.
2. Dan Bahat, ed., *Twenty Centuries of Jewish Life in the Holy Land, The Forgotten Generations* (Jerusalem: The Israel Economist, first edition 1975, second edition 1976) pp. 40-41.
3. Quoted in Bahat, ed., *Twenty Centuries of Jewish Life in the Holy Land, The Forgotten Generations,* p. 49.
4. Goeffrey Wigoder, ed., *Israel Pocket Library, Immigration and Settlement* (Jerusalem: Keter Publishing House Ltd., 1973) p. 40.
5. Solomon Grazel, *A History of the Jews* (Philadelphia: The Jewish Publication Society of America, 1947) p. 665.
6. Grazel, *A History of the Jews,* p. 667.
7. Grazel, *A History of the Jews,* p. 669.
8. Wigoder, ed., *Israel Pocket Library, Immigration and Settlement,* pp. 13-14.
9. Goeffrey Wigoder, ed., *Encyclopedia Judaica Vol 2,* (Jerusalem: Keter Publishing House Ltd.,) pp. 633-635.
10. Goeffrey Wigoder, ed., *Israel Pocket Library, History From 1880* (Jerusalem: Keter Publishing House Ltd., 1973) p. 14.
11. Grazel, *A History of the Jews,* p.670.
12. Grazel, *A History of the Jews,* p. 671.
13. Grazel, *A History of the Jews,* p. 672.

14. Quoted in Claude Duvernoy, *The Prince and the Prophet* (Jerusalem: Christian Action For Israel, First published in French 1966, English 1979) p. 58.

15. Robert St. John, *Tongue of the Prophets* (North Hollywood, CA: Wilshire Book Company, 1952) p.84.

16. Martin Gilbert, *Jewish Historical Atlas,* 4th edition (Jerusalem, Tel Aviv & Haifa, Israel: Steimatzky, Ltd., 1969, 1992) p. 85.

17. Wigoder, ed., *Israel Pocket Library, Immigration and Settlement,* p. 36.

18. Paul Johnson, *A History of the Jews* (New York: Harper & Row, 1987) p. 519.

19. Johnson, *A History of the Jews,* p. 526.

20. Hannah Hurnard, *Watchmen on the Walls* (Nashville, TN: Broadman & Holman Publishers, 1997) p. 154.

21. Cecil Roth, *A History of the Jews* (New York: Schocken Books,1954, fifth printing, 1966) p. 415.

22. Martin Gilbert, *The Arab-Israeli Conflict, Its History in Maps,* third edition, (London: Widenfeld and Nicholson, 1974) p. 46.

23. Wigoder, ed., *Israel Pocket Library, Immigration and Settlement,* p. 50.

24. Wigoder, ed., *Israel Pocket Library, Immigration and Settlement,* p. 56.

25. Mitchell G. Bard, and Joel Himelfarb, *Myths and Facts, A Concise Record of the Arab-Israeli Conflict* (Washington, DC: Near East Report, 1984, 1988, 1992) pp. 120-121.

26. Wigoder, ed., *Israel Pocket Library, History From 1880,* p. 151.

27. Gilbert, *The Arab-Israeli Conflict, Its History in Maps,* p. 60.

28. Gilbert, *The Arab-Israeli Conflict, Its History in Maps,* p. 62-63.

29. Wigoder, ed., *Israel Pocket Library, History From 1880,* p. 195.

30. Gilbert, *The Arab-Israeli Conflict, Its History in Maps,* p. 69.

31. Wigoder, ed., *Israel Pocket Library, History From 1880,* p. 200.

32. Wigoder, ed., *Israel Pocket Library, History From 1880,* p. 202.

33. Quoted in Charles F. Deloach, *Seeds of Conflict* (Plainfield, NJ: Logos International, 1974) p. 63.

34. Gilbert, *The Arab-Israeli Conflict, Its History in Maps,* p. 74.

35. Gilbert, *The Arab-Israeli Conflict, Its History in Maps,* p. 93.

-7-

Christians in Search of Their Roots

We live in a rootless society. Today many people live far from their physical roots, far from their families and sometimes even from their home countries. Thus, there is a great need in our society for people to be a part of something, to feel attached.

This need was expressed in the 70s by the American author Alex Haley, in his book *Roots*. In the book, Haley sought to portray his own roots, generations ago with his slave ancestors from Africa. The book gained wide popularity and was later turned into an eight-part TV mini-series. The mini-series became one of television's most-watched dramatic telecasts, with a reported 130 million viewers.[1]

The search for roots, whether it be Alex Haley, the average TV viewer, or modern Christians, is a very important endeavor. Today there are thousands of Christians who are seeking their spiritual roots. Many may be seeking them because of the deadness and disappointment they often find in the churches.

At present, the Gentile Church in many places is much like a bouquet of cut flowers. It may still look pretty, but it has no roots. There is little nourishment or sustenance. In early centuries, the Church's rich Hebrew heritage was subtly exchanged for a Greek one, for most of our early church fathers were Greek. In modern times, the church has gone to Madison Avenue, to rock music and to many other places to find its missing vitality. All these attempts have failed miserably.

What the modern church has not realized, is that the vitality has always been available. There is an unrecognized source of supply – a wellspring of life and learning for the taking. However, we should be forewarned that the continuation of this search may reveal some shocking facts about our own family tree!

SHOCKING FACTS ABOUT OUR FAMILY TREE!

The Bible makes it clear that Christianity does not stand on its own. It has been a long-hidden secret, but the secret is now out. In fact, the Apostle Paul actually revealed this secret centuries ago. What is the secret? It is this – Christianity is Jewish! Paul makes it plain that the Gentile Church is "grafted" into the Jewish olive tree and that it does not stand alone. Paul says in Romans 11:17-18:

> *If some of the branches have been broken off, and you, though a wild olive shoot, have been grafted in among the others and now share in the nourishing sap from the olive root, do not boast over those branches. If you do, consider this: You do not support the root, but the root supports you.*

This is an astounding statement. How could we have missed it for so many centuries? Paul is saying, that in a way unknown to us, Israel supports the whole Church and has always done so. This may be news even for those Israel boosters in the Church. They do not support Israel, but Israel supports them. Israel has been the support of the Church for almost two thousand years, despite the Church's anti-Semitism and outright persecution of Israel. It was God's plan that the sap or nourishing juices of the old Hebrew olive tree would supply the Church. In other words, we draw from a very rich heritage.

An old olive tree.

Let us stop a moment to consider the picture Paul is using here. The olive tree is one of the longest-living trees on earth. Some believe the giant, gnarled olives trees standing in the Garden of Gethsemane may have been alive at the time of Christ. The olive is also a very hardy tree, and it is practically indestructible. If cut down, it will probably grow back and live another thousand years.[2]

We see in Genesis 8:11, that the olive tree apparently withstood the flood quite well, because the dove brought Noah a freshly plucked olive twig after the deluge. The olive is a tree that gives great stability, for the gnarled trunk is often quite large and sturdy.

The tree grows in abundance over most of Israel. It seems to thrive in many different types of soil and in varied weather. The tree grows in the highlands or lowlands; it grows in the wet or dry, cold or hot; and even in the shallow rocky soil around Jerusalem.

The connection of the olive tree with Israel is an old one. The prophets Jeremiah and Hosea mention it (Jer. 11:16 and Hos. 14:6). In Hosea, God speaks of the beauty of the olive tree. It truly is an attractive tree with its silvery leaves blowing in the breeze. It is particularly delightful when loaded with fruit. The olive is a very fruitful tree, even when it receives a minimum of care. The amazing thing is that its fruitfulness can continue on for many centuries.

In ancient times the main product of the tree, olive oil, was used as a primary food source. It was also used for anointing, for healing and for light. Therefore the olive tree is literally the tree of light, and the light speaks of revelation. The Bible tells us that where there is no revelation, people perish (Prov. 29:18). The anointing and healing, like the light, speak of other greatly needed works of the Holy Spirit. Also, since the days of Noah, the tree has symbolized peace, reconciliation and restoration (Gen. 8:11).

Today the Church is in great need of all these things. We need the light of new and clear revelation to give us direction in the maze of this modern world. The churches are starving for true anointing and for physical and spiritual healing. We desperately need reconciliation. This is particularly needed in relation to the Jewish people. We must remember that these things are freely provided in our roots and are available for all believers today.

Gentile Christian pilgrims reap wheat in Israel at the Shavuot festival.

A RICH AND ANCIENT HERITAGE

Years ago when I went to college as a young man, I was immediately shocked by the remarks of some scholars. Some of them spoke about Christianity as being a very young religion. This information was devastating to me since I had always considered Christianity as being very old. My shock simply grew out of a misunderstanding of my own faith.

When we realize that Christianity is founded upon Judaism, it is then that we realize how ancient our faith really is. For instance, many Christians are now realizing that the Lord's Supper is a part of the ancient Passover seder. For this reason, thousands of Christians are lately participating in *seders* attempting to learn more about the roots and richness of their own faith.

For the same reasons Christians are now celebrating along with Israel in many of her feasts. Each year in Israel, thousands of Christians come from all over the world to join with Israel in celebrating the Feast of Tabernacles *(Sukkot)*. This celebration is sponsored by the International Christian Embassy in Jerusalem. Christians are also coming to Israel for the Feast of Pentecost *(Shavuot)* sponsored by Christian

Christian worshippers wave their sheaves near the Western Wall.

Friends of Israel. Participation in these festivals simply makes the old dusty pages of the Bible come to life in the present day.

There are many Christians who now celebrate the Sabbath *(Shabbat)* in order to learn more about God's rest. In Hebrews 4:9 we read, *"There remains, then, a Sabbath-rest for the people of God..."* For those many Christians living in Israel, this celebration is almost obligatory since the nation of Israel virtually shuts down for the Sabbath. Even some Christian worship services are held on this day as they may also have been in the first century.

Does this all sound strange? It shouldn't. After a long winter, the sap is simply rising from the old tree into the engrafted branches. When we carefully read our New Testament we realize that Jesus and the earliest Christians also celebrated these feasts, as well as the Sabbath. For instance, we have a record of Jesus celebrating the Feast of Tabernacles and giving important teachings during the celebration (John 7:14-44).

Thus Jesus and the earliest Christians celebrated the feast and kept the Sabbath as any good Jews would do. They were simply enjoying and appropriating their rich Hebrew heritage. When we read some of the New Testament books like Hebrews, for instance, we realize that the authors had understanding far beyond what we have today. They thoroughly understood the Hebrew scriptures and the Hebrew heritage. They drew their materials from a gold mine of Hebrew information.

We do not have to reflect long to realize that our Bible was both written and delivered to us by Jews. There is only one author, Luke, who is probably not Jewish. Our beloved Messiah was not only Jewish but was delivered to us by Jewish parents, announced by Jewish prophets, and he sprang from a totally Jewish culture and setting. Of course, the earliest Church was Jewish to the core. Our teachings and concepts are likewise Jewish.

When we cut ourselves off from the richness of our Hebrew heritage we become empty. We are left to improvise from the world and culture around us. Perhaps this is partly what the prophet is speaking of in those mournful words of Amos 8:11-12:

> *"The days are coming," declares the Sovereign LORD, "when I will send a famine through the land – not a famine of food or a thirst for water, but a famine of hearing the words of the LORD. Men will stagger from sea to sea and wander from north to east, searching for the word of the LORD, but they will not find it.*

WRONG IDEAS OF ISRAEL & THE JEWISH PEOPLE

The land of Israel for many Christians is just that place that the preacher visited last year with his tour and took all those lovely slides. Perhaps once in a lifetime some Christians might venture to the Holy Land, at least if things are peaceful and there is no trouble brewing there.

When the average Christian comes to Israel it is often primarily just to "see where Jesus walked." However, if Jesus is the Messiah, and the Messiah is the restorer of Israel as we read in Isaiah 49:6, we need to wake up to some new realities. We should not only want to see where Jesus walked, but we should want to see where he is walking, in the restoration of the nation. In fact, the land of Israel is called "Immanuel's land," as we see in Isaiah 8:8.

Christians also often come to Israel with a sense of pride, feeling that they have all the truth and the Jews have none. They express this condescending attitude in numerous ways. A particularly galling one is the disinterest they often express in the many Jewish historical sites. This betrays a misunderstanding of what it means to be grafted into Israel. If we share a common heritage, then we also share a common history and a common land.

"Unfortunately, the Church has often spiritualized the concept of land so that the earthly Canaan has evaporated into an ethereal, heavenly Canaan."[3] The Jews can teach us much here. For them it is a *mitzvah* or good deed to live in the actual land of Israel and to even be buried in the land. Jews have been instructed to leave a corner of their houses unpainted as a way of remembering and longing for Zion.[4]

When we spiritualize the land of Israel we cut ourselves off from our ancient roots. We separate ourselves from the people of Israel. In doing so we overlook hundreds of verses in the scriptures that talk of the actual land of Israel and its importance, even to us Christians. We forget that our Messiah is coming back to a literal place, a literal land, a literal people and he will set his feet down on a literal Mount of Olives.

Unfortunately we have looked upon the Jewish people as a people cursed and cut off from God's plan. Through our doctrines of trimuphalism we feel we have replaced the Jews entirely. Thus, the Jews per se are of little interest to the average Christian. We often feel that we have all the revelation and they have none. We forget that they were the only people in history to have a direct audience with God. They have much to teach us.

A Christian volunteer picks olives in the Galilee.

MAINTAINING A PROPER ATTITUDE

In Romans 11:18-21, Paul warns us about keeping the proper attitude toward Israel.

> *do not boast over those branches. If you do, consider this: You do not support the root, but the root supports you. You will say then, "Branches were broken off so that I could be grafted in." Granted. But they were broken off because of unbelief, and you stand by faith. Do not be arrogant, but be afraid. For if God did not spare the natural branches, he will not spare you either.*

After almost two thousand years of belittling, defaming, and persecuting Israel, it is difficult for us to understand and heed his instructions.

It might be good for us in light of the dismal history of Jewish Christian relations, to stop and consider a few cardinal truths about Israel. Our lineage goes back to Abraham as is pointed out in many places in scripture. We are

the seed of Abraham (Gal. 3:29). In Genesis 17:4, God promised that he would make Abraham the father of a multitude
of nations *(goyim)*.

God never removed all the natural branches (Israel), but
only some of them as we see in Romans 11:17. The root of
Israel is still holy, regardless of what anti-Semites have
taught for two thousand years (Rom. 11:16). Israel is loved on
account of the patriarchs (11:28). God's gift and call are
irrevocable (11:29). In Romans 9:4-5, we see that to the
Israelites pertain many things: *"...the adoption as sons; ...the
divine glory, the covenants, the receiving of the law, the temple
worship and the promises. Theirs are the patriarchs, and from
them is traced the human ancestry of Christ..."*

It might even shock us to realize that the New Covenant, in
which we take so much pride, is a covenant made with Israel.
In Jeremiah 31:31 it is said: *" 'The time is coming,' declares the
LORD, 'when I will make a new covenant with the house of
Israel and with the house of Judah.' "* We are beneficiaries of
this covenant solely because we are grafted into Israel and
have experienced the new work of God through the sending of
his Messiah. It is not a covenant made separately with
Gentile people.

GETTING TO THE ROOT OF THE ROOTS

There is, however, an inherent danger in today's "roots
movement." The danger is that we will look to natural Israel
and to the Jewish people totally for the roots of our faith. The
designation "roots movement" is not biblical in its essence,
since there is only one root. In fact, the word "root" is used in
the singular throughout Romans 11. The movement would
thus more accurately be called the "root movement," or better
still, the "Hebrew Heritage movement." We must always
remember that the true root is the Messiah. He is the root of
Israel and every good thing we see in Israel today is but his
disguised presence.

The scripture makes this plain. In Isaiah 11:10 we read,
"And in that day there shall be a Root of Jesse, Who shall stand

as a banner to the people; for the Gentiles shall seek Him, and His resting place shall be glorious." In Revelation 22:16 (cf. Rev. 5:5) Jesus is clearly named as the root: "I, Jesus, have sent My angel to testify to you these things in the churches. **I am the Root** *and the Offspring of David, the Bright and Morning Star" (emphasis mine).*

Although the Bible never specifically compares Jesus to the olive tree, the clear implication is there by the fact that He is the root. We know from another related picture that He is the vine.   In John 15:5 we read, *"I am the vine; you are the branches. If a man remains in me and I in him, he will bear much fruit; apart from me you can do nothing."*

The Apostle Paul gives us end-day Christians this sound advice in Colossians 2:6-10: *"As you have therefore received Christ Jesus the Lord, so walk in Him,* **ROOTED** *and built up in Him and established in the faith, as you have been taught, abounding in it with thanksgiving. Beware lest anyone cheat you through philosophy and empty deceit, according to the tradition of men, according to the basic principles of the world, and not according to Christ. For in Him dwells all the fullness of the Godhead bodily; and you are complete in Him, who is the head of all principality and power" (emphasis mine).*

A BEAUTIFUL BIBLICAL EXAMPLE

The beautiful story of Ruth expresses for us most clearly what a proper attitude toward Israel should be.[5] This lovely woman seems to illustrate in her life most all the fruit of the Spirit mentioned by Paul in Galatians 5:22-23.   Ruth was truly devoted to Naomi her Israelite mother-in-law. She loved Naomi with a deep love and commitment that led her to forsake her own heritage and even her own country, in order to be with her.

When Ruth arrived in Israel it was not with the feeling of superiority that so many Christians have today.   Instead, "…she bowed down with her face to the ground…"(Ruth 2:10). She was willing to abase herself to a position lower than a servant girl (2:13). Her attitude was one of continual mercy and generosity as she shared her meager gleanings with Naomi (2:18).

The life of Ruth was also marked with obedience (3:5), kindness (3:10), holiness (3:10), discretion (3:14), and true love and commitment to Israel (4:15). Ruth said to Naomi, *"...Don't urge me to leave you or to turn back from you. Where you go I will go, and where you stay I will stay. Your people will be my people and your God my God"* (Ruth 1:16).

Perhaps Ruth's life gives us some hints of what the engrafting spoken of in Romans 11 is all about. If we could see Israel as Ruth did, we could then consider ourselves only as wild branches grafted into the tree of Israel (Rom. 11:17). Ruth was grafted right into the Messianic line. Like Ruth, we would fully understand that it is not we who support the root, but the root supports us (11:18).

Like Ruth, we would then have no room for pride or triumphalism, or other ideas that we have replaced Israel. There would be no room for boasting and arrogance (Rom. 11:18-21), as our Christian brothers and sisters have been so prone to do. Instead, we would be left with godly fear, (Rom. 11:20) and thankfulness for the Lord's great mercies to us (11:33-36).

STUDY QUESTIONS:

What are some things that have cut us off from our Hebrew heritage?

What does the olive tree illustrate about our heritage?

Explain the difference between "roots" and "root."

What kind of attitude should we manifest as we approach Israel?

NOTES

1. Grolliers Interactive Encyclopedia, CD-Rom, 1992, 1993, 1994.
2. Clarence Wagner, *Israel Teaching Letter,* Bridges For Peace, July 1995.
3. Marvin R. Wilson, *Our Father Abraham* (Grand Rapids, MI: William B. Eerdmans Publishing Co., and Center for Judaic-Christian Studies, Dayton, OH., 1989) p. 260.
4. Wilson, *Our Father Abraham,* p. 261.
5. Jim Gerrish, "Exploring Our Jewish Roots," *Jerusalem Prayer Letter,* Bridges For Peace, August, 1990.

-8-

JESUS, BEFORE HE
BECAME A GENTILE

Jesus was a Jew. He was born of a Jewish mother, and for that reason alone he could qualify for *aliya* (immigration in Israel) by present standards. He was born in a Jewish town, circumcised according to Jewish law, worshipped in a Jewish synagogue, and read the Jewish law as was customary. He undoubtedly spoke the Hebrew language.[1] Joachim Jeremias remarks that Jesus was "a prophet who completely remained within the limits of Judaism."[2]

Jesus has been pictured in the garb and with the skin coloration of virtually every Gentile people on earth. However, prior to recent decades Jesus was seldom depicted with clearly Jewish features or in a religious Jewish context. The theologian Charlesworth states, "...if two facts are unassailable today, they are Jesus' deep Jewishness – he was a Jew – and his paradigmatic effect on Jews and Gentiles."[3]

It would shock many Christians today to see Jesus wearing a *tallit* (a garment with tassels or fringes). Yet, we can be assured that he wore one. Had he not done so, he would have broken the very Law that he came to uphold. The law concerning the wearing of such garments is found in Numbers 15:37-41. This type of garment was certainly still worn in Jesus time, because along with the discovery of the Dead Sea

Scrolls, a *tallit* was found almost intact. It can be seen on display today at the Shrine of the Book in Jerusalem.

On one occasion a sick woman came and touched what must have been the fringes *(tzitzit)* of this garment, and in so doing, she was healed (Mk. 5:25-34). Perhaps she was depending upon that phrase in Malachi 4:2, *"But for you who revere my name, the sun of righteousness will rise with healing in its wings. And you will go out and leap like calves released from the stall."* The word for "wings" is from the Hebrew root *"kanaph,"* and can also refer to the wings of the prayer shawl *(arba kenafyot)* or four wings.[4]

EVIDENCE OF HIS JEWISHNESS

There is much evidence of Jesus' Jewishness in scripture if we take time to search it out and consider it. Jesus was born of Jewish parents and into a devout Jewish home. He was circumcised on the eighth day (Lk 2:21). After Jesus' birth, his mother performed the required purification rites by presenting him at the Temple in Jerusalem and by making the necessary sacrifice (Lk. 2:22-24).

Jesus' parents were faithful in journeying to Jerusalem every year for the feast of Passover (Lk. 2:41). When we remember the distance between Galilee and Jerusalem, and when we consider most people traveled on foot, this was in itself a considerable demonstration of their devotion.

Even as a child, Jesus was deeply attracted to the Temple and was interested in the theological discussions carried on in its precincts. On one of his many trips to Jerusalem, he talked at length with the teachers (Lk. 2:42-49), both answering their questions and asking questions of them. The teachers were astounded at his wisdom since he was only a child of twelve years. His parents were also astounded when they discovered he was not on their caravan headed home. They made a panicky trip back to Jerusalem and were amazed to find him in the Temple.

We learn also from scripture that Jesus was no stranger to synagogue. In Luke 4:16 we read,

*The Synagogue at Capernaum. Some scholars think the black
basalt foundation belonged to the synagogue in Jesus' day.*

*He went to Nazareth, where he had been brought up,
and on the Sabbath day he went into the synagogue,
as was his custom. And he stood up to read.*

We learn that it was not only Jesus' custom to attend the
synagogue, but apparently it was quite customary for him to
participate in the public reading of scripture as well.

As an adult, Jesus kept the various Jewish holidays and
festivals. He ate the Passover meal with his disciples (Matt.

26:17, cf. John 2:23). In John 5:1, Jesus attends some unnamed feast in Jerusalem. We also read in John's gospel that Jesus went up to Jerusalem to keep the Feast of Tabernacles (John 7:2,14).

In fact, one of the truly beautiful teachings of the New Testament was made during this festival. It was the teaching related to the giving of the Holy Spirit to Jesus' followers. Apparently the teaching was based upon one important part of the Temple celebration in ancient times, known as the "Water-drawing Festival." In this celebration, a young *cohen* (priest) took a golden pitcher to the Pool of Siloam and filled it with water. He then led a large procession of people as they carried lighted torches and made their way up to the Temple. Upon arriving there, the water was poured upon the altar, and the people broke out into jubilant song and dance.

The rabbis have connected this celebration with Isaiah 12:3, where it is said, *"With joy you will draw water from the wells of salvation."* The rabbis also have said of the Water-Drawing Festival, "He that never has seen the joy of the *Beth ha-She'ubah* has never in his life seen joy." (*Mishnah, Sukkah* 5.1)[5]

Jesus seems to have used this feast as the backdrop for his teaching. We read:

> On the last and greatest day of the Feast, Jesus stood and said in a loud voice, "If anyone is thirsty, let him come to me and drink. Whoever believes in me, as the Scripture has said, streams of living water will flow from within him." (John 7:37-38).

The writer John tells us that Jesus was speaking about the Holy Spirit whom his followers would receive.

It seems that Jesus, being a devout Jew, also kept the lesser festivals. We see him in Jerusalem in winter at the Feast of Dedication (John 10:22). Today we know this winter festival as *Hanukkah*. Although it was a non-biblical festival, and although it was in winter, with its cold, rain and discomfort, Jesus showed up in Jerusalem for the festival.

Moses' Seat from the synagogue of Korazin.

We can be sure that Jesus honored the Law. He says of it in Matthew 5:17, *"Do not think that I have come to abolish the Law or the Prophets; I have not come to abolish them but to fulfill them."* Sometimes we get the idea that Christ brought an end of the Law. We probably get that idea by not reading far enough in Romans 10:4. In that verse Paul says, *"For Christ is the end of the law for righteousness to everyone who believes (NKJV)."* He was the end of the law for righteousness, but definitely not the end of the Law.

He no doubt honored the Sabbath. Had he not done so he would have broken the law. Jesus did have a running battle with the Pharisees concerning what could and could not be done on the Sabbath. It seems that Jesus made a special effort to heal people on the Sabbath, and that was strictly forbidden by the Pharisees and other religious leaders. However, among the Jews there is the teaching of *pecuach nephesh*. By this understanding, most laws can be set aside to save a life. Perhaps Jesus was operating under this principle or one similar to it in his healings.

Jesus seemed to have no argument with many Jewish customs. His argument was with the failure of some Jewish leaders to practice what they themselves taught. Jesus also attacked their prideful abuse concerning these customs. In. Matthew 23:2-3, Jesus instructs his followers to heed what the religious leaders are teaching:

> *The teachers of the law and the Pharisees sit in Moses' seat. So you must obey them and do every-thing they tell you. But do not do what they do, for they do not practice what they preach.*

In Matthew 23:5, Jesus speaks of phylacteries (tiny boxes containing God's word attached to the foreheads and arms of devout Jews), and he speaks about the borders on Jewish garments. Larsson remarks: "Does Jesus condemn the Jewish custom here? Does he say: 'They make phylacteries and put them on'? No, He says: 'They make their phylacteries broad.' "6 Their actions were a thinly disguised attempt to win the praise of men.

Yes, Jesus was a Jew. He was not a Gentile as we have supposed, and even as we have been taught. It is a rather surprising fact that Jesus avoided preaching and sending out his disciples to Gentiles. With rare exceptions, both he and his disciples ministered only to the House of Israel (Matt. 15:24).

In Jesus' early ministry we see him instructing his twelve disciples not to enter into the way of the Gentiles or go even into the cities of the Samaritans, but only to the people of Israel (Matt. 10:5-6). This is a surprising statement when we realize that much of the area around the Sea of Galilee was in Gentile hands. Virtually the whole eastern and southern shores of the lake were a part of the Decapolis, a Gentile-Greek area. Jesus seems to have confined his ministry to the northern and northwestern shores of the lake, primarily to three Jewish cities, Capernaum, Bethsaida and Korazin.

On one occasion Jesus traveled to the area of today's Lebanon, in the region of Tyre and Sidon. There he was encountered by a Syro-Phoenician woman who asked him to heal her child. The disciples roughly requested that she be sent away. Jesus replied to her bluntly in Matt. 15:26, *"...It is not right to take the children's bread and toss it to their dogs."* The woman persisted and finally Jesus granted her petition.

Near the close of his ministry when he was facing crucifixion, some Greeks came desiring to see Jesus (John 12:20-22). This was a simple request, but Philip to whom they first spoke had to consult with Andrew about it. Afterwards, both of them approached Jesus. It is interesting that Jesus did not give an answer to the Greeks. Instead he began to speak of his approaching death and how it was necessary for him to die in order to bring forth fruit (12:24). Jesus seems to be saying that his death and resurrection would be necessary before Gentiles would be able to come into the Church. Indeed, this proved to be the case.

Although we read the Bible, we Gentiles often picture Jesus as being totally Gentile. How mistaken we are.

HIS FAMILIARITY WITH JEWISH LEARNING

It appears that Jesus had a good understanding of rabbinic learning and methodology. David Flusser, Professor Emeritus of Hebrew University, remarks, "Jesus was part and parcel of the world of the Jewish Sages. He was no ignorant peasant, and his acquaintance with the Written and the Oral Law was considerable"[7] In another place Flusser points out that Jesus had a "...profound Jewish education..."[8]

Flusser mentions several areas of similarity between Jesus' teaching and that of certain Jewish Sages. In Matthew 5:27-30, Jesus connects committing adultery with the lustful eye. This is also reflected in the Sages teaching "that the word 'commit adultery' has four letters in Hebrew, since a man commits adultery with his eyes, hands, heart and feet."[9]

There was the concept present in Judaism at the time that to shame a neighbor is to shed his blood. A similar idea is reflected in Jesus teaching in Matthew 5:22, which states that one who insults his brother shall be liable to the council."[10]

In the Mishna, a saying of the great Hillel is repeated. Hillel lived before and slightly contemporary with Jesus. His words were, "What is distasteful to yourself, do not do to your neighbor; that is the whole law, the rest is but commentary." (*Talmud, Shabbat,* 31a) How similar is this statement with the words of Jesus in Matthew 7:12, *"So in everything, do to others what you would have them do to you, for this sums up the Law and the Prophets."*

In Luke 20:18 Jesus says, *"Everyone who falls on that stone will be broken to pieces, but he on whom it falls will be crushed."*   Brad Young points out how the rabbis have a similar story about a pot and a stone: "If a stone falls on a pot, woe to the pot! If a pot falls on a stone, woe to the pot! In either case woe to the pot!..."[11]

When Jesus told his parable of the Good Samaritan (Luke 10:30-37), he may have had some of the Jewish Oral Torah in mind. He spoke of a priest and a Levite who passed by a seriously wounded man on the road to Jericho. The man was spoken of as "half dead." He may have been beaten to unconsciousness and even have appeared dead. The poor man was later assisted by a despised Samaritan.

In the Oral Torah, a person is required to bury an abandoned corpse. This was such a stringent requirement that it even applied to the High Priest. Although he was not allowed to become ritually impure even for a death of a member in his own family, he was still required to become impure to bury an abandoned body *(met mitzvah* - i.e. commandment concerning the dead), or to give life sustaining assistance.[12] Jesus may have been chiding religious leaders over their failures to keep the Oral Torah.

We see a connection with Jesus and the teaching of the Jews in the episode of Jesus' temptation in the wilderness. The devil transports Jesus to the pinnacle of the Temple and tempts him to cast himself off that God may deliver him (Matt. 4:5). Young comments how in a later Jewish *midrash,* the Messiah is pictured as standing on the roof of the temple and proclaiming redemption to the humble.[13] Apparently the Jews expected this type of demonstration from their Messiah and therefore Jesus was tempted along these lines.

Jesus certainly followed in the tradition of the Hassidim, or the pious ones in the realm of miracle working. His miracles greatly exceeded all who had gone before him. However, he was a miracle worker in the tradition of Honi the Circle-Drawer and Rabbi Hanina ben Dosa and Abba Hilkia.[14] These men either preceded Jesus or were of the same general period in history. The last two of these miracle workers were also from the Galilee.

JESUS AND THE DEAD SEA SCROLLS

Since their discovery by a Bedouin boy in 1947, the Dead Sea Scrolls have fascinated the minds of Bible scholars. As more of these scrolls have been translated, scholars have realized that they provide us with unusual insights on Jesus and his times. Charlesworth remarks, "Now placed before our eyes are leather scrolls once written, held, and read by Jews contemporaneous with Jesus."[15]

The members of the Essene group who produced and preserved these scrolls were Jews. They were a very zealous sect of Jews for sure, but they believed some things that Jesus believed. The main body of this sect lived and worked at Qumran, in fairly close proximity to the highway between Jericho to Jerusalem. Thousands of other Essenes were scattered in various communities throughout Israel. It seems very likely that Jesus was acquainted with them and with their teaching.

Many of Jesus' teachings were similar to those of the Essenes. They shared the same adversaries, Romans, Sadducees, Pharisees, and Zealots. They emphasized the sinfulness of humanity, the need for God's grace, the approaching end of the age, and even the establishment of a new covenant.[16]

In the book of Matthew there is a whole Thanksgiving Hymn that is written in the style of the Essene Thanksgiving Hymns.[17] Jesus says in this hymn, "...*I thank You, Father, Lord of heaven and earth, that You have hidden these things*

from the wise and prudent and have revealed them to babes"
(Matt. 11:25 NKJV).

Jesus was much like the Esssenes in that he considered
humility, purity and simplicity of heart as supreme religious
virtues. He regarded all possessions as a threat to the holy
life.[18]   He believed that evil could be overcome with good
(Matt. 5:39-41), just as the Essenes before him had believed.[19]

Jesus, along with John the Baptist and the Essenes, also
practiced baptism. In the *Mishnah,* living water (water from
rivers or seas) was believed to have the highest grade of
cleansing for ritual immersion. It is interesting that John the
Baptist baptized in the Jordan River. Jesus and his disciples
did the same. The Dead Sea sect required repentance before
baptism, likewise the early Christians.[20]

There seem to be other teachings that Jesus and his disciples had virtually in common with the Essenes. The Essenes
spoke of themselves as "poor in spirit" and "poor."[21] Jesus also
admonished his disciples to be "poor in spirit" (Matt. 5:3). The
Essenes prohibited divorce.[22]   Jesus' teaching did the same
(Mark 10:2-9).

In recent years there has been the discovery of a small gate
at the southwest corner of the second wall in Jerusalem.
Some have connected it with the Essene gate mentioned by
Josephus. If this is truly the Essene Gate, then one may conclude that some Essenes lived in the southwest section of
Herodian Jerusalem. Charlesworth points out that it was in
this area according to early sources that Jesus probably held
his last supper. It was also possibly the home of Jesus' family.
Jesus' disciples and his family members may have shared the
same section of Jerusalem in close proximity with this Jewish
sect.[23]

A JEWISH MESSIAH

Jesus, or *Yeshua* as he is called in Hebrew, came to this
earth as God's promised Servant to the Jewish people. As a
part of his great mission to Israel, he also came to bring
judgment or deliverance to the Gentiles (Isa. 42:1). As

Matthew says: *"In his name the nations will put their hope"* (Mat. 12:21).

Thus, Jesus came first and foremost to the house of Israel (Matt. 10:6). The New Covenant was made with them and not with Gentile people (Jer. 31:31). Gentiles by the grace and mercy of God would be "grafted" into God's covenant with Israel.

We Gentiles in our pride and arrogance have done great violence to the scripture and to its proper understandings. We are guilty of greatly distorting the person of Jesus. We have robbed him of his Judaism. In doing so we have made him contemptible to the Jewish people. We have made him a Gentile like ourselves.

STUDY QUESTIONS:

What if Jesus appeared at your church door wearing a *tallit?* Do you suppose he would be admitted? Would he receive stares?

How many evidences of Jesus' Jewishness can you identify?

Was Jesus opposed to the bulk of Jewish customs of his day? Was he even opposed to the general teaching of the Pharisees? Can you find a scripture to illustrate this?

What are some things Jesus seemed to have in common with the Essenes?

NOTES

1. David Flusser, *Jewish Sources in Early Christianity* (New York: Adama Books, 1987) p. 11.
2. Quoted in Marvin R. Wilson, *Our Father Abraham* (Grand Rapids, MI: William B. Eerdmans Publishing Co., and Center for Judaic-Christian Studies, Dayton, OH., 1989) p. 54.

3. James H. Charlesworth, *Jesus Within Judaism, New Light from Exciting Archaeological Discoveries* (New York: Doubleday, 1988) p. 167.

4. See Clarence Wagner, Jr., "Hem of the Garment, " *Israel Teaching Letter,* January, 1995.

5. Herbert Danby, translator, *The Mishna,* (New York: Oxford University Press, 1933).

6. Goran Larsson, *"The Jews! Your Majesty"* (San Diego, CA & Jerusalem, Israel: Jerusalem Center for Biblical Studies and Research, 1989) p. 19.

7. Flusser, *Jewish Sources in Early Christianity,* p.19.

8. Flusser, *Jewish Sources in Early Christianity,* p.62.

9. Flusser, *Jewish Sources in Early Christianity,* p.25.

10. David Flusser, *Jesus* (Jerusalem: The Magnes Press, The Hebrew University, 1968 and 1997) p. 91.

11. Quoted in Brad H. Young, *Jesus The Jewish Theologian* (Peabody, MS: Hendrickson Publishers, Inc., 1995) p. 221.

12. Young, *Jesus The Jewish Theologian,* p. 167.

13. Young, *Jesus The Jewish Theologian,* p. 31.

14. Flusser, *Jesus,* p. 113.

15. Charlesworth, *Jesus Within Judaism, New Light from Exciting Archaeological Discoveries,* p. 56.

16. Charlesworth, *Jesus Within Judaism, New Light from Exciting Archaeological Discoveries,* p. 59.

17. Flusser, *Jewish Sources in Early Christianity,* p.41.

18. Flusser, *Jesus,* p. 94.

19. Flusser, *Jesus,* p. 98.

20. Young, *Jesus The Jewish Theologian,* p. 14-15.

21. Charlesworth, *Jesus Within Judaism, New Light from Exciting Archaeological Discoveries,* pp. 68-69.

22. Charlesworth, *Jesus Within Judaism, New Light from Exciting Archaeological Discoveries,* p. 72.

23. Charlesworth, *Jesus Within Judaism, New Light from Exciting Archaeological Discoveries,* pp. 116-117. For more detailed information please consult *Jesus and the Dead Sea Scrolls,* edited by Charlesworth and published by Doubleday, (N.Y.). See particularly pages 204, 207-208, and 215.

HOW DID A NICE JEWISH CHURCH BECOME GENTILE?

Jesus, the founder of the Church, was a Jew. Not only was Jesus a Jew, but his disciples were all Jewish. They were all born as Jews and they lived as Jews. They worshipped regularly at the Jewish Temple in Jerusalem (Acts 2:46).

The early church was a Jewish church, with a Jewish constituency and Jewish leaders.

Let us consider some evidences of these facts.

BACK WHEN CHRISTIANITY *WAS* ALL JEWISH

The earliest Jewish Christians were called Nazarenes (Acts 24:5). The biblical designation, Nazarene, is thought to have a connection to the word *"Netzer"* (branch) found in Isaiah 11:1. Later in the Talmud, Christians were called *Notzrim.*[1] The name *Notzrim* has persisted until the modern era, and is the name used to designate Christians in Israel today.

We know from scripture that Jesus' followers were first called "Christians" at Antioch during the New Testament era (Acts 11:26). After the first century there seems to have been a split in the group and we hear of some of these believers called Ebionites. Since this name means 'the poor' it is thought that they were probably an ascetic group. They made their abode in the region east of the Jordan River.

The first century synagogue at Gamla on the Golan Heights. This synagogue may have been visited by Jesus or by his disciples.

This split may have been doctrinal in nature, and the Ebionites may have been the remnants of the earlier circumcision party. They upheld the whole of the Jewish law and vehemently rejected the letters of Paul. They apparently had a flawed view of the deity of Jesus.[2] The sect continued on for several centuries.

The earliest Christians kept the Sabbath and Jewish festivals (Acts 13:13-15). Although the Apostle Paul was the disciple to the Gentiles, he was still thoroughly Jewish. He once hurried from Gentile lands to Jerusalem that he might arrive in time to keep the Jewish festival of Pentecost (Acts. 20:16). When he arrived in Jerusalem he underwent a Jewish ceremony of purification in the company of other Jews who had made vows to God (Acts 21:26). It is evident that the earliest Christians showed deep respect toward the requirements of the Jewish law (Acts 21:20).

The Church in Jerusalem continued as a Jewish Church for several generations. The Historian Eusebius reports that the first fifteen bishops of Jerusalem, until the time of Hadrian (AD 135), were all Hebrews. After the fifteenth bishop, Narcissus, we finally hear of Marcus, who is listed by Eusebius as being the first Gentile bishop of Jerusalem.[3] He also reports that the whole church consisted of Hebrews.[4]

The Jewish Church flourished in these early years. Lately, several artifacts have been uncovered to illustrate the presence of this Church. In Jerusalem early Christian sarcophagi have been discovered. On the Golan Heights, archaeological evidence of Christian/Jewish symbols has been found by French archaeologist, Dr. Claudine Dauphin.[5]

EARLY RELATIONS WITH GENTILES

The Church was so thoroughly Jewish from its earliest days that it greatly struggled with the problem of Gentiles. In Matthew 10:5-6, we see that this tension was also reflected in the ministry of Jesus and his disciples.

We see this problem regarding Gentiles continuing on for some time in the early Church. In Acts 8, we see the evangelist Philip going down to Samaria and proclaiming the Gospel. The Samaritans were a mixed people, the bulk of whom had been brought in by the Assyrians after the fall of the Northern Kingdom in 722 BC. These people believed Philip and many were converted by his preaching.

However, Philip's revival in Samaria seems to have provoked a mini-crisis in Jerusalem. The Church immediately dispatched Peter and John to Samaria (Acts 8:14). Peter and John prayed and the new converts received the Holy Spirit. The situation then apparently became acceptable to the Church in Jerusalem.

Later, Peter had an experience with Gentiles, and this was in relation to the Gentile centurion, Cornelius (Acts 10:1-11:18). The angel of God appeared to the devout Cornelius in Caesarea, and requested that he send for Peter. While Peter was in Joppa he himself had a vision, and in the vision God showed him many unclean animals and requested that he kill and eat of them. Although Peter was hungry, he still protested that he had never eaten of such non-kosher food. This vision of the unclean animals occurred to him three times. In the vision the Lord spoke to Peter that he should not call anything unclean that God had made clean (Acts. 10:15).

Just as Peter aroused from his vision, the emissaries of Cornelius knocked on the door. The Spirit instructed Peter that he was to go with them for they were sent by God. As he met the men, they told him about the supernatural events related to their coming. With all these preliminary preparations in mind it is surprising to see what Peter did later.

When he entered the house of Cornelius he related how it was against Jewish law for him to be in the house of a Gentile (10:28). He then stated how God had shown him not to call anything unclean that God had cleansed. Then Peter asked the very strange question of Acts 10:29: *"...May I ask why you sent for me?"* It seemed that Peter, steeped in Judaism, was still unable to comprehend that Gentiles were about to come to the faith.

As Peter preached, the Holy Spirit then fell on Cornelius and everyone who heard. At this point, the Jews who had accompanied Peter were astonished that the Holy Spirit had come upon Gentiles (10:45). After this episode Peter went to Jerusalem. There the circumcised believers criticized him saying, *"...You went into the house of uncircumcised men and ate with them"* (Acts 11:3). Peter then had to relate his whole experience to the believers in Jerusalem. After they heard it, they all agreed that God had indeed granted repentance to the Gentiles.

Later, Paul was called by the Lord specifically as an apostle to the Gentiles (Rom. 11:13). He made much of his ministry and defended the presentation of the gospel to the Gentiles whenever it was threatened. On one early occasion Peter came to Antioch where Paul was. Peter freely ate with Gentiles until some men came from James and the Church in Jerusalem. Then Peter withdrew himself and would not eat with the Gentiles any longer. Seeing his example, other Jews including Barnabas also withdrew. At this, Paul arose and publicly rebuked Peter for his hypocrisy (Gal. 2:14).

Perhaps the greatest confrontation concerning the Gentiles happened at the Council of Jerusalem mentioned in Acts 15:1-35 and in Galatians 2:1-10. Paul's ministry to the Gentiles had come under question and he, along with Barnabas and Titus, went up to Jerusalem to present his case before the leaders there. The question was whether or not Gentiles who believed would be required to become circumcised and keep all the requirements of the Law.

At this conference Peter was able to speak up on behalf of the Gentiles. After him, James, the leader of the Church, gave his opinion that the Church should not make it difficult for Gentiles coming to the faith (Acts 15:19). The question was resolved and it was determined that Gentiles would not have to become circumcised and keep the law. The leaders, James, Peter and John extended the right hand of fellowship to Paul and Barnabas.

We see that up until this time the Church in Jerusalem was very Jewish. This situation continued on throughout the first century and well into the second century. Gruber remarks about this saying, "In the first century, the most heated, controversial, doctrinal issue of all that the Church faced was: 'How do the Gentiles fit into all this?' ...Today the most heated, controversial, doctrinal issue that the Church faces is: 'How do the Jews fit into all this?' "[6]

GENTILE CHURCHES PATTERN AFTER JEWS

It is clear even in the early days of the Gentile church that it was closely connected to the Jewish Church in Jerusalem. Paul apparently patterned the Gentile churches after those in Judea (1 Thess. 2:14). He taught Gentile churches of their great debt to the people of Israel. He even insisted that because of this great debt, the Gentile churches should take an offering for believers in Israel (Rom. 15:27).

It is a surprising fact of church history that the first general offering mentioned in the New Testament is an offering taken among the Gentiles on behalf of Jews in Israel. It is also surprising that the bulk of stewardship teaching of the New Testament is based upon this offering for Israel.

Today the world-wide Church raises money for every conceivable program. Unfortunately, the modern Church seldom follows the biblical and blessed pattern of taking offerings for Israel.

A FINAL PARTING OF THE WAY

The decision of Jerusalem in Acts 15:5-29 concerning circumcision, undoubtedly helped to widen the growing rift between the Jew and Gentile Christians. Circumcision was, and is today, a critical matter for the Jews. However before AD 70, the Christians were still considered a sect of Judaism. We see this clearly in Acts 2:47, where the Church is described as *"...enjoying the favor of all the people..."* We see it again in Acts 24:5, where the "Nazarene sect" is mentioned.

The real problems began to develop somewhere around AD 66-70, with the Jewish revolt against Rome. At this time the Christians in Jerusalem fled to Pella in Perea. Pella was located in the present Jordanian foothills, about 60 miles northeast of Jerusalem. Later, Pella became an important center for Jewish Christianity.[7]

The Christians probably fled Jerusalem because of the specific instructions of Jesus. In his prophetic utterance regarding Jerusalem's destruction, he warned his followers to flee to the mountains when they saw the city being surrounded by armies (Luke 21:20-22). Although some from Jerusalem seem to have returned after the war, we can understand how Christians from this point on, must have been regarded as traitors to the Jewish cause.

Not only was there a change in the Christian situation, there was also now a drastic change in the Jewish situation. In AD 70, Jerusalem was conquered and the Temple was destroyed by the Roman general Titus. The Jewish Temple, the sacrificial system, and numerous customs and practices of Judaism had come to an abrupt end.

However, during the siege of Jerusalem, a noted Rabbi by the name of Yohanan ben Zakkai escaped. With Roman permission he began a school at Yavneh (Jabne or Jamnia) near the Mediterranean coast. Rabbi Yohanan, a student of the famous Hillel, began a reformulation of Judaism along Pharasaic lines. The Sanhedrin was re-instituted. Some rituals of the Temple were transferred to the home.

His school began to stress acts of charity and kindness as a replacement for sacrifice. The reforms brought about by him and his school insured the survival of Judaism, even without a temple or a sacrificial system. Yohanan attempted to base Judaism upon the spiritual and not upon the territorial.[8]

The reforms of the Yavneh school accomplished many constructive things. The Old Testament canon was defined there. Considerable work was carried on toward establishing the official text of the Hebrew Bible. However, Yavneh was also responsible for one other thing that made the division between Jew and Christian much deeper. Somewhere around AD 90, the *Birkat ha-Minim* (the Heretic Benediction) was adopted and made part of the *Shemoneh Esreh* (the Eighteen Benedictions), a prayer that is to be recited every day by devout Jews.

The Heretic Benediction, which was a condemnation of sects, may not have been drafted specifically against the Christians, but it certainly included them.[9] From this point on it would be exceedingly difficult for Jewish Christians to sit comfortably in the synagogue while their own faith was being cursed.

The final parting of the way was now close at hand. The stage was fully set with the Bar Kochba revolt against Rome in AD 132-135. Probably because Bar Kochba was looked upon as a messianic figure, and even acclaimed as such by the famous Rabbi Akiva, the Jewish Christians could not be involved. This war "was, for all essential purposes, the final major national blow that severed the two communities."[10]

After Rome's second conquest of the Jews, the Emperor Hadrian renamed the city of Jerusalem Aelia Capitolina, after himself. On the Temple Mount he constructed a temple to

Jupiter and forbade Jews to enter Jerusalem. Many of the surviving Jewish leaders went into hiding and eventually the Jewish center of learning was transferred to the Galilee. We can understand how contacts between Jews and Christians would become much more difficult after all this.

THE RIFT WIDENS

We can clearly trace the events within Judaism that separated Jews and Christians. However, there were also events and movements within Christianity itself that contributed to the separation and even widened it.

As Christianity rapidly moved out into the Gentile world, it began to adapt itself to the Gentile culture. Its Hebrew roots were at first forgotten and later they were despised.

This trend is clearly seen in an early controversy over the proper dates of the Passover and Easter celebrations. In primitive times these were celebrated together.

Early in Church history when Anicetus was bishop of Rome (c. 155-166), he was visited by Polycarp Bishop of Smyrna. Although their visit was cordial, it was apparently arranged to settle a disagreement that had broken out over the proper date for Easter. Polycarp represented the eastern and more ancient tradition of having Easter in connection with the Passover, beginning on the 14th of *Nisan*. His position carried much weight since he had celebrated these festivals with John the disciple of the Lord.[11] Anicetus represented the Roman and western idea of choosing a separate date for Easter. He was apparently unconvinced by Polycarp's arguments.

The Easter and Passover problem didn't go away. It flared up again about 167 in Laodicea. There was difficulty again in 190, and several church synods were held to try and reconcile the problem. Eventually the decisions were in favor of the Roman practice. The eastern churches of Asia Minor, led by Bishop Polycrates of Ephesus, refused to accept the decision. At this the Roman bishop Victor excommunicated the recalcitrant congregations.[12]

When Christianity finally gained the ascendancy in the Roman Empire, the Passover problem was legislated from the Roman or Gentile position.

THEOLOGICAL DEVELOPMENTS

Even with the earliest church fathers, there was a tendency to deprecate the Jewish people and the biblical position of Israel. Wilson remarks, "By the time of Justin Martyr (ca. AD 160) a new attitude prevailed in the Church, evidenced by its appropriating the title 'Israel' for itself."[13] Wilson carries this subtle theological trend to its conclusion by saying:

> A triumphalistic and arrogant Church, largely gentile in makeup, would now become more and more de-Judaized – severed from its Jewish roots. This de-Judaizing developed into a history of anti-Judaism, a travesty which has extended from the second century to the present day.[14]

In the theological arena, there is probably no other person who has done so much damage to the Hebrew roots of Christianity as Origen (185?-254?), the early church father from Alexandria. Origen has been credited as being the father of the allegorical method of interpreting the scriptures.[15]

This seems innocent enough at first glance. After all, there is such a thing as allegory in the word of God. In Galatians 4:21-31, Paul speaks of the allegory of the slave woman Hagar and her representation of the covenant of Sinai. It is contrasted with the Jerusalem above, which is free.

Unfortunately, Origen did not stop with these allegories of scripture. He insisted upon seeing almost all scripture in the allegorical sense. Much like some modern preachers, he could take an Old Testament text out of context and virtually preach whatever he wanted from it. For instance, when Origen saw "Israel" in the scripture, he knew it was a reference to the Church.[16]

Gruber remarks, "It is Origen's system of interpretation that produces the anti-Judaic 'New Israel' theology where the church replaces the Jews in the plan and purpose of God."[17] "He lost no opportunity, in his sermons, to attack Jewish literalism, and his powerful invective no doubt made its contribution to the later tragic persecution of Jews by Christians."[18]

He looked upon anyone who did not accept his system as a "Jew," and as someone who did not belong in the Church.[19] When he spoke of "Jewish myths," he was speaking of the Jews and their supposed literal interpretation of the Bible. He felt that "Jewish" and "literal" were virtually synonymous.[20]

It is sad when we consider that Origen had a great deal of interaction with the Jews and undoubtedly knew that the Jews did not always rely upon a literal interpretation. It was, in fact, the Hellenistic Jew, Philo of Alexandria, who had greatly influenced Origen with his allegorical interpretation.

Although Origen was considered a heretic in his lifetime and was later officially branded as such by the Church, his influence lived on and greatly increased.

Later, Pamphilus led the churches of Palestine to begin a theological school dedicated to promulgating Origen's views throughout the whole Church. Pamphilus was the esteemed teacher of Eusebius, the church historian. Eusebius, in turn, devoted himself wholeheartedly to defending the views of Origen. Soon at the Council of Nicea, Eusebius helped ensure the triumph of Origen's heresy.[21]

THE COUNCIL OF NICEA

With the supposed conversion of the Roman Emperor Constantine, the nature of Christianity began to undergo a rapid and radical transformation. Constantine was eager to consolidate his gains and was determined to quell the various divisions within Christianity. Two problems were particularly difficult, the Arian Controversy, which contested the divine nature of Christ, and the continuing divisions over the proper date and celebrations of Easter.

Constantine

In the year 325, the Council of Nicea was called together by the new Emperor. Christian leaders, who a few short years before were persecuted and fed to lions, now traveled at state expense and with great fanfare to Nicea. The Emperor himself presided at the council. Eusebius, who was in favor with the Emperor, had great influence in the outcome of the discussions.

The Arian controversy was dealt with and also a conclusion was finally reached on the Easter celebration. The Church decided to accept the Roman custom of designating a separate day for Easter, quite apart from when the Passover would be celebrated by the Jews. We can understand the embarrassment of this now proud Gentile Church in having to consult the despised Jews on when to celebrate Easter.

The anti-Semitic and anti-Hebraic flavor of this council can best be understood by taking a brief look at some of the statements in the letter of Emperor Constantine to the churches. Here are a few of his statements:

> ...it seemed to every one a most unworthy thing that we should follow the custom of the Jews in the celebration of this most holy solemnity, who, polluted wretches! having stained their hands with a nefarious crime, are justly blinded in their minds. It is fit, therefore, that, rejecting the practice of this people, we should perpetuate to all future ages the

> celebration of this rite, in a more legitimate order.
> ...Let us then have nothing in common with the
> most hostile rabble of the Jews. ...In pursuing this
> course with a unanimous consent, let us withdraw
> ourselves ... from that most odious fellowship.[22]

The opinion of the Council was not to be taken lightly. Now the Church had behind it the full power of the Roman Empire. Any dissent would be looked upon as criminal. From this point on the sword of the Empire and not the sword of the Spirit would determine church doctrine and practice.

Gruber remarks that this council was a turning point in the history of the Church. He states that since this council, all Church theology has been built upon this anti-Judaic foundation. Israel was cast aside and the Church officially became the "new Israel."[23] The teaching of contempt for Israel, along with haughty triumphalism would now be the norm – the only proper Christian attitude.

The early church historian, Eusebius, continued to make the rift wider between Christianity and Judaism. Eusebius in his writings promoted the heresy of Origen. In fact, Eusebius wrote a six volume defense of Origin in an attempt to convince the Church of Origen's orthodoxy.[24]

Eusebius believed that in Constantine, the fullness of the kingdom had come, and that the "new Israel" of the Church would now replace the old Israel. For instance, although there was much evidence in the primitive Church for belief in a literal millennium in Israel, Eusebius ignored the evidence and taught that the millennium was a carnal concept. This fit much better with his own views. He thought that this Jewish doctrine was unacceptable for Christians.[25]

By his writings and influence, he did much to set the theological tone for coming generations. In fact, for the most part, the Greek fathers continuing through the third and fourth centuries would stand generally under the influence and spirit of Origen.[26]

THE CHURCH CUT OFF FROM ITS ROOTS

The Church of Constantine was now effectively cut off from its Jewish heritage. It would receive its sustenance from the Greco-Roman and pagan culture around it. It could no longer be truly biblically-based. As Wilson points out, "It is impossible to be anti-Semitic or anti-Judaic and take the Bible seriously; otherwise one engages in a form of self-hatred."[27]

The trend would continue to modern times. The de-Judaizing of Christianity is clearly evident in some of our Bible translations. One may open the King James version of the Bible and be astonished to see how clearly the Church has replaced Israel. As a general rule the Church is substituted for Israel in the headings at the top of the pages. Even in the beautiful passages speaking of the restoration of Israel in Isaiah 49, the heading reads, "Restoration of the Church."

In its attempt to appropriate the heritage of Israel, the Church has been the real loser. In its bungled attempt, it has almost lost the heritage of Israel altogether. Today the modern Church tries to draw its life from every possible source, yet it withers; it fades; it starves for true nourishment.

STUDY QUESTIONS:

What are some evidences that the earliest Christians followed Jewish practices?

Were Gentile believers readily accepted into the earliest Christian assemblies? Give a scripture to back up your answer.

Name three events that may have contributed to the final separation of Judaism and Christianity.

What were some positive achievements of the Yavneh (Jabne) school?

How did the choosing of the date for Easter help separate the Christian church from its Hebrew heritage?

How did the allegorical method of interpreting scripture aid in the growing Christian anti-Semitism?

In what way was the Council of Nicea a watershed in the Church's relation with Israel?

NOTES

1. Marvin Wilson, *Our Father Abraham, Jewish Roots of the Christian Faith* (Grand Rapids, MI and Dayton, Ohio: William B. Eerdmans Publishing Company, Grand Rapids, MI and Center for Judaic-Christian Studies, 1989) p. 41.
2. Michael Walsh, *Roots of Christianity* (London: Grafton Books, 1986) p. 101.
3. Isaac Boyle, trans. *The Ecclesiastical History of Eusebius Pamphilus* (Grand Rapids, MI: Baker Book House, eighth printing 1976) p. 192.
4. Isaac Boyle, trans. *The Ecclesiastical History of Eusebius Pamphilus,* p. 130.
5. See *Dispatch From Jerusalem,* July/Aug. 1994 Vol. 19. No. 4, p. 1.
6. Daniel Gruber, *The Church and the Jews, The Biblical Relationship* (Springfield, MO: General Council of the Assemblies of God, Intercultural Ministries, 1991) p. 2.
7. Wilson, *Our Father Abraham, Jewish Roots of the Christian Faith,* p. 76.
8. Wilson, *Our Father Abraham, Jewish Roots of the Christian Faith,* p. 77.
9. Wilson, *Our Father Abraham, Jewish Roots of the Christian Faith,* p. 69.
10. Wilson, *Our Father Abraham, Jewish Roots of the Christian Faith,* p. 81.
11. Philip Schaff, *History of the Christian Church, Vol 2, Anti-Nicene Christianity* (Grand Rapids, MI: Wm. B. Eerdmans Publishing Company, MI, 1910) p. 213.

12. Williston Walker, *A History of the Christian Church* (New York: Charles Scribner's Sons, 1959) p. 62.

13. Wilson, *Our Father Abraham, Jewish Roots of the Christian Faith,* p. 83.

14. Wilson, *Our Father Abraham, Jewish Roots of the Christian Faith,* p. 84.

15. Gruber, *The Church and the Jews, The Biblical Relationship,* p. 11.

16. Gruber, *The Church and the Jews, The Biblical Relationship,* p. 11.

17. Gruber, *The Church and the Jews, The Biblical Relationship,* p. 12.

18. Nicholas DeLange, *Origen and the Jews, Studies in Jewish-Christian Relations in Third-Century Palestine* (London, New York , Melbourne, Cambridge University Press, 1976) p. 135.

19. Gruber, *The Church and the Jews, The Biblical Relationship,* p. 15.

20. DeLange, *Origen and the Jews, Studies in Jewish-Christian Relations in Third-Century Palestine,* pp. 105-106.

21. Gruber, *The Church and the Jews, The Biblical Relationship,* p. 17.

22. Quoted in Gruber, *The Church and the Jews, The Biblical Relationship,* p. 30.

23. Gruber, *The Church and the Jews, The Biblical Relationship,* p. 1.

24. Gruber, *The Church and the Jews, The Biblical Relationship,* p. 9.

25. Gruber, *The Church and the Jews, The Biblical Relationship,* p. 18.

26. Gruber, *The Church and the Jews, The Biblical Relationship,* p. 12.

27. Wilson, *Our Father Abraham, Jewish Roots of the Christian Faith,* p. 20.

- 10 -

THE SICKNESS OF ANTI-SEMITISM

Since the days of the Patriarchs, the world has suffered a low-grade fever. At given intervals this fever has become a burning sickness inflaming peoples and nations.[1] This lingering, unexplainable, and irrational sickness was only given a name in 1879. It is called anti-Semitism. The disease may be defined simply as prejudice, discrimination, or persecution against the Jewish people. It has been called "...the longest and deepest hatred of human history."[2]

Obviously, the persecution of Israel was not possible before the covenant was fully established with Abraham, Isaac and Jacob. But since those ancient days, peoples and nations have come repeatedly against the people of God in order to destroy them. The Bible is replete with evidence of these attacks.

ATTACKS IN ANCIENT TIMES

While sojourning in Egypt the Hebrews were mightily oppressed by Pharaoh. In his attempt to destroy God's chosen, he commanded that all the newborn males be slain (Exo. 1:15-16). Had this plan succeeded, it would have ultimately amounted to genocide for the Hebrews.

Pharaoh oppressed and enslaved God's people until at last they were miraculously delivered by the hand of the Almighty.

After this, the Amalakites, Edomites and Moabites all oppressed Israel as she was just a newborn babe, toddling on her way to Canaan. What makes this strange, is that all these ancient peoples were actually blood relatives of the Hebrews.

Of particular interest are the attacks of Amalek and Edom. It seems that the roots of present-day anti-Semitism may be traceable back in some degree to these two nations. We will speak more about these nations, but let us here consider their possible impact upon the seething anti-Semitism of Arab nations in the Middle East today.

The Amalakites were likely the first nation on earth to persecute Israel (Num. 24:20). As the nation of Israel was birthed from Egypt, these relatives attacked them without cause (Exo. 17:8-16). These wicked enemies preyed upon the stragglers, undoubtedly the old and infirm who were tired and weary (Deut. 25:17-18). They set ambushes for Israel (1 Sam. 15:2-3). God's fierce wrath was therefore aroused.

Later, God sent King Saul on a special mission to avenge these hateful acts and to utterly destroy Amalek (1 Sam. 15:2-3). He disobeyed, and the seed of Amalek survived. It is ironic that Saul was later killed by an Amalakite.

God knew that the hate virus in Amalek was extremely dangerous to humankind. He therefore commanded that the whole nation be wiped off the face of the earth (1 Sam. 15:3). Centuries later in Persia, wicked Haman arose to persecute Israel. He almost put an end to the Jewish people in all 127 provinces of this vast kingdom. Persia controlled the Holy Land at that time, and had the plan succeeded, the Jews would have suffered a massive destruction. Jewish tradition declares that Haman was of Amalakite origin.

The Edomites are another ancient nation needing close scrutiny in this regard. This people may also be a source of modern anti-Semitism in the Middle East.

The Edomites apparently received the lineage of hatred intact from their father Esau, who had sworn to kill his brother Jacob (Gen. 27:41). Edom continued the tradition of virulent hatred for Israel.

As Israel was coming out of Egypt, the Edomites refused them passage and came against them with swords (Num. 20:14-21). They later attacked Israel on several occasions and finally assisted in the destruction of Jerusalem in 586 BC. At that time they stood at the crossroads and cut down the people of Judah (Obad. 1:14). It appears that this act may have sealed Edom's doom.

But does the spirit of Edom live on? We read in scripture that the Edomites stifled all compassion. The anger of Edom *"...raged continually and his fury flamed unchecked,"* (Amos 1:11). Edom *"...harbored an ancient hostility..."* (Ezek. 35:5). All this sounds strangely familiar to the sentiments toward Israel of surrounding Arab and Muslim countries today.

In Obadiah 1:10, God says, *"Because of the violence against your brother Jacob, you will be covered with shame; you will be destroyed forever."* It is surely interesting that the word for "violence" used here, is the Hebrew word *"hamas."* Since a group by this very name is now one of the leading antagonists of Israel, we realize how little things seem to change over the thousands of years.

The birth of Jesus gives us a most enlightening insight into the hatred of Edom. King Herod was absolutely enraged with the news of Jesus' birth. He even ordered the massacre of all the infants of the Bethlehem area in a vain attempt to kill the Christ child. He was determined to put a quick end to this one who was to be King of the Jews. It should not surprise us in the least to learn that King Herod was not a Jew, but was of Idumean or Edomite origin.

As proof that the spirit of Edom still lives on today in the Middle East, we should look at a strange passage of scripture in Isaiah 34:5-16. In verse eight we read: *"For the LORD has a day of vengeance, a year of retribution, to uphold Zion's cause."*

This is a future prophetic event. In this passage he tells us that Edom's streams will be turned into blazing pitch, that her smoke will go up forever and that the land will lie desolate with no one passing through it. There is trouble coming in the future for these Israel bashers even though Edom as a nation has long since ceased to exist.

In some popular eschatology today, Edom and its city of Petra, are strongly pictured as a place of refuge for the Jews as the Day of the Lord nears. Perhaps this may be a reason why some Christian pilgrimages now include Petra. The spiritual types and patterns for this conclusion seem mistaken. The scripture makes very plain that Edom is a place of eternal cursing, not a place of refuge and blessing for God's people.

Many of the other prophets elaborate on the Edom theme. Ezekiel speaks of Edom as harboring an ancient hatred. Then he says something that should send a shiver up the spine of all Israel bashers today.

> *Then you will know that I the LORD have heard all the contemptible things you have said against the mountains of Israel...* (Ezek. 35:12)

We understand by this statement that the God of the Universe still hears all the slanders that nations speak against Israel today. He still hears all the slanders spoken by writers and newscasters, and he will recompense them all.

The Messiah at his coming will deal harshly with Edom, or with its spiritual descendants, whoever, and wherever they are. This account is found in Isaiah 63. In this passage we see the Messiah's garments stained with blood. By his own confession he says:

> *"I have trodden the winepress alone; from the nations no one was with me. I trampled them in my anger and trod them down in my wrath; their blood spattered my garments, and I stained all my clothing* (Isaiah 63:3).

The Messiah at his coming seems amazed at the nations (and perhaps at the Church) that there was no one who gave support (v.5). Perhaps the nations and even the Church have been too busy trying to justify and support the enemies of

Israel to realize that these modern enemies of that nation may well be God's enemies just as they were in biblical times.

We should learn one thing from the Amalek and Edom episodes in the Bible. When God decrees that a nation should be destroyed, we better believe that such destruction is absolutely necessary.

LATER ATTACKS

Once they were in the land of Canaan, the attacks against tiny, struggling Israel were virtually endless. The long centuries were filled with wars brought about by all the surrounding nations. Time and again the Edomites, Moabites, Amalekites, Ishmaelites, Ammonites, Midianites, and Philistines came against the people of God.

The persistent attacks upon Israel made no sense. King David often wondered about them. He could never understand why he had so many enemies. One other Psalmist certainly wondered about them. We have his recorded musings in Psalm 2:1-3. Although this Psalm speaks primarily about the Lord and his Messiah, we can see why it would also apply to the Jews and their law:

> *Why do the nations conspire and the peoples plot in vain? The kings of the earth take their stand and the rulers gather together against the LORD and against his Anointed One. "Let us break their chains," they say, "and throw off their fetters."*

The presence of the Jewish people in the world brings fetters to those who are lawless. These chains represent law, righteousness and holiness. The world wants none of these things, but instead desires to cast off these "chains" of Israel.

There is another and much deeper reason behind anti-Semitism. Anti-Semitism has behind it the secret mystery of iniquity. It is a part of Satan's diabolical plan to come against the heritage and the people of God. Thus, anti-Semitism is anti-God and anti-Christ in its essence.

Throughout the painful saga of Israel's history she was also bitterly attacked by the stronger empires in the area, such as the Egyptians, Assyrians, Babylonians, Greeks, and finally the Romans. The attacks of Antiochus IV (Epiphanes) during the Greek era had such demonic overtones that Antiochus became a type of the Beast or antichrist ruler who would arise to persecute the Jews mightily at the end of days (Dan. 8:19-26).

The spiritual and diabolical roots of this awful disease of anti-Semitism are pointed out for us clearly in the book of Daniel. In Daniel 10:20, when the angel appeared to the prophet, he made an interesting comment:

...Soon I will return to fight against the prince of Persia, and when I go, the prince of Greece will come;

This mighty angel of God had been struggling with extremely powerful spiritual entities. The prince of Persia had already delayed him by twenty-one days due to his opposition. Now we learn that the prince of Greece was waiting in the corridors to take his turn at destroying Israel. We see clearly by this that the nations who oppose Israel are driven by mighty supernatural forces.

PAGAN ATTACKS

Once the nation of Israel was destroyed by the Romans, and its people dispersed in the wars of AD 70 and 135, one would think that the "Israel problem" would be put to rest, and that the world would go on to other concerns.

Such was not to be the case. The fever and agitation were unabated. Even the pagan writers of that period, such as Lysimachus, Apion, Tacitus, and Juvenal, continued to attack and slander the dispersed Jewish people.[3] Riots and persecutions erupted in various cities of the pagan world.

All this could be understood much more readily than the attacks that came from another quarter – from the newly founded Christian Church.

EARLY CHRISTIANS INFECTED

Perhaps it first stemmed from jealousy or fear, or from some of both. Nevertheless, shortly after Apostolic times, the Church allowed itself to become infected with the ancient virus of anti-Semitism.

From the second century on, the early Church fathers such as Ignatius, Justin, Irenaeus, and Cyprian began to make inflammatory statements concerning the Jews. Their statements were made in contradiction to what seems to be clear biblical admonitions in Romans 11:17-18, and in many other passages of the New Testament.

This tendency, although mild at the outset, especially when compared with that which would come later, quickly laid the foundations for early triumphalism. This was the idea that the Church has superseded Israel entirely.

Ignatius of Antioch may have been the first Father of the Church to slander the Jews. He wrote to the Magnesians in the early second century that "Christianity... did not believe in Judaism, but Judaism in Christianity."[4]

Ignatius lived in a time when Christianity was still closely connected to the faith of Israel. Just shortly before his days, the Apostles had celebrated Jewish feasts and kept the Jewish Sabbath. Yet Ignatius has stern words for Christians who would pattern after the Apostles. He remarked:

> if anyone celebrates the Passover along with the Jews, or receives emblems of their feast, he is a partaker with those that killed the Lord and His apostles.[5]

Later, Justin Martyr (100-165? AD) in his lengthy *Dialogue with Trypho,* said of Trypho the Jew, "You hate and (whenever you have the power) kill us."[6] Justin also in speaking of the writings of Moses said to Trypho:

> They are contained in your Scriptures, or rather not yours, but ours. For we believe them; but you, though you read them, do not catch the spirit that is in them.[7]

Justin also remarked:

> For the prophetical gifts remain with us, even to the present time. And hence you ought to understand that [the gifts] formerly among your nation have been transferred to us.[8]

Later, Irenaeus, Bishop of Lyon (AD 130-202), declared the Jews "disinherited from the grace of God."[9]

Beginning as early as the days of Justin Martyr there had been a continuing dispute between Christians in the eastern and western areas of the Roman Empire. This dispute concerned the proper date for the observance of Easter. The disagreement became so acute about 190 that synods were held both in the east and in the west.

The decision was finally made in favor of the western Roman custom and against the ancient custom of celebrating Easter with the Passover. The churches of Asia Minor refused to accept this decision, whereupon Victor, the Bishop of Rome, excommunicated Polycrates, bishop of Ephesus.[10] It was a precedent favoring Roman understandings and practices that would bode ill for future Church decisions.

The trend toward triumphalism continued. Cyprian, Bishop of Carthage (200?-258) was bold enough to demand that all Jews leave his diocese or die.[11] We can see that in a very short time, triumphalism had taken on deadly proportions.

CONSTANTINIAN CHRISTIANITY

The fourth century was a critical one for establishing the nature of all future Christian anti-Semitism. Constantine, the new Roman emperor, declared himself a Christian. There is some question as to just how deeply Constantine's Christianity ran. He continued to use the pagan title *Pontifex Maximus* on his coins. He also used images of some of the pagan gods, along with the Unconquered Sun, his own favorite deity. In 321, Constantine made the first day of the week a holiday. He named it for his deity, Sunday.[12]

In the year 325, the first general council of the Church was called together to deal with the heresy of Arianism and to finally establish a uniform date for Easter. Constantine, the new "Christian" emperor exerted great influence upon this council. The resulting work, the famous Nicene Creed, was defined and accepted. The Church also moved to distance itself from Judaism in regard to the celebration of the Lord's resurrection. Constantine's letter to the churches is very instructive concerning the spirit of this council. In his letter he referred to the Jews as "...polluted wretches... blinded in their minds... (a) most odious fellowship... parricides and murderers..."[13]

Constantine made clear the intent of this council by quickly forbidding Jews to proselytize. He also forbade them to live in their own city, Jerusalem.[14]

Following in the spirit of Nicea, John Chrysostom (347?-407), one of the most popular preachers of these times, began his tirades against the Jews. Chrysostom was such a persuasive preacher that he was labeled the "Golden Tongue." In a series of eight sermons he used his golden tongue to attack the Jews. Chrysostom called the Jews "most miserable of all men" "lustful, rapacious, greedy perfidious bandits." He described them as having "the manners of the pig and the lusty goat." He said "they have surpassed the ferocity of wild beasts, for they murder their offspring and immolate them to the devil." Chrysostom went on to say, "...I hate the Jews also because they outrage the law..."[15]

At the end of his sermon series, Chrysostom demanded that his hearers pay him interest, apparently meaning that they go out and do something to actually persecute the Jews.[17]

"The language of anti-Semitism is the devil's native tongue; it quickly becomes the second language of the devil's disciples, and soon it takes command of their original language... (the Devil) is the god of anti-Semitism."[16]

The questionable teachings offered by these early fathers and preachers continued to inflame the Church in its formative centuries. Church and state also were now working hand and hand toward the systematic isolation and persecution of the Jews.

Following the example of Constantine, Emperor Constantius set a pattern by confiscating the property of a Christian who dared convert to Judaism.[18] In following years, the Byzantines disrupted synagogue services and forbade Jews to hold governmental posts. Jews were not permitted to beautify or repair their synagogues without permission. They were barred from public functions. Marriage of Jews to Christians was seen as "shameful," and such marriages were prohibited under penalty of death.[19]

Later Byzantine rulers such as Heraclius, Leo III, and Basil I promoted forced conversions of the Jews. The trend went on in both the eastern and western portions of the empire. In the west, sixth and seventh century Frankish kings, such as Chilperic I and Dagobert I, also promoted forced conversions and baptisms.[20]

THE CRUSADES

Soon after the end of the first millennium a crowning tragedy developed for the Jews. It came as a result of agitation caused by the Crusades. This tragedy began shortly after the Council of Clermont in 1095, and lasted almost two hundred years. In this council, the Pope called for crusades to liberate the Holy Land from the hand of the Muslims.

At the beginning of the First Crusade, restless adventurers started testing their swords on the Jews in their midst. In many cities such as Speyer, Worms, Cologne, and Prague, Jews were massacred. It is estimated that from January to July in 1096, some 10,000 Jews died. This would have probably amounted to about one fourth to one third of the Jewish population of Germany and Northern France.[21]

When the Crusaders finally reached Jerusalem in 1099, they rounded up its remaining Jews and burned them alive in their own synagogue. While the Jews screamed in the flames, the Crusaders held their crosses high and sang "Christ We Adore Thee!"[22]

Unfortunately, many more crusades were to come, and they all would tend to follow the same destructive pattern as the first.

NEW WEAPONS OF ANTI-SEMITISM

In the 12th and 13th centuries, the Church doctrine of transubstantiation gained wide acceptance. This doctrine affirmed that the actual flesh and blood of Christ became present in the consecrated Host and wine. Miraculous tales in connection with the Host began to circulate and soon the Jews began to be charged with desecration of the Host.

Another common charge of the Church in this period was that the Jews kidnapped Christian children, killing and torturing them in order to obtain blood for their Passover ritual. No one seemed to know or even care that partaking of blood was totally forbidden by Jewish law, yet the myth persisted even as late as 1936 in Nazi Germany.

After each blood libel, the Church would rise up in hysterical rage to avenge itself upon the Jews. Blood libels became one of the most vicious weapons used against the Jews, and they left a trail of Jewish blood through the centuries.

Anti-Semitism continued to take its toll with expulsions of whole Jewish populations from many European states. In the period between the 11th and 19th centuries the Jews were expelled at least 34 times from major Christian cities and states.

In the year 1215, the Church at its Fourth Lateran Council, ordered Jews to wear distinctive garments. These garments took many forms such as patches of cloth sewn to clothing or the forced wearing of funny hats.

Jews were at various times forbidden to engage in trades, to own land, to intermarry with Christians, and even to live in the midst of Christians. As a final insult they were not even allowed to die in the midst of Christians, and Jewish graves were commonly desecrated.

---

34 Times when Jews were expelled from their homes
(Often they were expelled, invited back and then expelled again)

1012	Mainz	1492	Italy
1182	France	1496	Portugal
1276	Upper Bavaria	1496	Naples
1290	England	1498	Nuremberg
1306	France	1510	Brandengurg
1322	France	1515	Genoa
1394	France	1533	Naples
1420	Lyons	1541	Naples
1424	Cologne	1541	Prague
1438	Mainz	1550	Genoa
1439	Augsburg	1551	Bavaria
1442	Upper Bavaria	1557	Prague
1446	Brandenburg	1569	Papal States
1462	Mainz	1649	Hamburg
1483	Mainz	1669	Vienna
1483	Warsaw	1744	Bohemia and Moravia
1492	Spain	1891	Moscow[23]

By 1240, the Jews were being forced into disputations with the Christians. As a result of these disputations, the Talmud was burned in Paris in 1242. Jews were also forced to listen to Christian sermons, a practice not abolished until 1848.

As a result of the Black Death in Europe, the Jews suffered much in what is referred to as the Black Death Massacres. These massacres continued from 1348 to 1350. In this plague, the Jews were the usual scapegoat and were accused of poisoning the wells of Christians.

THE INQUISITION

The Jews had experienced a "golden age" in Spain, which produced some of the greatest poets, thinkers and inventors in the history of the country. Nevertheless, in 1391 a storm of anti-Jewish persecution swept over the nation. This storm was provoked by certain Christian preachers. As a result, thousands of Jews were killed. For the first and only time in history, the spirit of a whole Jewish people broke, and when faced with the choice of conversion or death, many chose the former.[24]

Churches were filled with these "new Christians." Unfortunately, the "old Christians" now looked upon the new Jewish converts with suspicion. This was partly due to their rapid rise to important positions in the country, even into the royal court. They were soon given a name of contempt, *marrano*, which meant "swine." Judaism and marranism were looked upon as having a common source – bad blood. Jews were considered perverse and defiled, whether or not they were baptized.[25]

Certainly, some continued to be crypto-Jews, who secretly held on to elements of their former faith. This fact also aroused suspicion and helped hasten massive persecution.

As a result, in 1480 Pope Sixtus IV gave permission for the Inquisition to be established. With the rise of the Christian rulers, Ferdinand and Isabella to the throne, and the defeat of the Moors (Muslims), the situation rapidly turned against the Jewish population. Soon the infamous Thomas de Torquemada became the Grand Inquisitor.

Many citizens, including a large proportion of *marranos*, fell into the hands of the Inquisition. The first act of the Inquisition upon arrest was generally to seize all property of the accused. This, of course did a great deal to prejudice the outcome of any trial. The accused was also forbidden to know the names of his accusers or to use a counsel for defense.

Almost any innocent act could bring down the wrath of the Inquisition upon a person or a whole family. Simply a regard for personal cleanliness, or special culinary tastes could get one accused of Judaism and cost the person's life. The failure to wear one's best clothes on Sunday, failure to eat pork, the lighting of candles on Friday, changing linens for Sabbath, or calling children by Old Testament names, could consign one of the flames.

The inquisition used the most cruel forms of torture to induce a confession. Roth describes some of them for us:

The commonest modes were the pulley or *strappado*, and the water-torment of *aselli*. In the former, the victim's wrists were tied behind his back and attached to a pulley, by means of which he was hoisted from the floor. If this did not prove sufficient to make him speak, weights were attached to the feet... The water torture was more ingenious, and more fiendish. The prisoner was fastened almost naked on a sort of trestle with sharp-edged rungs and kept in position with an iron band, his head lower than his feet, and his limbs bound to the side-pieces with agonizing tightness. The mouth was then forced open and a strip of linen inserted into the gullet. Through this, water was poured from a jar *(jarra)*, obstructing the throat and nostrils and producing a state of semi-suffocation. This process was repeated time after time, as many as eight *jarras* sometimes being applied. Meanwhile, the cords round the sufferer's limbs were continually tightened until it seemed as though every vein in his body was at bursting-point.[26]

When the confessions were made, the *auto de fe* was then arranged. There were times when as many as fifty persons were burned at the stake in one day. It was a gala event for the people and the nobility, with sometimes as many as fifty thousand spectators on hand. Not all the accused were burned at the stake. Some were reconciled to the faith. Roth states, "A man might leave the Inquisition without being burned, the proverb ran, but he was certain to be singed."[27]

From the time the Spanish Inquisition was founded to the year 1808, one estimate is that 31,912 heretics were burned. Another estimate sets the total of those burned between 1482 and 1525 at 28,540.[28] This does not include the number of those burned in Portugal where the Inquisition also spread.

Both Spain and Portugal ultimately expelled their Jews. Spain expelled its Jews in 1492, as Columbus was sailing from her harbor to the new world. Expulsions continued on until 1615, with the numbers running somewhere between 300,000 and 3,000,000.

Roth adds a sad commentary: "Spain was rid at last of that section of her children who, in the ninth and tenth centuries, had raised Spanish culture to its greatest heights."[29]

MODERN ANTI-SEMITISM

It would relieve us somewhat if we could say that Christian anti-Semitism was confined only to the dark ages of Christian history. Unfortunately this was not the case.

Even the great 16th century reformer, Martin Luther, had a few things to say about the Jews.

> What shall we Christians do with this rejected and condemned people, the Jews?... I shall give you my sincere advice. First, to set fire to their synagogues or schools and to bury and cover with dirt whatever will not burn, so that no man will ever again see a stone or cinder of them. This is to be done in honor of our Lord and of Christendom... Second, I advise that their houses also be razed and destroyed... Third, I advise that all their prayer books and Talmudic writings, in which such idolatry, lies, cursing, and blasphemy are taught, be taken from them... Fourth, I advise that their rabbis be forbidden to teach henceforth on pain of loss of life and limb... Fifth, I advise that safe-conduct on the highways be abolished completely for the Jews. For they have no business in the country-side... Sixth, I advise that usury be prohibited to them, and that all cash and treasure of silver and gold be taken from them and put aside for safekeeping... Seventh, I recommend putting a flail, an ax, a hoe, a spade, a distaff, or a spindle into the hands of young, strong Jewesses and letting them earn their bread in the sweat of their brow.[30]

These were just a few of his suggestions. It is of note that Luther's remarks were used in the defense of Nazi war criminals at the Nuremberg trials.

Anti-Semitism raged on in Christianity until modern times. Jews were finally placed under lock and key in the Ghetto. There were accusations, blood libels, pogroms, slanders. Early in the twentieth century there was the publication of the infamous fabrication *Protocols of the Elders of Zion*. The stage was being perfectly set for the most horrendous persecution of all.

THE HOLOCAUST

The bitter seed that had been sown in Christendom for almost two thousand years became ripe during the Holocaust, culminating in World War II. In the midst of enlightened Europe, even in the very cradle of the great Reformation, six million Jews were coldly and cruelly murdered while most Christians simply shrugged.

The Holocaust or *Sho'ah* began in Germany on January 30, 1933 as Adolph Hitler and his Nazi party rose to power. Hitler immediately began to implement the radical anti-Semitism that he had earlier expressed in his book, *Mein Kampf.*

First of all, the Jews were eliminated from public office, from professions, and from intellectual and artistic life. Even children were barred from public schools. The Nuremberg Laws of 1935 stripped Jews of their citizenship. There were boycotts against Jewish businesses and enforced sales of property and businesses.

On November 9-10, 1938, *Kristallnacht,* "the night of broken glass," was staged by the Nazis. Jewish businesses and properties were attacked, synagogues were burned, and in the aftermath, thousands of Jews were rounded up and sent to concentration camps.

During this period, the Church in general did not raise its voice. The dissident Confessing Church did resist and many of its ministers were arrested.[31] Somehow the Church had

Several women and a girl in Latvia stand partially undressed, as they await the firing squad. (Courtesy Yad Vashem)

forgotten the biblical admonition to love its neighbor. It had also forgotten the admonition of Proverbs 24:10-12 which reads:

> *If you falter in times of trouble, how small is your strength! Rescue those being led away to death; hold back those staggering toward slaughter. If you say, "But we knew nothing about this," does not he who weighs the heart perceive it? Does not he who guards your life know it? Will he not repay each person according to what he has done?*

The Church not only remained passive to the Jewish plight, but it also on occasions assisted the Nazis. Some diocesan chancelleries actually supplied data from their church records as to the religious background of their parishioners.[32]

With Hitler's invasion of Poland in 1939, millions of Jews came under his demonic power. Jews were herded to the ghettoes and into concentration camps. At first, the Nazis envisioned total emigration of the Jewish population from

Doom seems written on the faces of women and children at Auschwitz. (Courtesy Yad Vashem)

Europe. Later, at least by the beginning of 1941, the decision was made for genocide.

When the Nazis invaded Russia, Hitler gave the order to kill all Jews as well as Communist officials. The Nazi advance into Russia trapped 1,500,000 Jews and the newly formed *Einsatzgruppen,* set at work on the extermination project. The grisly work was first accomplished through firing squads and mass burials. Later, gas trucks were used, and finally even these were not sufficient for the task.

The Nazis finally turned to extermination camps, equipped with fake shower rooms for gassing, and with giant furnaces for cremation. One such extermination camp was Auschwitz, an enormous facility in southern Poland. At this one installation, it was possible to cremate 10,000 corpses a day. A total of two million Jews died there. Because of the brutality in the camp, many of the Jews died before they reached the gas chambers.[33]

The Nazis made a very thorough sweep of Jews in the areas of their control. Johnson remarks:

> There were about 8,861,800 Jews in the countries of Europe directly or indirectly under Nazi control. Of these it is calculated that the Nazis killed 5,933,900, or 67 per cent. In Poland, which had by far the largest number, 3,300,000, over 90 per cent, were killed.[34]

As six million Jews died in the Holocaust most nations of the world turned their heads. Great Britain, a supposedly Christian nation, had already aided Hitler by closing the doors to Palestine. The Jews were thus locked out of their homeland.

Even "Christian" America, although it knew of the gassing of millions of Jews, would not intervene to bomb the facilities. Nor would America raise its stingy immigration quotas. On one occasion the SS St. Louis with 907 Jewish passengers tried to enter US waters. It was turned away, as "Christian" America shut its eyes and sent these Jewish refugees back to the gas chambers. Based on the actions of America and other "Christian" nations, Goebbels could write in his diary, "I believe both the British and the Americans are happy that we are exterminating the Jewish riff-raff."[35]

Some countries did help the Jews. Denmark refused to cooperate with the Nazis and saved 99 percent of its 7,000 Jews. The people of Holland saved thousands of Jews by hiding them in their homes. The late Christian leader, Corrie Ten Boom, who wrote *The Hiding Place,* had a part in this great effort.[36]

The Holocaust, more than any other event in history, illustrates for us the demonic and other-worldly aspect of anti-Semitism. For instance, the trains carrying Jews to their death in Nazi Europe were given priority over everything else, even during the Russian offensive when every train was desperately needed.[37] Although Hitler was conducting a war on many fronts, this illustrates that his most important war was the one against Israel. It also again vividly illustrates the true nature of the awful sickness of anti-Semitism.

SYMPTOMS STILL PERSIST TODAY

One would think that after the horrors of the Holocaust, the world in general and Christians in particular would have learned about the evils of anti-Semitism and would have eradicated it.

Strangely though, even today in the modern Church and in the "enlightened" modern world, the disease of anti-Semitism still persists and even flourishes.

Now that the Jewish people are being re-gathered to their land, anti-Semitism often takes the form of anti-Zionism, of anti-Israel or pro-Arab sentiment. One can note this trend by the numerous times Israel is condemned in the press or on TV, or the times she has been censured by the United Nations.

Israel, whose population constitutes only one-thousandth of the world's total, has been the object of an amazing one-third of all UN Security Council resolutions. This international "Israel bashing" reached one of its zeniths in 1975 when the UN declared Zionism to be racism. In effect, it declared illegal the biblical hope of returning to Zion. This hope had been nurtured through the ages, both by Israel and by many in the Church.   Fortunately, this resolution was rescinded a few years after it was passed.

As the Jewish people return to their ancient home and become more and more concentrated in their land, this trend toward anti-Zionism will undoubtedly increase.

The prophet Zechariah declares that someday all the nations of the earth will be whipped into one last frenzy and will surround the tiny nation of Israel in order to take care of this "problem" once for all (Zech. 14:1-3). At that point God himself will personally intervene and demonstrate to the nations their folly.

We would think that surely now the Church would separate itself from this madness. Yet, even today in the modern Church there remains a persistent coolness and an unexplainable hardness toward the Jewish people and toward the nation of Israel.

Various new strands of triumphalism, today named Replacement Theology or Restoration Theology are on the upswing. Although it seems almost incomprehensible, some Christian groups in recent years even have gone so far as to express open support for the PLO. How could such attitudes prevail in light of biblical teaching?

Perhaps my query in this regard is summed up best in these simple lines written by two different people. The first part was written by William Norman Ewer, a British writer. Later the sequel was written by Cecile Brown, an American businessman. The little lines go:

> How odd
> Of God
> To choose
> The Jews
>
> But not so odd
> As those who choose
> A Jewish God,
> But spurn the Jews[38]

STUDY QUESTIONS:

Who were the first people to persecute the Jews after they became a nation? Why was this ironic?

Was it fair for God to curse Amalek and to order the obliteration of that nation? What would have likely happened if he had not done so?

In what way does the hatred of Amalek and Edom possibly live on today?

Briefly describe how the tiny and seemingly harmless seed of anti-Semitism grew from the days of the church fathers, through the era of Constantine and into the Middle Ages.

How did the new church doctrine of transubstantiation become a threat to the Jewish people?

Can you name two church-sponsored persecutions of the Jews?

A great teacher or leader may be correct in many beliefs but wrong in others. What great church leader illustrates this fact?

What was the basic sin of the church during the Holocaust?

Now that the Holocaust is over and the nation of Israel is established, how does anti-Semitism best express itself?

NOTES

1. See Jim Gerrish, "The Sickness of Anti-Semitism," *Jerusalem Prayer Letter,* July, 1991.
2. Edward H. Flannery, *The Anguish of the Jews, Twenty-Three Centuries of Antisemitism* (Mahwah, New York: Paulist Press, 1985) p. 285.
3. Goeffrey Wigoder, ed., *Encyclopedia Judaica,* vol. 3 (Jerusalem: Keter Publishing House Jerusalem, Ltd., 1971-72) pp. 95-96.
4. Quoted in Flannery, *The Anguish of the Jews, Twenty-Three Centuries of Antisemitism,* p. 35.
5. David A. Rausch, *A Legacy of Hatred: Why Christians Must Not Forget the Holocaust* (Chicago: Moody Press, 1984) p. 20.
6. Quoted in Flannery, *The Anguish of the Jews, Twenty-Three Centuries of Antisemitism,* p. 35.
7. Quoted in Rausch, *A Legacy of Hatred: Why Christians Must Not Forget the Holocaust,* p. 21.
8. Quoted in Rausch, *A Legacy of Hatred: Why Christians Must Not Forget the Holocaust,* p. 21.
9. Rausch, *A Legacy of Hatred: Why Christians Must Not Forget the Holocaust,* p. 22.
10. Williston Walker, *A History of the Christian Church* (New York: Charles Scribner's Sons, New York, 1959) pp. 61-62.

11. Rausch, *A Legacy of Hatred: Why Christians Must Not Forget the Holocaust,* p. 22.
12. Dr. Tim Dowley, ed., *A Lion Handbook: The History of Christianity* (Tring, Herts, England & Sutherland, Australia: Lion Publishing, & Albatross Books Pty Ltd., 1977) pp. 130-131.
13. Daniel Gruber, *The Church and the Jews: The Biblical Relationship* (Springfield, MO: General Council of the Assemblies of God, 1991) pp. 28-30.
14. Rausch, *A Legacy of Hatred: Why Christians Must Not Forget the Holocaust,* p. 23.
15. Quoted in Flannery, *The Anguish of the Jews, Twenty-Three Centuries of Antisemitism,* pp. 50-52.
16. Quoted in Michael L. Brown, *Our Hands are Stained With Blood, The Tragic Story of the "Church" and the Jewish People* (Shippenburg, PA: Destiny ImagePublishers, 1992) pp. 50-51.
17. Rausch, *A Legacy of Hatred: Why Christians Must Not Forget the Holocaust,* p. 25.
18. Rausch, *A Legacy of Hatred: Why Christians Must Not Forget the Holocaust,* p. 23.
19. Flannery, *The Anguish of the Jews, Twenty-Three Centuries of Antisemitism,* p. 58.
20. Goeffrey Wigoder, ed., *Encyclopedia Judaica,* v. 7 (Jerusalem: Keter Publishing House Jerusalem, Ltd., 1971-72) p. 9.
21. Flannery, *The Anguish of the Jews, Twenty-Three Centuries of Antisemitism,* p. 93.
22. Rausch, *A Legacy of Hatred: Why Christians Must Not Forget the Holocaust,* p.27.
23. Richard Siegel and Carl Rheins, *The Jewish Almanac* (New York: Bantam Books, Inc., 1980) pp. 127-129.
24. Cecil Roth, *The Spanish Inquisition* (New York: W.W. Norton & Company, 1964) pp. 22-23.
25. Flannery, *The Anguish of the Jews, Twenty-Three Centuries of Antisemitism,* p. 136.
26. Roth, *The Spanish Inquisition,* p. 95.
27. Roth, *The Spanish Inquisition,* p. 107.
28. Roth, *The Spanish Inquisition,* p. 123.
29. Roth, *The Spanish Inquisition,* p. 161.

30. Quoted in Rausch, *A Legacy of Hatred: Why Christians Must Not Forget the Holocaust,* p. 29.

31. Goeffrey Wigoder, ed., *Israel Pocket Library, Holocaust* (Jerusalem: Keter Publishing House Jerusalem Ltd., 1974) p. 13.

32. Wigoder, ed., *Israel Pocket Library, Holocaust,* p. 137.

33. Flannery, *The Anguish of the Jews, Twenty-Three Centuries of Antisemitism,* p. 223.

34. Paul Johnson, *A History of the Jews* (New York: Harper & Roe, 1987) p. 497.

35. Quoted in Johnson, *A History of the Jews,* p. 503.

36. Flannery, *The Anguish of the Jews, Twenty-Three Centuries of Antisemitism,* pp. 149-151.

37. Paul Johnson, *A History of the Jews* (New York: Harper & Roe, 1987) p. 490.

38. *The Macmillan Dictionary of Quotations* (New York: Macmillan Pub. Co., 1987) p. 294.

- 11 -

BLESSING OR CURSING!

When God called Abraham long ago he said to him in Genesis 12:2-3:

> *I will make you into a great nation and I will bless you; I will make your name great, and you will be a blessing. I will bless those who bless you, and whoever curses you I will curse; and all peoples on earth will be blessed through you.*

Not only will God keep his covenant with Abraham and Israel, but he will also bless the nations through Israel. This is a fact that has been little understood by the nations, or even by Gentile Christians for that matter. We sometimes realize how the Jewish Bible and the Jewish Messiah are blessings to us and to the nations. However, we are not often aware how the Jews themselves have been a blessing to the nations by their very presence.[1]

HOW THE JEWS BLESSED ANCIENT NATIONS

We do not have to look far in history to see that some ancient nations were blessed by the Jewish people. We may never fully know the impact of Jewish or Hebrew influence in antiquity because records of this nature are virtually nonexistent. However, we do have biblical records that substantiate some of this influence.

First of all, we see that Jacob the Patriarch blessed Pharaoh (Gen. 47:7). Then there was the story of Joseph. This son of Jacob was sold into slavery by his own brothers, and later arose to dizzying heights of power in Egypt. Soon he became second-in-command in one of the consistently strongest monarchies of the ancient world. He wore Pharaoh's own signet ring and was put in charge of the whole land of Egypt (Gen. 41:41-45).

Joseph rose to this position because of the providence and plan of God. God had enabled him to accurately interpret Pharaoh's dreams, telling of an awful seven-year famine that was to come upon the land. Joseph was thus appointed as Pharaoh's right-hand-man to insure that bountiful provisions were stored up in the seven plentiful years, which Joseph had also foreseen.

We can confidently say that because of Joseph, Egypt was spared from seven years of terrible famine that might have brought an end to the nation. In Genesis 41:57, we see how the surrounding nations were also blessed and spared, for they came to Egypt to buy grain.

We can certainly say that at least one Jew brought great blessing to the land of Assyria in biblical times. His name was Jonah. This prophet was commissioned by God to go the mighty capital city of Nineveh. His task was to warn the people of the disaster about to overtake them because of their sins. Jonah ultimately went, even though Assyria was a bitter enemy of Israel. We read in Jonah 3:5, that *"The Ninevites believed God. They declared a fast, and all of them, from the greatest to the least, put on sackcloth."* Because of their repentance, God spared the capital city of Assyria.

It is also interesting to note that Jews rose to the highest positions of authority in ancient Babylonia and Persia. The result was that these nations were blessed.

One sterling example of this influence is seen in the life of Daniel the prophet. As a young man, Daniel was carried away from his home in 605 BC by the Babylonians. He gained influence very rapidly in Babylon. Daniel interpreted dreams for kings (Dan. 2:31-45; 4:9-27); he, along with his three

Hebrew companions, sat as advisors to the king of Babylon. In Daniel 1:20, we read that their wisdom was *"ten times better"* than all his other advisors.

Daniel publicly rebuked kings for their idolatry (Dan. 5:22-24); he was so miraculously delivered by God that a whole nation stood in awe of him and the king made a proclamation that all the vast empire should acknowledge the God of Daniel (6:26-27). He foretold historic events down to the end of time with uncanny and amazing accuracy. He even predicted that the Messiah of Israel would come before the Second Temple was destroyed in AD 70 (9:24-27).

Daniel did something that probably not too many people accomplished in the ancient world. He survived the fall of one nation and immediately rose to great power in the political framework of the succeeding nation. This was by the will of God, but we learn from Josephus, the Jewish historian, that it may have been facilitated by the fact that Cyrus the Persian had read portions of Isaiah.[2] In that prophetic work Cyrus is mentioned by name and even referred to as "the Lord's anointed" (cf. Isaiah 44:28 and 45:1).

It would certainly impress any ruler to learn that a prophet had called him by name several hundred years before he was born. Probably this information caused Cyrus to have warm feelings toward the Jewish people in general, and perhaps toward Daniel in particular. In all likelihood, Daniel may even have had something to do with Cyrus reading Isaiah.

When we consider his remarkable life, we are forced to conclude that Daniel was an incredible person and that he was a blessing to both ancient Babylonia and Persia.

The Media-Persian Empire became one of the mightiest empires in the ancient world. We read in the Bible that ancient Persia stretched over 127 provinces from India to Ethiopia (Esth. 1:1). It is almost incredible how much influence the Jews continued to have in this vast empire.

Ezra the Scribe, a Jew, was able to have great favor in the court of Artaxerxes I (Longimanus: 465-424 BC). By royal decree Ezra was given permission to lead a contingent of the

202 DOES GOD PLAY FAVORITES?

Lord's people back home to Israel. Ezra was able to take along a considerable amount of treasure offered by the king himself and his advisers. He went with a good deal of political power to appoint magistrates and judges over the land of Israel (Ezra 7:12-26). Not only did Ezra teach and help establish the people of God, but he also probably helped bring order in the far-flung kingdom. At that particular time, Egypt represented a threat to Persia, and the Jews may have helped to bring stability in the area.[3]

Another interesting Jewish person connected with the Persian court was actually the cupbearer to king Artaxerxes. He was an able administrator by the name of Nehemiah (Neh. 1:11). Probably of all the men of influence in Persia, the cupbearer might have been the greatest. Nehemiah would have been "...one with the closest access to the king, and one who could well determine who got to see the king."[4] He used this great opportunity to guide the king, so that the monarch might work together with God, and allow the city and wall of Jerusalem to be rebuilt.

Much Jewish influence for good in ancient Persia had probably come about a few years earlier by the Cinderella-type marriage of a young Jewish girl named Hadassah. In God's unbelievable plan, little Hadassah, or Esther, was elevated to great heights to become the Queen of Persia during the reign of Ahasuerus (Xerxes I, 486-465 BC).

She used God's wisdom to guide the nation away from the disastrous course of xenophobia and civil turmoil. How interesting it is that in the next generation, her stepson issued the famous decrees that sent both Ezra and Nehemiah on their missions to restore Israel.

There are probably other stories of Jewish influence for good in the ancient world. Many of these stories will not likely be told until the great books are opened in the next world. However, let us turn our attention to more recent centuries. In modern times the influences of Jews and their blessings to the nations can be readily documented as they are often preserved in historical records.

SOME NATIONS BLESSED IN MODERN TIMES

The Ottoman Empire

In modern times, we can clearly see a pattern, that those nations who have blessed Israel have been blessed. For instance, in 1492, when the Jews were expelled from Christian Spain, many of them were accepted in what we call Turkey today. It was then called the Ottoman Empire. Later, in 1497 and 1498, they were joined by Jews fleeing Portugal.

It is interesting indeed that as the Jews arrived in the Ottoman Empire, it began to experience the apex of its political power and expansion. This trend continued on through the reign of Suleiman I (The Magnificent: 1520-1566). Suleiman is known for building the present wall around the Old City of Jerusalem. It is noteworthy that the Ottoman Empire began with such momentum that it lasted until our era, coming to its demise at the end of World War I.

According to the famed Jewish historian, Cecil Roth, the Jewish exiles from Spain found a warm welcome in the Ottoman Empire. Roth quotes a remark supposedly made by Sultan Bajazet: "What! call ye this Ferdinand 'wise' – he who depopulates his own dominions in order to enrich mine?"[5] The Sultan then went on to greatly encourage Jewish immigration.

Roth continues to describe how the Jewish influence grew in the fast-rising Ottoman Empire. He mentions that because the Turks were essentially a military and agricultural people, they were not interested in the sedentary life style. Thus, the trade of the vast empire was left in the hands of Jews, Armenians and Greeks.

The Jews were exceptionally well equipped in this area. The Jewish immigrants brought with them their skill in languages, their knowledge and their fortunes. Soon Jews controlled much of the international trade in the eastern portion of the Mediterranean basin.

The Jewish artisans quickly made a name for themselves as they introduced trade secrets brought from Spain. Soon gunpowder was introduced to the army and navy of the

Ottoman Empire. There were also other armaments manufactured by Jews.[6]

The Jews first settled in Constantinople, and rapidly that Jewish community grew to be the largest Jewish settlement in that part of the world. Soon it was rivaled and passed by Salonica, which because of Jewish enterprise, went on to become the greatest mercantile center of the Mediterranean.

The Jews were thoroughly experienced in European languages and were quite familiar with conditions on the continent.

Thus the Jews began to play a very important and even crucial role in international politics. One person to gain international prominence was Joseph Nasi. He was not only influential in the Ottoman Empire, but he was solicited by the powers of Europe as well. He was powerful enough in international politics that he was able to avenge the Jewish expulsion from Spain by encouraging the Netherlands to revolt.[7]

As Roth states,

> The Jewish people must always remember the Turkish Empire with gratitude because, at one of the darkest hours of its history, when no alternative place of refuge was open and there seemed no chance of succor, Turkey flung open its doors widely and generously for the reception of the fugitives, and kept them open.[8]

The obvious lesson of the Ottoman Empire is that when the Jewish people are received, blessing to the nation ensues. We see this pattern clearly repeated in other modern nations.

The Netherlands

In 1497, Portugal followed the lead of Spain, and also expelled its Jewish population. These Portuguese Jews along with some of the dispersed Jews from Spain made their way to the Netherlands. These Jews were known as *Marranos* (a derogatory term for converts to Christianity). Again, as in the case of the Ottoman Empire, there were many merchants, industrialists, and scholars in this group, and the Netherlands was enriched by their coming.

The Jews of the Netherlands, like their relatives in the Ottoman Empire, were very knowledgeable in languages, administrative experience, and also in international relationships. They began to play an expanding role in the economy of the rising nation.[9]

It seems very curious that the tiny Netherlands began about this time to explode into a worldwide commercial empire, even rivaling England. It became a great colonizing influence in the new world, far out of proportion to its size. Its centers of influence reached from New Amsterdam, Brazil and Guyana in the Americas to Africa, India and the Dutch East Indies.

Martin Gilbert in his *Jewish Historical Atlas,* remarks that:

> The most active period of Jewish commercial enterprise coincided with the widest expansion of the Dutch empire 1600-1700... Within two hundred years of their expulsion from Spain, the Jews who settled in Amsterdam had built up a trading empire on a scale previously unimaginable. Their successes made an important contribution to the golden age of Dutch commercial enterprise.[10]

Amsterdam continued to become an established center of world trade. The city's Jews held an important place as shareholders in the famous East India Company. The Jews also gained prominence in industries such as printing, sugar refining, tobacco, silk and diamonds. In time, the diamond industry became an exclusively Jewish one in the Netherlands.[11]

Generations later, during the time of the Holocaust, many people in Holland stood by the Jews and sheltered them from the Nazis. A stroll down the Avenue of Righteous Gentiles at the Holocaust Museum in Israel reveals this. There are more memorials to citizens of Holland than any other nation.

Today it seems that Jews, as well as Christians from Holland, make up an unusually large and influential representation in the land of Israel.

The U.S.

An outstanding example of Jewish influence for good has been seen in the United States. No doubt, because of its strong Puritan influence in the colonial period, the Jews were looked upon with admiration. The Puritans felt that "...the interests of the Gentiles themselves are bound up with God's designs toward Israel."[12] The Puritans studied Hebrew and longed for the restoration of Zion.

This warm feeling of the Puritans toward the Jews affected many areas within the rising nation. Even today, this influence can still be seen in the seals and insignias of the great early American universities, Columbia, Dartmouth and Yale. At the top of Columbia's seal is the Tetragrammaton (four letter name of God) in Hebrew. Dartmouth displays the Hebrew *"El Shaddai"* the name of God. Yale's seal is virtually covered with the biblical Hebrew words *"Urim Ve-thummim"* (Light and Truth).[13]

Early American colonists began to name their children after biblical characters. Also their cities, such as Bethlehem and Salem, began to take on biblical names. Their preachers spoke often of Zion and their political leaders began to make pronouncements concerning the Jews.

America's initial warmness to the Jews soon paid rich dividends. This began to happen even by the time of the American Revolution. At that dark hour Washington's troops were languishing in the cold and snow. To make matters worse, the new congress did not yet have power to raise taxes, so the war effort tottered on the brink of disaster.

At this low ebb in American history, it was a Jew who stepped forward to rescue the nation. His name was Haym Salomon. A few years ago in 1975, the US Post Office issued a commemorative stamp in honor of this great but almost forgotten man. The stamp printed on front and back read:

> Financial Hero – Businessman and broker Haym Salomon was responsible for raising most of the money needed to finance the   American Revolution and later to save the new nation from collapse.

Salomon not only made loans to the new government, but he made them to several of its statesmen as well, like James Madison, Thomas Jefferson and James Monroe. Salomon loaned the government at least $600,000. Other estimates range as high as $800,000. The loans were never repaid to the Salomon heirs. Should they be repaid today with interest, these loans on the higher figure would come to over two and a half trillion dollars.[14]

Haym Salomon, the Jewish immigrant to the colonies, was so devoted to his new adopted land that he invested all his fortunes in it. He died leaving his small family without financial means.

As the doors of America were flung wide open to Jewish immigration in coming years, the nation was greatly blessed by the Jewish presence. Ironically, many other nations who had themselves persecuted the Jews, were also blessed from the overflow of Jewish blessings to America.

In merchandising, names like Levi Strauss, Sears Roebuck, Gimbels and Macys eventually sprang up on the American scene. There was Edwin Land with his development of the instant Polaroid picture. There was Emile Berliner with his development of the Grammaphone, that made the modern recording industry possible.[15]

In entertainment the Jew, David Sarnoff, was a pioneer in radio network broadcasting and founded the National Broadcasting Company. He went on to pioneer in television broadcasting and was later awarded the title "The Father of American Television" by the Television Broadcasters' Association.[16] William S. Paley built the mighty Columbia Broadcasting System. "Between 1941 and 1945, CBS devoted over six thousand hours to war reports and dramatizations. For this Paley was awarded the Legion of Merit and the French Croix de Guerre."[17]

In the field of movie entertainment there were names like Samuel Goldwyn, co-founder of MGM Studios, and Adolph Zukor, founder of Paramount Picture Corporation. Other Jewish names in the early movie industry are Louis B. Mayer, Lewis Selznick, William Fox and Marcus Loew.

America and the world began to be soothed by the sweet music produced by its Jews. There was Irving Berlin who wrote what has been called the nation's second national anthem, "God Bless America."

It may be a little embarrassing for some Christians to realize that the top-selling song of all times, "White Christmas" was written by Berlin, the Jewish composer. An additional embarrassment is that Berlin also wrote our most popular Easter, song entitled "Easter Parade."[18]

The song of the old south, "Swanee" was written by the Jew, George Gershwin, and popularized by another Jew, Al Jolson.[19]   There were Rogers and Hammerstein with their "Oklahoma," "Sound of Music," South Pacific," and "Carousel." America could also boast of greats like Benny Goodman, the "King of Swing."   She could boast of great violinists like Jerome Kern and Fritz Kreisler.   Americans and the world could enjoy the orchestral directing of Bruno Walter, Arthur Fiedler and Leonard Bernstein.

Because of Jewish skill and learning, America was able to launch the world into the Nuclear Age. The brilliant physicist, Albert Einstein, helped convince the US President to launch the Manhattan Project, which ultimately brought about the development of the atomic bomb. It was the Jew, J. Robert Oppenheimer, who successfully directed this project. Another Jew, Edward Teller contributed greatly to the project, and later went on to develop the Hydrogen bomb. Later, the Jew, Hyman Rickover developed the *Nautilus,* the world's first atomic powered submarine.

Many of these Jewish discoverers and inventors agonized greatly over the potential for destruction in nuclear weapons. However, they consoled themselves that such weapons of mass destruction would possibly limit future wars. The discoveries in the nuclear field have spurred the peaceful usage of atomic energy and thus have blessed many nations.

On the political and judicial scene in the US, many Jewish people have been outstanding. These names include New York Mayor LaGuardia, advisor to presidents, Bernard Baruch, Senators Abe Ribicoff, Jacob Javits, Rudy Boschwitz,

Howard Metzenbaum and Barry Goldwater. They also include Secretary of State, Henry Kissinger and Chairman of the board of governors of the Federal Reserve System, Arthur Burns. There were the famous Supreme Court justices Benjamin Cardozo, Louis D. Brandeis and Felix Frankfurter.[20]

America has truly been blessed by the presence of Jewish people in the nation!

JEWISH BLESSINGS TO THE WHOLE WORLD

The Jews, at present, account for less than one percent of the earth's population. Yet, they have had a profound effect upon modern civilization in all areas. The Jews have been responsible for the rise of the three great monotheistic religions in our world. Their thinkers like Einstein and Freud have had a great influence upon the modern era.

It seems that in every age the Jews have had to acquire skills that were transportable. They never knew when they would be forced to leave a city or a country and flee to parts unknown. Thus the Jews have leaned heavily upon academic skills, including science, mathematics and medicine.

This tendency among the Jews has brought great blessing to the nations. Although the Jews are such a tiny fraction of the earth's population, from 1901 to 1990 they won an astonishing 22 percent of the Nobel Prize awards in science.[21] Their endeavors in the area of medicine are even more astonishing. (see inset)

It is ironic that while the Jews have been generally treated as parasites by their host nations, they have nevertheless managed to bring blessings to their begrudging hosts as well as to the whole world.

The Jews throughout history have provided the philosophers, musicians, scientists, physicians, financiers and statesmen to bless their host nations. Someone once said that other ancient peoples left only monuments but the Jews have left ideas. They seem to have done this wherever they have gone. These ideas have greatly influenced history.

For instance, the great age of exploration in the fifteenth century, launched primarily by Spain and Portugal, was

---

Jews and the age of exploration

Because of their great emphasis upon learning, the Jewish people did much to bring the age of exploration into being. There were many Jewish mathematicians, astronomers, and cartographers who made possible the voyages into the unknown. Here are a few of these greats:

Moses de Leon (1250-1305) - Stated that the earth is round and that it rotates, two hundred years before Columbus.

Isaac B. Solomon Sahula - In a book written about 1281 and not published until 1490, claimed that the globe beneath us is inhabited by people.

(Note: even the Palestinian Talmud written centuries earlier had also claimed that the earth is round)

Judah ben Moses and Moses Cohen between 1262 and 1272 prepared the famous *alphonsine tables* for King Alfonso of Castile. These were lists of planetary movements, and they continued to be used for centuries afterward. Moses and Cohen wrote many books and constructed numerous astronomical instruments

Levi Ben Gerson also known as Gersonides (1288-1344) - Invented the Jacob's staff, which enabled early sailors to plot their positions. His thinking developed later by others formed the basis of trigonometry.

Abraham Crescas and son Judah (fourteenth century) - Abraham served as Master of Maps and Compasses to the King of Aragon. As cartographer, he produced what was called the world's best map in 1377. His son Judah also a famous cartographer helped chart the voyages of the Portuguese explorers.

Abraham Zacuto (1450-1525) - The noted astronomer who produced the navigational guides later used by Columbus, Vasco da Gama, and others. The vessels of da Gama were fitted with astrolabes designed by Zacuto.

Pedro Nunes (1492-1577) - The most distinguished of Portugal's nautical astronomers and the founder of scientific navigation.

Note: Many think today that Columbus himself was Jewish. He had at least five Jews accompanying him on his first expedition. His Jewish interpreter, Louis de Torres, was one of the first two men to set foot on American soil.[22]

---

largely made possible by Jewish contributions. (see inset) We must remember that ocean exploration was a frontier just as new in that day as space exploration is in our day.

The Jews through the ages have been outstanding in many fields of science, mathematics and medicine. (see inset) In Modern times the German mathematician, Karl Jacobi (1804-1851) developed the theory of elliptic functions. Georg Cantor

(1845-1918), also of German origin, founded the theory of sets, and also the theory of transfinite numbers. He revolutionized the whole area of mathematics and is known as one of the greatest mathematicians of all time.

Sir William Herschel (1738-1822) was one of the great astronomers of the modern era. He not only discovered the planet Uranus, but was the founder of modern stellar astronomy. Eugene Goldstein (1850-1930) is associated with the discovery of gamma rays. Austrian physicist Lise Meitner (1878-1968) shared in the discovery of nuclear fission, with her primary work being in the relationship between beta and gamma rays. Albert Michelson (1825-1919) established the speed of light. The paradoxical results of his experiments led to Einstein's formulation of the general theory of relativity in 1916.

Leo Arons (1860-1919) invented the mercury vapor lamp. Gabriel Lipman (1845-1921) developed color photography. Charles Gerhardt (1816-1857) was the developer of the molecular theory and also was first to make an effective classification of organic compounds.

One of the many ironies of Jewish history occurred in Germany. That nation had produced an unusual amount of Jewish chemists. There was Adolf Frank (1834-1916) founder of Germany's potash industry. Frank was also influential in developing the nitrogen fixation industry by forming calcium cyanide. There was Adolf von Bayer (1835-1917), who discovered the phthalein class of dyes and passed his patents to the giant I.G. Farben-industrie, which became infamous in the Holocaust. Lastly there was Fritz Haber (1868-1934), who developed the synthetic production of ammonia. This was a great benefit to Germany's supply of nitrates for the war. For his efforts Haber was later exiled. Nevertheless, it was Jewish genius that formed a large basis of the German chemical industry, and it was particularly that industry which was used to destroy the Jews.[23]

In the modern era, Jewish names have stood behind the development of many inventions. Unfortunately, Jews did not always get the credit for their work. Consider the airplane for

---

Some Jewish contributions in the field of medicine

Jews have particularly stood out in the field of Medicine. In the Middle Ages it is estimated that over one-half of the rabbis and other Jewish intellectuals were physicians by occupation. From the sixteenth to eighteenth centuries in Europe, Jews of *Marrano* descent made up an astonishingly high percentage of the physicians.

Andreas Vesalius (1514-1564) is considered the founder of the study of anatomy.

Garcia da Orta (1498-1568) pioneered the study of tropical diseases and is one of the fathers of botanical science. Unfortunately, in 1580 the Inquisition found out that he was a Jew and although he had been dead for twelve years, the church ordered his bones burned.

Ferdinand Cohn (1828-1898) is considered to be the father of bacteriology.

Simon Baruch (1840-1921) made the first diagnosis and successful operation of appendicitis.

Alexander Marmorek (1865-1923) produced a serum to protect against streptococcal infection.

Oscar Minkowski (1858-1931) was first to demonstrate the relationship between the pancreas and diabetes, thus leading to the discovery of insulin.

Casimir Funk (1884-1967) while doing research with the anti-beriberi substance in polished rice coined the word "Vitamin."

Selman Abraham Wakman (1888-1973) discovered streptomycin.

Jonas Salk (1914-) virtually brought an end to the dreaded disease of Polio by developing the Polio vaccine.

Albert Sabin (1906-1993) American medical microbiologist developed the oral Polio vaccine.[24]

---

instance. The Wright Brothers greatly relied upon the experiments of a German Jewish inventor named Otto Lilienthal. In his experiments, Lilienthal had made more than two thousand powerless glider flights. He died in 1896, while making another of these flights.

When we think of the gas-filled airship, we usually think of Zeppelin. However, Count Zeppelin bought his patents from the widow of an Austrian Jew by the name of David Schwartz. Schwartz had devised the idea of a gas-filled airship earlier in 1890.

Another Jew, Heinrich Rudolph Hertz, by his discovery of electromagnetic radiation paved the way for the development of radio, television and radar. Guglielmo Marconi, a non-Jew, using the discoveries of Hertz, patented the wireless telegraph in 1896. Later he further developed the concepts into the invention of the radio.

When we think of the telephone, we automatically think of Alexander Graham Bell. However a Jewish inventor, Johann Philipp Reis was the first to publicly demonstrate the telephone as early as 1861. Bell, who did not demonstrate his device until 1876, gave some credit for his invention to Reis.

Again, when we think of the motorcar, we think of Ford. Yet as early as 1864 a German-born Jew by the name of Sigfried Marcus is said to have patented a motorcar powered by an internal combustion engine. The vehicle ran four to five miles per hour.[25]

There is probably no other area in our modern world where Jews have had so much influence as in the entertainment industry. When we look at the industry we realize that it has been Jews who have made us listen, watch, laugh and cry. They have tugged our heartstrings and enthralled us in drama.

The list of entertainment greats past and present goes on and on, all the way from Joey Adams to Shelly Winters (see inset). Although we cannot applaud the excesses of Hollywood and the entertainment industry, we can say that it has been one of the most influential medias in our world. Not only does it have the potential for great evil, it also has the potential for great good.

THEIR REAL BLESSINGS ARE SPIRITUAL

Although the Jews have brought great physical blessing to our world, their greatest accomplishments are, and will continue to be, in the spiritual realm. It cannot be denied that the Jews are the one people on the face of this earth who have had a direct audience with the Creator. They have faithfully delivered this revelation to us in the form of the Old Testament or *Tanakh*. In the fullness of time the Messiah was also delivered to the world through Israel and the Jewish

A List of Jewish entertainment greats past and present
(includes radio, TV, movies and other entertainment media)

Joey Adams	Paulette Goddard	Mike Nichols
Mel Allen	Samuel Goldwyn	Leonard Nimoy
Woody Allen	Elliott Gould	Jan Peerce
Ed Asner	Cary Grant	Tony Randall
Lauren Bacall	Lee Grant	Harry Reems
Theda Bara	Lorne Greene	Joan Rivers
Rona Barrett	Buddy Hackett	Harold Robbins
Gene Barry	Goldie Hawn	Edward G. Robinson
Jack Benny	Dustin Hoffman	Billy Rose
Milton Berle	Judy Holliday	Barney Ross
Joey Bishop	Harry Houdini	Mort Sahl
Fanny Brice	John Houseman	Soupy Sales
Mel Brooks	Leslie Howard	George Segal
Dr. Joyce Brothers	Lou Jacobi	Peter Sellers
Lenny Bruce	David (Meyer) Janssen	William Shatner
George Burns	Al Jolson	Artie Shaw
Dyan Cannon	Madeline Kahn	Dick Shawn
Eddie Cantor	Danny Kaye	Dinah Shore
Al Capp	Alan King	Beverly Sills
Kitty Carlisle	Jack Klugman	Phil Silvers
Jeff Chandler	Ted Koppel	Steven Speilberg
Joan Collins	Bert Lahr	Irving Stone
Howard Cosell	Michael Landon	Barbra Streisand
Jamie Lee Curtis	Linda Lavin	Jill St. John
Tony Curtis	Pinky Lee	Mike Todd
Howard Da Silva	Battling Levinsky	Sophie Tucker
Kirk Douglas	Jerry Lewis	Mike Wallace
Bob Dylan	Hal Linden	Barbara Walters
Werner Erhard	Peter Lorre	Nathaniel West
Douglas Fairbanks	Jay Lovestone	Gene Wilder
Peter Falk	Tony Martin	Debra Winger
Bonnie Franklin	Marx Brothers	Henry Winkler
John Garfield	Paul Muni	Shelly Winters[26]
Jack Gilford	Arthur Murray	
Paul Michael Glaser	Paul Newman	

people. As a result of his coming into the world we have also received the New Testament. All of the writers of the New Testament except Luke, were Jewish.

The Isaiah Scroll at the Shrine of the Book in Jerusalem.
(Courtesy Israel Information Office)

Many people think that the contribution of the Jews in the realm of religion has drawn to a close. That idea is false on many counts. The Jews have an extremely rich heritage upon which to draw. Their tradition and learning continues even today, springing as a well from its ancient roots in Sinai. They still add color and dimension to our understanding of the Bible.

But the real accomplishments and blessings of the Jewish people will come in the future. In the beautiful servant songs of Isaiah 41:8-10, God says of Israel:

> *But you, O Israel, my servant, Jacob, whom I have chosen, you descendants of Abraham my friend, I took you from the ends of the earth, from its farthest corners called you. I said, 'You are my servant'; I have chosen you and have not rejected you. So do not fear, for I am with you; do not be dismayed, for I am*

your God. I will strengthen you and help you; I will
uphold you with my righteous right hand.

Isaiah is speaking of a future day and time, and it is interesting that Israel is still called the "servant" of the Lord.

In Isaiah 43:4-7, we see the continuing special relationship
between God and Israel in the future:

Since you are precious and honored in my sight, and
because I love you, I will give men in exchange for
you, and people in exchange for your life. Do not be
afraid, for I am with you; I will bring your children
from the east and gather you from the west. I will say
to the north, 'Give them up!' and to the south, 'Do not
hold them back.' Bring my sons from afar and my
daughters from the ends of the earth – everyone who
is called by my name, whom I created for my glory,
whom I formed and made.

In Isa. 43:21 the Lord says: *"the people [the Jews] I formed*
for myself that they may proclaim my praise." Be not deceived,
God will still show forth his praise through Israel. It is
written in his word and will not fail.

As we approach the end of history, the Jews and Israel will
take on a much greater significance. This is clear even when
we look at the book of Revelation. When we carefully examine
Revelation, we see that it is a picture of the *Day of the Lord.*
A day that was often spoken of by the prophets of Israel. We
sense a strangely Jewish flavor to these last days.

We are first introduced to Jesus, who is pictured in the
garments of the High Priest of Israel. Next, we see what are
surely Jewish *menorahs* placed right in the middle of the first
chapter (Rev. 1:12). It is even more surprising that these
menorahs are said to represent the seven churches.

Then, we are introduced to the 144,000 overcomers from
the tribes of Israel (Rev. 7:1-8). We began to hear much more
about Jerusalem and its restoration as a spiritual reality. In
Revelation 21:2, 9-10, we learn that this heavenly Jerusalem
is the true bride of Christ.

We hear of Jewish apostles whose names are now written on the twelve foundations of Jerusalem (Rev. 21:14). Interestingly, the gates of the city through which we all long to pass have written on them the names of the twelve tribes of Israel (Rev. 21:12). Imagine how the Christian persecutors of Israel will feel when they attempt to enter through those gates!

There may even be some surprises for us when we begin to sing those heavenly choruses with the angels.[27] In Revelation 15:3-4, the redeemed sing the "Song of Moses." Whether this song is taken from Exodus 15 or from Deuteronomy 32, one thing is clear: the redeemed will be singing about Israel and God's faithfulness to that nation. It may take some Christians a while to get in tune with that particular heavenly hymn.

We see that according to God's great plan of restoration, the Jews will have a very prominent place in the end days. In Isaiah 61:6-7 it is said of them:

> *And you will be called priests of the LORD, you will be named ministers of our God. You will feed on the wealth of nations, and in their riches you will boast. Instead of their shame my people will receive a double portion, and instead of disgrace they will rejoice in their inheritance; and so they will inherit a double portion in their land, and everlasting joy will be theirs.*

Yes, in the end days the Jews will be priests and ministers of God. We read in scripture that they will also be called *"the Holy People"* and *"the Redeemed of the LORD"* (Isa. 62:12). The Lord describes them as *"jewels in a crown"* (Zech. 9:16). We Gentiles have happily applied Malachi 3:17 to ourselves, however, this verse lets us see that God is primarily speaking of the Jewish people:

> *"They will be mine," says the LORD Almighty, "in the day when I make up my treasured possession. I will spare them, just as in compassion a man spares his son who serves him."*

In the last days, the Jews will be as though they were never cast off by God (Zech. 10:6).

Perhaps one of the most interesting pictures of the Jews in future ages is given to us in Zechariah 8:23. It is a verse that should demolish our triumphalistic and replacement theologies. We read in this passage:

> *This is what the LORD Almighty says: "In those days ten men from all languages and nations will take firm hold of one Jew by the hem of his robe and say, 'Let us go with you, because we have heard that God is with you.'"*

Let us pause to get the picture here. In the last days people from all over the world will cling to the Jewish people and beg to go with them because of the presence of the Lord will be with them. One would think that it would be Gentile Christians to whom the world is clinging in the last days. But alas, in God's plan it is the Jews.

This is only a sampling of the many verses in scripture that speak of the elevation of the Jews in the end times, and their blessing to the nations. But with even these few verses in mind we would have to conclude with Moses in Deuteronomy 33:29:

> *Blessed are you, O Israel!   Who is like you, a people saved by the LORD?...*

SOME NATIONS WHO WERE CURSED

The nations who have been blessed for favoring Israel are not numerous. We could count them on our fingers, possibly on the fingers of one hand. However there is a long list of nations, both ancient and modern, who have cursed Israel, and who have thus been cursed.

Pharaoh of ancient Egypt certainly got his share of cursing for meddling with God's elect. The ten plagues that are recorded in Exodus would have worked havoc on the economy of any nation, ancient or modern. It appears that Pharaoh's choicest legions were also lost in the depth of the sea. What an unmitigated disaster to befall this nation.

Then there were the Amalakites, who attacked the Israelites soon after their exodus from Egypt. God took a very dim view of this attack. He arose in *"fierce wrath"* (1 Sam. 28:18) and swore to blot out the name of Amalek from under heaven (Deut. 25:14).

Of course, King Saul failed to destroy Amalek as he was instructed. We might ask, how Amalakites are doing today? The answer is that God wiped their nation off the face of the earth and closed the book on their history. He cursed them out of existence as a nation, although various people of Amalakite origin undoubtedly are scattered throughout the Middle East, and probably continue to corrupt the area with their vicious anti-Israel hatred.

Edom is another ancient kingdom that came under an eternal curse for its hatred of Israel. Edom was the nation founded by Esau, the brother of Israel, and the kingdom was initially blessed by God. This nation was located in the southern area of present day Jordan. Because they kept alive an ancient hatred God cut them off. The prophets, Isaiah, Ezekiel, Joel, Amos and Obadiah, all elaborate on this theme.

The ancient nation of Edom has long since disappeared from the earth, never to rise again. However, as in the case of Amalek, individual Edomites surely live on.

We have seen how many of the mighty empires of the past have come against Israel. As we look at these mighty nations of the past, we might ask, where are they today? All have disappeared from the stage of history. Rome exists, but the Roman Empire is gone – it fell in AD 476. Egypt is still present, but the ancient nation was overcome and its culture obliterated by the Muslim invasion of the seventh century. They are gone, but Israel remains.

Now let us move on to more recent centuries. Shortly after the turn of the first millennium, a great crusading excitement swept over much of Europe. Ostensibly, the Crusaders were intent on going to the Holy Land to drive away the Muslims. In truth, they were generally a reckless band of adventurers.

Their lack of discipline and understanding cost the Jews dearly. The Crusaders became a great curse upon Israel. It should not surprise us that it was the Crusaders who returned home with a form of the bubonic plague, known as the Black Death. Before the plague ended, it killed a fourth of the population of Europe.[28]

By 1492, Spain and Portugal were fast becoming two of the mightiest sea powers on earth. Their mariners were beginning to sail unexplored waters the world over. Soon this momentum would enable them to establish colonies in the ends of the earth and returning with shiploads of gold. We mentioned earlier in this chapter the almost unknown fact that the Jewish people had helped make this great exploration possible by their contributions to astronomy and mapmaking. Spain and Portugal would go on to amass tremendous wealth and build vast colonial empires spanning the globe.

However, in 1492, the Christian rulers of Spain decided to expel the Jews from that realm. The Jews of Spain had lived there for centuries, and had produced a "golden age" of Jewish civilization in that country. The Jews were nevertheless expelled. Soon in 1497, the Jews of Portugal were also expelled.

When the Jews left Spain and Portugal in a very real sense, the "lights went out" for these civilizations. In a short period of time the vast influence of these two nations climaxed and went into a rapid and permanent decline. Both countries sank into dismal degradation as they were plagued and haunted by the specter of the Inquisition. This lasted until the nineteenth century. Interestingly, in 1996, five-hundred years to the day after their expulsion, Portugal apologized to Israel and sought to make atonement for their act.[29] Spain had done a similar thing in 1993.

It should be noted that in 1588, the mighty Spanish Armada was destroyed by the British, who later took control of the seas.

It is quite interesting that at almost the time of this great sea victory, there was beginning to arise a strong and favorable Zionist sentiment in Britain.[30]

There are many other modern nations who have opposed Israel and have reaped bitter cursing. Consider Germany for instance. Despite the recent unification of East and West Germany, the Berlin wall stood for 45 years as a testimony of judgment upon this nation. Her great cities were also bombed and turned into ashes by allied raids. Her people suffered.

Consider Russia and the other countries of the former Soviet Union. Until 1989, the people of these countries languished under the cruel heel of Communism. These are vast lands of great natural resources. The people of these lands should have enjoyed a great abundance of food and of all other natural products. Yet, when the new immigrants from the former USSR came to Israel, they told many tales of standing in long lines in order to purchase the bare necessities of life, even to purchase rotten potatoes. The people suffered by oppression, wars and purges. Stalin killed millions of his own people. Today these nations grope in a political and financial quagmire that seemingly defies solution.

It is certainly possible that the whole land is under a divine curse brought about by centuries of anti-Semitism. One writer has remarked: "Antisemitism is as perennial in Russia as the snow...and it lurks beneath the surface the rest of the time as stubbornly as permafrost."[31] The Russians were murdering Jews long before Hitler was born. In fact, the first *aliya* to Israel began in 1882, as a result of Russian anti-Semitic pogroms. Today Russia and other former Soviet countries are penalized by the brain-drain of their highly skilled Jewish scientists, engineers, teachers, physicians and others who have immigrated to Israel.

Consider Poland. There has hardly been a nation in modern times more dedicated to the destruction of the Jews than Poland. Rausch says of the Polish people, "...we cannot deny that their anti-Semitism over the decades grew into a Jew-hatred that fashioned them into key collaborators with the Nazi regime."[32] Of the six million Jews who died in the Holocaust, it is almost inconceivable that half of them died in Poland. Even after the war ended, the Poles continued to murder Jews. The historian Johnson puts the number of murdered Jews after the war at 350.[33]

Could Poland's sorrows as a modern nation be traced back to its Jew hatred? It seems plausible.

The list of modern nations following the evil path of entrenched anti-Semitism certainly includes many Middle Eastern countries. Consider the horrors of Lebanon for instance. This once beautiful nation attacked Israel in 1948. Later she opened her doors to the PLO when they were expelled from Jordan. Lebanon opened her doors so that fire could devour her beautiful cedars (Zech. 11:1).

In Lebanon, the PLO built a vast infrastructure of terror from 1975 to 1982. They destroyed, murdered, and raped as they chose. They kidnapped Lebanese children and trained twelve year-olds to kill. In their rage they shelled hospitals, turned churches into weapons and garbage dumps. They turned beautiful Lebanon into a war zone.

Consider the lot of the Palestinians, who have despised Israel with an intensity unrivaled in modern times. During the Gulf War the Palestinians literally danced on their roofs as Saddam Hussein's missiles fell on Tel Aviv.[34] Later as Gaza was being turned over to them in the ceremonies of the Oslo peace accord, they could not stifle their hatred for a moment, but stoned the Israeli soldiers who were participating in the ceremony. One expert, Ruth Wisse, comments on this incredible hatred saying, "The Palestinians are the first people whose nationalism consists primarily of opposition to the Jewish people."[35]

It appears that the Palestinians have certainly become heirs of the ancient hatred of Amalek and Edom. They have hardly noticed that their Druze brethren in the northern parts of Israel have received great blessing for their cooperation with Israel. Their beautiful and peaceful cities dot the areas of Carmel in the north and also the Golan Heights.

As a result of their support of Saddam Hussein in the Gulf War, 350,000 Palestinians were expelled from Kuwait. Their own Muslim brothers would not take them in, although Israel accepted many of them.[36] They have gone from woe to woe, always blaming Israel for their plight.

But perhaps the most obvious example of inheriting a curse in modern times is Great Britain. Probably because of Puritan influence, there arose a strong support for Zion in Great Britain. This support had been expressed among her writers and poets. It was also expressed in the highest levels of government.

God honored Britain by allowing her to be the guardian of the newborn child, Israel. Britain was in an excellent position to do this since she had greatly assisted in the defeat of the Ottoman Empire in 1918, and was left to carve up Palestine virtually as she wished. At that time, Britain ruled a quarter of the earth's surface.

Interestingly, Britain's military efforts had been greatly helped during World War I by a Jewish chemist and states- man, Chaim Weizmann. In the dark days of the war, Britain had turned to him desperately in need of a synthetic acetone for her munitions industries. Weizmann discovered a process for producing this acetone in 1916.[37] Britain was able to continue her war efforts and gain vast land holdings in the Middle East.

In 1917, Britain produced the noble Balfour Declaration, that looked favorably to a home for the Jews in Palestine. At the end of the war, Britain was one of the mightiest powers on earth with colonies stretching over the world.

In spite of her noble beginnings, Britain failed miserably. Although she was charged by the League of Nations in 1920 to aid the establishment of a state for newly emerging Israel, one of her first acts was to take 75% of the territory allotted to Israel and establish the Palestinian Emirate of Transjordan (today's Jordan). That area was immediately closed to all future Jewish settlement, and even today with the present peace process in force, no Jew is allowed to become a citizen of Jordan.

Britain then proceeded to hinder all Jewish settlement in the land of Israel, while at the same time encouraging Arab settlement there from the surrounding nations.[38] Britain shut the door on Jewish immigration at precisely the time that millions of Jews were fleeing from the coming Holocaust.

The British then for their own selfish political purposes, did much to help create the myth of Palestinian nationalism. It is a long and complicated story filled with many intrigues. Finally, in 1948, the British were forced to turn the now sticky problem of the Jewish homeland back over to the United Nations. Britain was then forced to withdraw her once proud forces from Palestine in shame. Britain not only quit its mandate over Palestine. She also quit Iran in 1951, and Sudan in 1953. Britain then quit Egypt in 1954-56, Jordan in 1957, Iraq in 1958 and Aden in 1967.[39]

The once mighty British Empire began to unravel. At the very time she was abusing her sacred trust in Palestine, her capital city began to be bombed nightly by the Nazis. Britain survived, but lost most of her vast worldwide holdings. Great Britain like many other nations before her, learned the high price of seeking to curse those whom God has blessed.

So to this very hour, the blessing of Abraham is available to the nations. The curse is also available. Many nations today continue walking in the "valley of decision" concerning Israel (Joel 3:14). The New Testament teaches us that the nations of the world will someday line up before God as sheep and goats. The sheep nations will then be blessed eternally, while the goat nations will be eternally cursed.

We learn in Matthew 25:32-46, that the criteria for this great judgment will be none other than how nations have treated the brothers of the Lord. The brothers of the Lord are Jewish.

STUDY QUESTIONS:

Name three Jews who blessed Gentile nations in biblical times.

List some blessings brought to the Ottoman Empire and the Netherlands by the expelled Jews of Spain and Portugal.

What great blessing did the American Colonies receive from one devoted Jew?

Name some Jews who helped usher in the Atomic Age.

Why do you think Jews would lean so heavily toward academic skills, including the sciences and medicine?

What other event was happening as Columbus was sailing from Spain to discover the new world? Why was this especially ironic?

Based upon what we have learned in this chapter, why do the Palestinians always seem to have such a difficult time?

NOTES

1. See Jim Gerrish, "Blessing or Cursing," *Jerusalem Prayer Letter,* Nov. 1990. I have drawn heavily from this previous published article.
2. William Whiston, trans., *The Works of Josephus, Complete and Unabridged* (Peabody, MS: Hendrickson Publishers, 1987) p. 286.
3. Edwin M. Yamauchi, *Persia and the Bible* (Grand Rapids, MI: Baker Book House, 1990) p. 254.
4. Yamauchi, *Persia and the Bible,* p. 259.
5. Quoted in Cecil Roth, *A History of the Jews* (New York: Schocken Books, 1954) p. 252.
6. Roth, *A History of the Jews,* p. 252.
7. Roth, *A History of the Jews,* pp. 253-254.
8. Roth, *A History of the Jews,* p. 256.
9. Goeffrey Wigoder, ed., *Encyclopedia Judaica, Vol 12,* (Jerusalem: Keter Publishing House Jerusalem, Ltd., 1971-1972) p. 977.
10. Martin Gilbert, *Jewish History Atlas, 4th Edition* (Jerusalem, Tel Aviv & Haifa: Steimatzky Ltd., 1969,1976, 1985, 1992) p. 52.
11. Wigoder, ed., *Encyclopedia Judaica, Vol 12,* p. 977.

12. Iain H. Murray, *The Puritan Hope* (Edinburg, Scotland and Carlisle, Pennsylvania: The Banner of Truth Trust, 1971) p. 66.
13. Richard Siegel and Carl Rheins, editors, *The Jewish Almanac* (New York: Bantam Books, Inc., 1980) pp. 482-483.
14. David Allen Lewis, *Israel and the USA, Restoring the Lost Pages of American History* (Springfield, MO: Menorah Press, 1993) pp. 168-19.
15. Leonard C. Yassen, *The Jesus Connection* (New York: The Crossroads Publishing Co., 1985) pp. 92-94.
16. M. Hirsh Goldberg, *The Jewish Connection* (New York: Bantam Books, Inc., 1976) p. 171.
17. Yassen, *The Jesus Connection,* pp. 101-102.
18. Goldberg, *The Jewish Connection,* pp. 23-24.
19. Goldberg, *The Jewish Connection,* p. 171.
20. Yassen, *The Jesus Connection,* pp. 97-105.
21. John Hulley, Comets, *Jews & Christians* (New York & Jerusalem: The Root and Branch Association, Ltd., 1996) p. 60.
22. Louis Finkelstein, ed., *The Jews: Their History, Culture, and Religion, Vol III,* (Philadelphia: The Jewish Publication Society of America, 1949) pp. 1057-1064.
23. Finkelstein, ed., *The Jews: Their History, Culture, and Religion, Vol III,* pp. 1083-1084.
24. Goldberg, *The Jewish Connection,* p. 187-196. For this information I have also used the valuable and interesting materials in Louis Finkelstein, The Jews: Their History, Culture, and Religion, Vol III, pp. 1067-1068 and 1085-1088.
25. Goldberg, *The Jewish Connection,* p. 85-104.
26. Siegel and Rheins, editors, *The Jewish Almanac,* pp. 14-16. A portion of this material was taken from Yassen, The Jesus Connection, pp. 109-127.
27. Dr. Goran Larsson, *"The Jews Your Majesty"* (San Diego, CA and Jerusalem, Israel: The Jerusalem Center for Biblical Studies and Research, 1989) p. 37.
28. *The World Book Encyclopedia* (Chicago, Frankfurt, London, Paris, Rome, Syndey, Tokyo, and Toronto, Vol 2, World Book-Childcraft International, Inc., 1978) p. 545.
29. See *The Jerusalem Post,* 6 December, 1996

30. Lawrence J. Epstein, *Zion's Call, Christian Contributions to the Origins and Development of Israel* (Lanham, MD: University Press of America, Inc., 1984) p.7.
31. See *The Jerusalem Post,* 24 November, 1998
32. David A. Rausch, *A Legacy of Hatred: Why Christians Must Not Forget the Holocaust* (Chicago: Moody Press, 1984) p. 109.
33. Paul Johnson, *A History of the Jews* (New York: Harper & Roe, New York, NY, 1987) p. 513.
34. See *Dispatch From Jerusalem,* 2nd. qtr. 1991, p. 7.
35. See *The Jerusalem Post,* 28 January, 2000
36. See *Dispatch From Jerusalem,* 1st. qtr. 1992, p10.
37. Siegel and Rheins, editors, *The Jewish Almanac,* p. 179.
38. Joan Peters, *From Time Immemorial, The Origins of the Arab-Jewish Conflict Over Palestine* (New York: Harper & Row, Publishers, 1984) p. 295.
39. Charles F. DeLoach, *Seeds of Conflict* (Plainfield, NJ: Logos International, 1974) p. 68.

IS THE MESSIAH
RESTORING ISRAEL?

Many Jews today believe that only the Messiah can re-establish the nation of Israel. Several ultra-orthodox groups now living in Israel do not believe that the present nation is even legitimate, because they believe the Messiah has not yet come. These groups happily receive benefits from the nation but refuse to fight for its defense.

Where does such a belief regarding the Messiah come from? Perhaps these groups get some of their ideas originally from the Bible, in scriptures such as Isaiah 11:10-12. However, their interpretations seem faulty. Since the 1880s there has been a gigantic move within worldwide Judaism to return home to the biblical land. This fact seems to be ignored by such groups.

The many waves of Jewish immigration to the land began in 1882. Once the nation was established in 1948 there was massive immigration from many parts of the world. The people of Israel have now returned home from some one hundred nations. In fact, there are many nations where Jews have lived for centuries that are now almost empty of their Jewish populations.

The likelihood of some future return to Zion from these nations is virtually nil, unless, of course, there would be a totally new modern dispersion. The return to Zion in our era seems to be the true fulfillment of scripture. We cannot close our eyes to these biblical and historical facts. The Jews have come home!

With this in mind we must ask a pertinent question. Could it be that the Messiah is actually leading the Jews home and restoring Israel today?

SECRETS IN THE SERVANT SONGS

One of the most interesting and puzzling sections of scripture is known as the Servant Songs of Isaiah. This unusual section is introduced with a burst of Messianic glory in Isaiah chapter 40. This chapter begins with words of great comfort to Israel. In verse three, we are introduced to the ministry of the Messianic forerunner (cf. Luke 3:4-6). We are given a quick picture of the Messianic Servant, who *"...gathers the lambs in his arms and carries them close to his heart..."* (Isa. 40:11).

Beginning with Isaiah 41:8, the Servant is formally introduced. Scholars feel these servant passages continue through much of the remainder of Isaiah, possibly even into the 63rd chapter.

This section of scripture "has exercised the minds of scholars perhaps more than any other single Old Testament question."[1] Scholars have been baffled over exactly who this Servant is. Sometimes the Servant appears to be Israel, at other times he appears to be an individual. We know that the Servant of Isaiah 53 has been interpreted as an individual at least since the days of Philip and the Ethiopian eunuch, in Acts 8:34.[2]

In speaking of these songs and of the Servant, Westermann says: "One thing at least is obvious; their language at once reveals and conceals the Servant. He is not described in the terms used elsewhere in the Old Testament of a king, a prophet, Israel, or an individual righteous man, although there are reminiscences of each of these."[3]

Also, his mood is fainthearted and despondent at times, when the Servant appears to be Israel. At other times he seems to be acting as a lone individual and his mood is totally

*Sunrise on the Sea of Galilee. The Prophet Isaiah
once spoke of a light arising in the Galilee.*

victorious. He even becomes the savior of faltering Israel. Let us look briefly at these interesting passages.

In Isaiah 41:8, Israel is definitely named as the Servant. We see that Israel is called from the four corners of the earth for God's purposes (v.9). God vows to help, strengthen and uphold Israel (vs.10, 14). However, in Isaiah 41:28-29, we see that Israel has failed as God's Servant.

In Isaiah 42:1 ff., we are introduced to the true Servant. He is called a "delight," and God affirms that he has put his Spirit on him (v.1). It is stated here that this Servant will not fail or be discouraged until he has established justice and law on earth (v.4). This Servant will be a covenant to the people and light to the Gentiles (v.6). Interestingly, in Matthew 12:15-21, this passage is applied to Jesus.

Once more God switches back to Israel and upbraids the people as blind and deaf. God says, *"Who is blind but my servant, and deaf like the messenger I send?..."* (Isa. 42:19) God speaks of Israel as plundered and looted (v. 22). Because they did not follow his ways, he sent war and violence upon them (v.25). However God does not give up. In Isaiah 43:1ff., God promises to be with Israel in the fire and floods of water (v.2). God promises to ransom Israel (v.3), and to gather her from the nations (vs. 5-7). He promises to lead Israel although the people are blind (v.8). God reaffirms that Israel is his witness (v. 10).

God tells Israel to forget the past, and not to dwell upon it (v.18). He tells them that he is doing a new thing (v. 19). That new thing is involved with making streams in the desert, or undoubtedly the restoration of the ancient land. God once more assures the people of Israel that they will ultimately show forth his praise (v. 21).

But from Isaiah 43: 22-24, we see again the cycle of Israel's doubting and disobedience. They have not called upon God. They have not kept the covenant and have burdened God with their sins.

In Isaiah 44:1 ff., God once more helps and encourages Israel. He tells her not to be afraid (v.2), that he will restore her land and even pour out his Spirit upon the people (v.3). Again they are called God's witnesses (v.8). In verse 21, Israel is again identified by name as God's Servant. God assures her that he will not forget her and that he will forgive her sins (v.22).

God also promises that Jerusalem shall be inhabited and the ruins of Judah shall be restored (v.26). As a part of this redemptive program God mentions Cyrus, who first restored Jerusalem and allowed its Temple to be built (v.28).

In Isaiah 46:3 ff., God encourages Israel once more. He promises to sustain and carry Israel even in old age (v.4). God promises to grant salvation in Zion and to place his splendor on Israel (v.13).

THE SERVANT REVEALED

However, it is in Isaiah 49 that the prophet returns to the theme of the true Servant. This is one of the most interesting chapters in the whole Bible. Now we have the clear introduction of the Servant Messiah. He is one who is formed in the womb to be God's Servant and to bring Israel back to himself (v.5). Thus, it is no longer possible to confuse this figure with Israel because the Servant is now the one redeeming Israel.[4] How well this corresponds with the jubilant song of Mary in Luke 1:54. In her song, she praises God who *"...has helped his servant Israel..."*

We see now that the Messianic Servant will do for Israel what Israel was powerless to do for herself. He will restore the tribes of Jacob and bring back those kept of God. This is not all. God says an astounding thing to his Servant. He says that it is too small a job for him just to re-gather Israel from all the nations and to restore them. In Isaiah 49:6, we see that God's Servant will also bring light to the Gentiles (cf. Luke 2:32). Westermann comments, "This much... is certain: the Servant has a task imposed on him by God and it embraces the Gentiles as well as Israel." [5]

It actually is an incredible thought, that the one restoring Israel is the very same one bringing light to the Gentiles! This idea is probably also pictured in Isaiah 11:10, where we read, *"In that day the Root of Jesse will stand as a banner for the peoples; the nations will rally to him, and his place of rest will be glorious."* Now God shares some sad news with us. The one before whom kings rise and princes bow down will be *"...despised and abhorred by the nation [Israel]..."* (Isa. 49:7).

Nevertheless, God will help his Servant Messiah (v.8) He will be a covenant for the people. He will restore the desolate land of Israel and release the captives (vs. 8-9). Israel's exiles will be brought home from the various parts of the earth.

Israel now feels forsaken and forgotten by the Lord (v.14). However God promises Israel that he could no more forget her than a mother could forget her child (v.15). Indeed, Israel is engraved on the palms of his hands (v. 16). God challenges dejected Israel to look as her sons are gathered home (v. 18). The land of Israel will become too small to contain them all (v.20). Even the Gentiles who were once captors will come bringing the children of Israel in their arms (v.22).

Once more God deals with Israel's failure to heed him. God says in Isaiah 50:2, *"When I came, why was there no one?*

When I called, why was there no one to answer? Was my arm too short to ransom you? Do I lack the strength to rescue you...?" Then again God turns to his true Servant Messiah in 50:4ff. This Servant has an instructed tongue (v.4) and open ears (v.5).

THE SUFFERING SERVANT

From Isaiah 50:6, we see the theme of the Suffering Servant developed. This theme will later find its completion in Isaiah 53. Note in Isaiah 50:6, that the Servant suffers abuse: *"I offered my back to those who beat me, my cheeks to those who pulled out my beard; I did not hide my face from mocking and spitting."* The Servant is one who suffers, however he knows that the sovereign Lord is his help (v.7).

Again we are treated with the pleasant scenes of Israel returning from captivity, entering Zion with songs and gladness (Isa. 51:11). Even those who had lived in constant terror, *"the cowering prisoners"* are brought home. They did not perish in their dungeons (v. 14).

Isaiah goes on to relate the failure and discouragement of Israel even after God's restoration (51:17-18). He also relates the glory of their restoration in some of the most beautiful passages in the Bible: *"Burst into songs of joy together, you ruins of Jerusalem, for the LORD has comforted his people, he has redeemed Jerusalem"* (Isa. 52:9).

Beginning with Isaiah 52:13 and running through Isaiah 53:12, we have the fully developed theme of the Suffering Servant. His appearance is disfigured beyond that of any man and marred beyond human likeness (52:14). The message about him is not believed (53:1). He is despised and rejected, a man of sorrows and not esteemed (v.3). However, he bears the infirmities and sorrows of the people, although they consider him stricken by God for his own sins(v.4). He is pierced for the sins of the people, but with his wounds the people are healed (v.5). Although the people have gone astray like sheep their sin is laid upon him (v.6).

Like a lamb, he is led to the slaughter (v.7). He is cut off from the land of the living for the transgression of the people (v.8). All this is the Lord's will, that his life can be a guilt offering (v. 10). Yet although the Messiah is cut off, he will still see his offspring (v.10). By his knowledge this righteous Servant will justify many because he will bear their sins (v.11).

The idea of a suffering Messiah is not a strange idea to the Jewish people. A prevalent idea among the Jews to this day is the concept of Messiah ben-Joseph, who actually suffers and dies at the hand of the enemy and is raised up in the last days. There are also the concepts of a Leper Messiah and even a Beggar Messiah.[6] The suffering Messiah in Jewish tradition is pictured as suffering for the sins of Israel.

CAN THE SERVANT BE JESUS?

Who is this Servant? Can it be that this Servant is Jesus? Jesus surely thought he was the Servant spoken of in Isaiah. The authors of the Gospels certainly thought so. Christians through the centuries have thought so, although they have been very careful to pick and choose which passages they want to apply to Jesus. Most all Christians would quickly apply Isaiah 53 to Jesus, without realizing that if that particular servant passage applies to him, the others probably do so as well.

The *Interpreters Bible* lists several events in Jesus life that are directly related to these Servant passages. There are the messianic words at his baptism drawn from Isaiah 42:1 (Mark 1:11). Then when Jesus reads from the scroll in his home town of Nazareth he reads from Isaiah 61:1ff., and states, *"Today this scripture has been fulfilled in your hearing"* (Luke 4:16 ff.).

The Gospel writer, Matthew, interprets Jesus' miracles as fulfillment of Isaiah 42:1-4 (Matt. 12:15-21). Also at Jesus' transfiguration (Mark 9:2-8; Matt. 17:1-8; Luke 9:28-36), the same words of Isaiah 42:1 that were sounded from heaven at his baptism are sounded again.

In Mark 10:45 the Lord says, *"For the Son of man came not to be served but to serve, and to give his life as a ransom for many."* Jesus also says in Luke 22:37, *"For I tell you that this scripture must be fulfilled in me, 'And he was reckoned with transgressors'; for what is written about me has its fulfillment."*

References to the suffering Servant also appear in 1 Corinthians 15:3 and Acts 8:26-39.[7]   The Apostle Paul in speaking of Jesus says that he *"...made himself nothing, taking the very nature of a servant, being made in human likeness"* (Phil. 2:7).

WHAT DOES IT MEAN IF JESUS IS THE SERVANT?

Perhaps we Christians have not fully thought out the implications of Jesus being the true Servant. If Jesus is the Servant, several shocking facts immediately manifest themselves.

If Jesus is the Servant, it was he who helped Israel even when the Church was happily persecuting and killing the people of God. If Jesus is the Servant, it is he who is now gathering the people of Israel from all the nations and bringing them back home. If Jesus is the Servant, it is he who is presently restoring the land of Israel - planting trees and rebuilding ancient cities.

What astounding implications for the Church! We have never pictured our Jesus doing such things. If Jesus is the Servant Messiah in Isaiah we need to fall on our faces in repentance and sincerely beg his forgiveness.

We have sinned an awful sin! Not only have we refused to help him in his program, but we have done everything possible to hinder it for almost two thousand years.

God help us!

STUDY QUESTIONS:

What are the primary differences between the Servant as a nation and as an individual?

In Isaiah 49:8-13, what are some things the true Servant will do?

What are some New Testament scriptures identifying Jesus as the Servant?

How has the Church failed to recognize the Servant?

How has Israel failed to recognize Him?

NOTES

1. George Arthur Buttrick, ed., *Interpreter's Bible,* Vol. 5 (New York & Nashville: Abingdon Press, 1956) p. 406.
2. R.N. Whybray, *The Second Isaiah* (Sheffield, England: JSOT Press, Department of Biblical Studies, The University of Sheffield, 1983) p. 66.
3. Claus Westermann, *Isaiah 40-66* (London: SCM Press Ltd., 1969) p. 20.
4. Buttrick, ed., *Interpreter's Bible,* Vol. 5, p. 408.
5. Claus Westermann, *Isaiah 40-66,* p. 21.
6. Raphael Patai, *The Messiah Texts, Jewish Legends of Three Thousand Years* (Detroit: Wayne State University Press, 1979) pp. 104-105.
7. Buttrick, ed., *Interpreter's Bible,* Vol. 5, p. 413.

- 13 -

CHRISTIANS REMEMBER ZION

Perhaps one of the first people since early Christian centuries to realize and proclaim the restoration of the Jews, was an Englishman by the name of Francis Kett. Kett had apparently read his Bible, and he came to the conclusion that the Jews would return to Zion. For espousing this view, the Church burned him at the stake in 1589.[1]

Others followed in his direction, including, Edmund Bunny (the traveling preacher 1540-1619), Thomas Draxe, Giles Fletcher, William Gouge, and Sir Henry Finch, all of the same general period. It is believed that Finch was the first person to bring forth a genuine plan for the restoration of Israel to the land.[2] The efforts of Finch and Gouge brought them the wrath of England's King James I. They were arrested and imprisoned.

Another prominent thinker and theologian of the era was Thomas Brightman (1562-1607). Brightman has been credited as being the "father" of the British concept of Jewish restoration.[3]

Christian Zionism, or the Restoration movement as it was called in those early days, was spawned by the pietistic Protestants, and later aided by certain groups of the English Puritans.[4] In 1611, the King James Version of the Bible was published, and with it there came a new accessibility of the common man to the Word of God. This accessibility to Israel's ancient prophets stirred Restorationism.

The movement was also soon heavily influenced by millennialism. The millenarians looked for the coming of Christ followed by his thousand-year-reign on earth. According to this understanding, the Jewish return to the land was a necessity prior to the millennial reign. The millenarians also looked for the conversion of the Jews prior to Christ's second advent and reign.

The Restoration Movement was championed not only in England but in other countries in these early years. In Holland, Johanna Cartwright and her son Ebenezer were Puritan writers and activists for the cause of Restoration. In France, there was the scholar Isaac de la Peyrere (1594-1676) and Marquis de Langallerie (1656-1717). A most famous French Restorationist of a slightly later period was Charles-Joseph Prince de Ligne (1735-1814).

In America, the Puritan fathers were great boosters of restoration. They named their children and their towns with Hebrew names. Hebrew letters graced the seals of their early colleges. Hebrew was taught at Harvard from 1636 onward, and was at certain times an obligatory course.[5] Roger Williams (1604-1683), founder of Rhode Island, was a champion of religious liberty and outspoken in the cause of the Jews.

RESTORATIONISM TAKES A POLITICAL TURN

Although Restorationism is not basically political, it was necessary for it to take a political stance. The Bible almost presupposes some political activity in the return to Zion with these words: *"Nations will take them and bring them to their own place..."* (Isa. 14:2). It was in God's plan for the nations of the earth to be involved with this project, and nations are political. Soon an agitation began for political leaders do something for the cause of Zion.

A pietist Dane, Holger Paulli (1644-1714), worked incessantly dispatching memoranda to the kings of England and France. He boldly called upon them to conquer Palestine and provide a home for the Jewish people.

However, with the rise of Napoleon, Restorationist ideas were propelled fully into the political arena. When Napoleon attacked the Holy Land in 1799, he made an offer to restore the Jews to their homeland. [6] Unfortunately, the enthusiasm was short-lived as Napoleon failed to conquer Acre and was forced to retreat to Egypt.

It is of note that even after Napoleon's military reverses he continued to support the Jewish return. In 1806, Napoleon drew together various rabbis and community leaders from throughout his empire. This meeting has been described as "the first organized Jewish political meeting in over 1700 years."[7] Although his political plans failed, Napoleon may have done a great deal to give Restorationism a political basis, and to free it from purely theological considerations.

The next political shock affecting Europe and indirectly affecting Restorationism was the rise of Mohammed Ali in Egypt in the 1830s. Ali's revolt against the Turkish Empire raised Europe's fears about its isolation in the Middle East and the loss of trading routes to the Far East. Suddenly the Restorationist viewpoint, with Jewish control of the Holy Land, began to make a lot of political sense.

At this time, especially in England, there was a rising tide of Zionist sentiment and political activity toward this end. The Christian statesman, Lord Palmerston (1784-1865), served as a member of the House of Commons, as Foreign Secretary and as Prime Minister. He was active in seeking to obtain an agreement with the Turkish Sultan allowing the Jews to return to Palestine.

A deeply religious political figure of this era was Lord Shaftsbury (1801-1885). Shaftsbury fought for the return of Israel to the Holy Land and saw it as a fulfillment of prophecy. On his ring, which was worn on his right hand, his daily prayer was engraved: "Oh, pray for the peace of Jerusalem."[8]

Restorationism received a political shot in the arm with the rise to power of Benjamin Disraeli (1804-1887). Disraeli, popular politician and writer for the Jewish cause, arose to become Prime Minister of England. He served in that capacity for many years. Disraeli, who was probably the most powerful politician in the world, became a sort of model to influence other politicians in the cause of Zion.[9]

Following in the political train, a British industrialist, Edward Cazalet (1827-1883), advocated a Restorationist approach concerning the Jews. It is of note that Cazalet even proposed a university devoted to Hebrew studies in Jerusalem.[10] His vision came to pass in 1918, as the Hebrew University was established.

Political activity was blossoming also in America during this period. In 1825, US President John Quincy Adams wrote on behalf of the Jews with these words: "I really wish the Jews again in Judea, an independent Nation..."[11] Years later in 1878, William E. Blackstone published a book entitled *Jesus is Coming*. The book attracted much attention, in that it called for a restoration of the Jews to their homeland. Blackstone did not confine himself to writing. In 1891, he presented a petition to US President Harrison. The petition entitled, "Palestine for the Jews" was signed by some four hundred prominent US personalities, both Christian and Jewish.

ZIONISM COMES OF AGE

From the 1880s onward, there was a growing movement within Judaism for the return to Zion. This movement was partly spurred by the horrible pogroms in Russia during the period. At this time of persecution and slightly before it, a philosophical and theological groundwork was laid as several prophetic voices arose to encourage the Jewish people.

Moses Hess (1812-1875) with his work *Rome and Jerusalem* encouraged the nations to assist the Jews as they sought to re-establish their own nation. After Hess there were other prophetic voices like Orthodox Rabbi, Zevi-Hirsch Kalischer, who in 1862 advocated the establishment of agricultural colonies in Palestine. Another who spoke out from among the Jews were Leo Pinsker, an Odessa physician. His pamphlet, *Auto-Emancipation* (freeing oneself), challenged the Jews to free themselves, and not wait on others to do it for them.

As the century closed, Jewish aspirations of return began to focus on one man, Theodore Herzl. Herzl, a man of great literary skill and personal charm, became the prophet of Zionism. In a fever of inspiration, Herzl wrote his classic book, *Der Judenstaat* (The Jewish State). The effects of Herzl and his book were electrifying. Soon the Jewish Zionist movement was in full bloom. In 1897 the First Zionist Congress was held in Basel. The political movement that would re-establish the Jewish nation had truly begun.

A CHRISTIAN PROPHET

Not only were there Jewish prophetic voices raised in support of Zion at this time, but one such prophetic voice was raised from Christian quarters. William H. Hechler (1845-1931) was a minister living in Vienna. Hechler was certain that God was about to restore the Jews to their land. When this Christian minister heard of Herzl and his book, he instantly became an enthusiastic supporter. The two became life-long friends.

It was through this Christian minister that Herzl was able to secure many contacts with political leaders in Europe, even with the powerful Kaiser of Germany.[12]

Had we known Hechler, we might have looked at this Christian prophet askance. He was a fanatic with all of his time tables and charts spread out before him. From his calculations he became certain that God would move to restore the Jewish nation in 1897. Unlike so many of his kind, he was absolutely correct.

INTO THE TWENTIETH CENTURY

Zionism was catapulted into the twentieth century, and not just as a political movement, but also a movement with strong spiritual foundations. These spiritual foundations were reflected in several political leaders of the century. Perhaps one of the most outstanding was Lord Balfour of England

(1848-1930).   He learned from his Scottish mother that Christians owed a great debt to the Jewish people, and that the debt had been shamefully repaid.[13]

Balfour personally did a great deal to repay this debt. He served as Britain's Prime Minister and later as her Foreign Secretary. Through his efforts the now famous Balfour Declaration of 1917 came into being. The Balfour Declaration formed the political basis for the re-establishment of the nation of Israel. Pragai remarking on its importance states: "This document was the first governmental sanction of the Jewish Return since the historic Cyrus edict (Ezra 1:2-4) in the sixth century BC, which allowed the Jews to return from their Babylonian Exile."[14]

Working along with Balfour was Britain's David Lloyd George (1863-1945), who also served as Prime Minister of the country.   Like Balfour, Lloyd George also came from a religious background. He once commented, "I was taught far more about the history of the Jews than about the history of my own people,"[15] Although the political aspect of Zionism was important, it probably could never have succeeded without the deep biblical background of men like these.

Another strong and consistent supporter of Israel in Britain was Winston Churchill (1875-1965).   Although as Colonial Secretary Churchill issued the White Paper that severed Trans-Jordan from Palestine, he nevertheless remained a true friend of Israel. He spoke out for the Jewish return to the land and finally insisted that his nation be among the first to recognize the newborn state of Israel.

The Zionist cause was also supported in this period by US President Wilson.   He not only played a vital role in the Balfour Declaration, but again, it was his rich Christian background that made him sympathetic to the needs of the Jewish people. In 1922, the US congress got into the act with a Joint Resolution declaring their favor toward the establishment of a Jewish national home in Palestine.[16]

Christians all over were stirred with the great significance of the events unfolding before them. In November, 1945, the International Christian Conference for Palestine was held in

Washington, with representatives from over thirty nations in attendance. The conference called for an easing in British immigration restrictions in Palestine as well as a repeal of anti-Jewish land laws. The conference also called for the establishment of a Jewish state. Pragai remarks, "This was the first-ever assembly of Christians to call for a Jewish State."[17]

In the political arena it was left for US President Harry Truman, a Baptist, to give newborn Israel the political lift it needed. Truman, who previously had close associations with a Jewish businessman, rushed to give defacto US recognition to newborn Israel in the first half-hour of its existence.[18] Truman did so over the strong objections of his own Secretary of State.

FAMOUS NAMES IN SUPPORT OF ZION

Through the centuries, the love of Zion has pulled at the heart strings of many of the world's most famous people, and not just the political leaders we have mentioned. Dr. Joseph Priestley, (1733-1804), a clergyman turned teacher and scientist, is best known for his discovery of oxygen. It is little known that Priestley was also a strong supporter of Zion and member of the London Society for Promoting Christianity among the Jews.

George Gordon, Lord Byron (1788-1824), the English poet and popular romantic figure, was greatly influenced by the plight of the Jews. In his collection entitled, *Hebrew Melodies,* Byron pens his famous lament, "The wild dove hath her nest the fox his cave, Mankind their country – Israel but the grave."[19]

Another famous figure in the literary field to support Zion was Mary Ann Evans, known as George Eliot (1819-1880). Pragai says of her contribution, "she demonstrates deep insight into Jewish life, its mainsprings and its aspirations, and in it she forecasts with much accuracy the force which political Zionism was to become at the turn of the century."[20] Eliot's work apparently had a profound effect upon Eliezer

Ben Yehudah, father of the modern Hebrew language, as well as upon Lord Balfour. [21]

The love of Zion reached from politicians to poets to the outstanding Swiss Protestant, Jean Henri Dunant (1828-1910). Reeling from his own battlefield experiences in Solferino, Italy in 1859, Dunant became the driving force to found the International Red Cross (1863) and the Geneva Convention (1864). Dunant was also a friend of Zion and founded the Association for the Resettlement of Palestine. He was once referred to by Herzl as a "Christian Zionist,"[22] this being the first time the term was ever used.

CHRISTIAN ZIONISM COMES HOME TO THE HOLY LAND

It is one thing to remain safely in one's home country and espouse the Zionist cause, but it is quite another thing to put feet to that theology. It was a big step for Gentile believers to live in the Holy Land and actually assist in helping the Jews in the early years. Yet by the nineteenth century, several had done just that.

Colonel George Gawler (1796-1869) was a senior commander at the Battle of Waterloo and later first governor of the new colony of South Australia. From his experience in Australia, Gawler realized that it was possible to settle uninhabited land within a period of a few short years. Gawler published a series of pamphlets wherein he sought to provide a solution to the Jewish problem in Europe and the unrest in the Middle East by urging Jewish settlement in Palestine.

Gawler accompanied Sir Moses Montefiore to the land in 1849, and has been credited with persuading Montefiore to begin agricultural settlements in the country.[23]   Without Montefiore's help the settlement of Israel would have been a near impossibility.

James Finn (1806-1872) was the British Consul in Jerusalem from 1845 to 1862. He with his wife Elizabeth were Anglicans with a genuine love of the scriptures. They both felt a deep attachment to the land and began to institute several works to aid the newly arriving settlers. With

---

Isa 14:1 *The LORD will have compassion on Jacob;*
once again he will choose Israel and will settle them
in their own land. Aliens will join them and unite
with the house of Jacob.

---

practical projects they trained the Jews in farming and in the
building trades.   Finn has been called "A pioneer for the
resettlement of the Jews in *Eretz* Israel."[24]

Another important figure who put his beliefs to work was
Laurence Oliphant (1829-1888). Oliphant rose to become the
most important Christian Zionists figure of his time.[25]   He
was a many-talented man, a writer of travel books and a
member of the English parliament.   With his political
connections he worked hard with the Turkish government to
negotiate a place of settlement for the Jews in Gilead (later
Transjordan). His practical plans never materialized due to
the suspicions of the Turkish government, nevertheless,
Oliphant was unfazed. He moved to Haifa, and from that
place he continued to assist Jewish settlers.

Today many aspiring Christian Zionists are encouraged by
the story of Lydia Christensen (1890-1975).   This young
Danish schoolteacher forsook the comforts of her home and
profession, partly in pursuit of a haunting vision that she had
received. It was a vision of an unknown dark-eyed baby girl.

Lydia moved to Jerusalem at God's urging. After settling
there and getting used to the harsh life in the Holy City, Lydia
was approached by a Jewish couple named Cohen. This poor
couple begged Lydia to take their dying baby girl named
Tikva (hope). Lydia was appalled at the prospects and at first
refused. Then driven by the word of God and the Holy Spirit,
she accepted the challenge. *Tikva* was nursed back to health
through much love and prayer. That little dark-eyed girl
became the first of approximately seventy orphaned and
abandoned children Lydia would take in.

In the midst of a siege in the city this Danish pioneer
realized why Jerusalem was so important. She describes her

feelings: "I began to see Jerusalem as the stage upon which this cosmic conflict between good and evil would come to its climax – a climax long foreseen by the prophets, now seemingly close at hand."[26]

Lydia later married the world-renowned Bible teacher, Derek Prince. Her visionary and fruitful life may well represent for us those myriads of unknown individual Christians who have come to the land of Israel. Like Lydia, they have come to love, to learn, to serve and to invest their lives for the sake of the Jewish people.

Christian Zionists serving in the military also made their contribution to the Jewish homeland. Lt. Col. John Henry Patterson (1867-1947) came from a devout Irish family. His Bible background aided him in being selected to command the Zion Mule Corps of World War I. The unit that this Christian led was made up of Jewish volunteers from *Eretz* Israel. "By an ironic twist of history a Christian officer commanded the first Jewish fighting brigade since Bar Kochba."[27] One of Patterson's associates would later become a national hero of Israel as he fell fighting at Tel Hai. His name – Joseph Trumpeldor.

Charles Orde Wingate (1903-1944) hailed from a Puritan family of missionaries and soldiers. In 1936, Wingate was assigned to Palestine by the British as an intelligence officer. At that time Arab rioters had the initiative. They were not only posing a serious threat to the Jews but to the British as well, as they attempted to disrupt the flow of the Iraqi oil pipeline. Wingate proposed the establishment of Special Night Squads made up of Jews. Their task was to counter Arab terror and to take away the initiative. The squads became very successful, but most important was the example and encouragement of Wingate, affectionately called by the Jews *"hayedid"* (the friend).

Although the British superiors were not amused, Wingate firmly espoused the cause of Zionism. He was one of the very first to say that the Jews would make good soldiers. He perceived that his work was laying the foundations for the Jewish military. In 1939, the British abruptly dispatched

Orde Wingate
(Courtesy, Jerusalem Post Archives)

Wingate back to England. In his final address to his troops, Wingate said to them in Hebrew: "You are the first soldiers of the Jewish army."[28]   Later "the friend" was killed in a plane crash in Burma.

Now we turn from fighting men to men of the soil and the cloth. Prof. Walter Clay Lowdermilk, eminent soil conservation expert and Bible lover, was sent by the US Department of Agriculture in 1939 to survey Palestine.   Lowdermilk's work, *Palestine Land of Promise,* later became an important document regarding the restoration of the nation. Also, Lowdermilk testified before the Anglo-American Palestine Committee in 1946, concerning the ability of the land to support its growing population.

One Christian clergyman was an eyewitness and alert observer of the momentous events of Israel's rebirth. Canadian, Rev. William L. Hull recorded these events for us in his book *The Fall and Rise of Israel.*   His book reveals Hull was a strong believer in the fulfillment of biblical prophecy. He was also a man of some connections. Through his friendship with Justice I.C. Rand, a Canadian member of UNESCOP, Hull unknowingly was able to exert a great deal of influence toward the founding of a Jewish State.[29]

One of the true pioneers of Christian Zionists was Dr. G. Douglas Young (1910-1979). Young was born of Presbyterian missionary parents. He received his Ph.D. from Dropsie College and after time in the pastorate, became a seminary dean and professor of Old Testament. Dr. Young became enamored with the newly established state of Israel. In 1958

Dr. G. Douglas Young
(Courtesy, Bridges For Peace)

he founded the Institute of Holy Land Studies on Mt. Zion in Jerusalem (now Jerusalem University College). Dr. Young felt it necessary for pastors and individual Christians to get better acquainted with Israel, to come to the land, to study, and to get involved with the land and its people.

After retiring from the Institute in 1978, Young devoted himself to the work of Bridges For Peace, a Christian organization he had founded several years earlier. Through Bridges he began to publish his *Dispatch From Jerusalem,* a small monthly pamphlet designed to disseminate good news from Israel. In 1978, for his long and fruitful work in the city, Dr. Young received Jerusalem's highest award, the *Yakir Yerushalayim* (Worthy of Jerusalem).

The influence of Dr. Young has been enormous on the Israeli people as they saw in him a very different kind of Christian. The institutions he founded continue to thrive in Jerusalem.

CHRISTIAN ZIONIST ORGANIZATIONS IN ZION

Since Israel has become an independent nation, and since she has scored remarkable victories in several wars, Christian interest in Israel has greatly increased. It has now become virtually impossible to even catalogue the worldwide organizations and churches that are in support of Zion. Even an enumeration of the larger ones would reach into scores. Small organizations and individual efforts on behalf of Zion could easily run into the hundreds today.

For this reason, we will limit our endeavors to listing some of the most notable Christian Zionist organizations actually based in Israel and at work in the land today.

Bridges For Peace

In founding Bridges For Peace, Dr. G. Douglas Young envisioned that he would accomplish several important goals. Among these goals, he wished to interpret Israel to Christians abroad by means of connecting biblical prophecy to current events. He hoped to encourage and give counsel to pro-Israel groups within Christianity. He also hoped to counter anti-Semitism within the church.[30] Dr. Young's small publication, the *Dispatch From Jerusalem,* became the primary tool for his work.

In 1978, Bridges For Peace was introduced in the US and later in Canada. Upon Dr. Young's untimely death in 1980, Clarence Wagner, Jr. assumed the directorship of Bridges. The work soon began a period of rapid growth and expansion into many other countries.

The small *Dispatch From Jerusalem* was greatly enlarged and changed from a quarterly to a bi-monthly publication. In 1985, Bridges began Operation Ezra ("Ezra" means "help" in Hebrew), a social assistance program allowing Christians everywhere to become personally involved in helping Israelis, particularly new immigrants.

In the ten-year period beginning with 1990, Bridges assisted more than 20,000 new immigrant families upon their arrival in Israel. These families were supplied from the Bridges Food Bank with food baskets, blankets, kitchen utensils and many other items. As Bridges entered the twenty-first century the organization was assisting 2400 families each month and distributing 31 metric tons (31,000 kilos) of food each month. Through Bridges programs, hundreds of families have now been "adopted" for regular support by Christian families abroad. Hundreds of homes of Holocaust survivors, new immigrants and the poor, have been repaired by the Bridges home repair team.

The Bridges For Peace Food Bank in Jerusalem. (Courtesy, Bridges For Peace)

On two occasions, Bridges has received special recognition by the city of Jerusalem for outstanding work in the area of social assistance.

The International Christian Embassy Jerusalem

In July 1980, Israel declared Jerusalem as its eternal, indivisible capital. Under threat of Arab oil embargo, all 13 national embassies in Jerusalem representing western nations relocated to Tel Aviv. Two months later, in solidarity with Israel, Christians from 23 nations founded the International Christian Embassy Jerusalem.

Under the leadership of Johann Luckhoff, Jan Willem van der Hoeven and Timothy King, the Embassy has challenged the Church regarding its responsibility towards Israel, while comforting the Jewish people in practical ways:

- Helping Jews immigrate from the former Soviet Union and cope with absorption difficulties in Israel. To this end the Embassy has sponsored numerous new immigrant flights to Israel;

Hundreds of Christians from all over the world march through Jerusalem. The march is sponsored each year by the International Christian Embassy, Jerusalem. (Courtesy, International Christian Embassy)

- Providing social assistance to needy Jews, Arabs, Druse and Bedouin;

- Proclaiming Israel's prophetic significance to the Christian world, and countering anti-Israel bias in the media.

Each year since its inception, the Embassy has hosted an eight-day Feast of Tabernacles celebration in Jerusalem, bringing thousands of pilgrims from more than 100 countries to what has become Jerusalem's largest annual tourist event.

Isaiah 49:22: *This is what the Sovereign LORD says: "See, I will beckon to the Gentiles, I will lift up my banner to the peoples; they will bring your sons in their arms and carry your daughters on their shoulders.*

Jay Rawlings sounding a shofar in Red Square prior to the fall of the USSR.
(Courtesy, Jerusalem Vistas)

Christian Zionism, the prophetic vision underpinning the Embassy's work, entails a commitment to comfort Israel, pray for her peace and be a part of what God is doing among his ancient people in the land today. The Embassy has hosted three Christian Zionist Congresses, bringing together Christian and Jewish leaders for theological and political discussions and seminars. The first was held in Basel, Switzerland in 1985, 88 years after Theodore Herzl held the first Zionist Congress at the same venue. Subsequent congresses have been held in Jerusalem, in 1988 and 1996.

Today the Embassy has representation in more than 100 nations, and a staff of 60 multi-national volunteers based at its Jerusalem headquarters.

Jerusalem Vistas

Jay and Meridel Rawlings forsook their careers in hospital administration and nursing and pursued their vision, moving their family to Israel in 1969. Their burning desire was to become "fishers" (Jer. 16:16), assisting Jewish people dispersed abroad in their return to Israel. In this cause, they visited Jewish communities in some 120 countries. Their remarkable story was later related by Meridel in her book entitled *Fishers and Hunters*.

Jay turned down a job offer as Administrator of the second largest hospital in Israel in order that he could bring the story of Israel to Christians on film. His production, *Apples of Gold* was shown worldwide and was even placed in Israeli Foreign Ministry offices around the globe. The film was followed in 1986 by *Gates of Brass*, a documentary making known the plight of Jews behind the Iron Curtain. Within three years of the film's release, the Rawlings' were able to rejoice as thousands of Soviet Jews began making their way home to Israel.

As the tool for their work, Jerusalem Vistas was established in Jerusalem in 1982. The work is now called Jerusalem Vistas and Israel Vision. Israel Vision is their regular television program that reaches 130 million viewers in 60 countries.

The Rawlings family continues to be great friends of Israel. Two of the Rawlings' sons have proudly served in the Israel Defense Forces (IDF).

Christian Friends of Israel

Christian Friends of Israel (CFI), is an evangelical parachurch ministry also with its headquarters in Jerusalem and affiliate offices throughout the world. Christian Friends was established in 1985 by its co-founders, Ray and Sharon Sanders.

During the Gulf War of 1991 when great numbers of new immigrants were arriving, CFI went into action to provide help in the resettling process for these immigrants. Clothing, both new and used was secured from abroad and transported to Israel by loving Christian hands. The clothing was then sorted and distributed at the CFI center. To date, Christian Friends has supplied over 200 tons of clothing to more than 130,000 new immigrants.

A new immigrant selects clothing from the CFI Distribution Center
(Courtesy, Christian Friends of Israel)

A very important part of the CFI Distribution Center is that of lending new immigrant brides their wedding gowns free-of-charge. The entire wedding party is often outfitted. All wedding garments are donated by Christians from the nations.

CFI sponsors other outreach projects to Israel. Holiday gift parcels are made up for IDF soldiers who are defending the nation. A Holocaust Fund helps hundreds of needy survivors with financial aid. An annual Holocaust Remembrance Day is sponsored in order to share the healing balm of God's love with many who suffered in the Holocuast.

An invisible Wall of Prayer continues to be built as Christians from over 87 nations intercede for the cities, towns and villages of Israel. There are 1,800 locations in Israel that are continually covered in prayer around the world.

Christian Friends also sponsors the Annual Pentecost *(Shavout)* Conferences in Jerusalem. This conference brings Christians from the nations and believers in the land together. They receive relevant, in depth teaching on God's plans for Israel and the Jewish people. They also participate in intercession on Israel's behalf.

The churches in the nations are kept informed through the many publications of CFI. Among these are the monthly Watchman's Prayer Letter for intercessors and news on current issues through the Israel News Digest.

THE STORY CONTINUES

Like Ruth of old, Gentile believers continue to arrive on the shores of Israel in increasing numbers. They come to share, to serve, to learn, to live and at times to even suffer hardship with the people of God. They work as Israel's vine-dressers and plowmen (Isa. 61:5). They come as servants to joyfully take the lowly jobs, and that most often without remuneration.

They come as practical souls, as gentle praying types, as starry-eyed visionaries, as fiery prophets. Still they come. They unknowingly fulfill the words of the prophet: *"The Sovereign LORD declares – he who gathers the exiles of Israel: 'I will gather still others to them besides those already gathered'"* (Isa. 56:8).

Increasingly, Gentile believers are realizing the Messianic nature of Israel's restoration as well as the eschatological necessity of a restored Israel before the Lord returns. They are gaining a better understanding as to how Jew and Gentile will be completely united as the scriptures emphatically declare in Ephesians 2:15-16. They are realizing that the Church must return home to Zion as the end-days approach, that it must gain a Zionist orientation. The prophet Isaiah declares:

> *The ransomed of the LORD will return. They will enter Zion with singing; everlasting joy will crown their heads. Gladness and joy will overtake them, and sorrow and sighing will flee away* (Isa. 51:11).

STUDY QUESTIONS

List two religious movements that had great influence upon the Restoration Movement.

What thing in their backgrounds united famous politicians like Lord Balfour and David Lloyd George?

Name two people in the literary field who had great influence on Zionism.

In your words, what is the difference between Christian Zionists and ordinary Christians?

NOTES

1. Lawrence J. Epstein, *Zion's Call, Christian Contributions to the Origins and Development of Israel* (Lanham, MD: University Press of America, Inc., 1984) p. 7.
2. Epstein, *Zion's Call, Christian Contributions to the Origins and Development of Israel,* p. 8.
3. Michael J. Pragai, *Faith and Fulfilment, Christians and the Return to the Promised Land* (London: Valentine, Mitchell and Company, Ltd., 1985) p.12.
4. Goeffrey Wigoder, ed., *Encyclopedia Judaica, Vol. 16* (Jerusalem: Keter Publishing House Jerusalem, Ltd., Israel, 1971-1972) p. 1154.
5. Pragai, *Faith and Fulfilment,* pp. 32-33.
6. Epstein, *Zion's Call, Christian Contributions to the Origins and Development of Israel,* p. 20.
7. Epstein, *Zion's Call, Christian Contributions to the Origins and Development of Israel,* p. 21.
8. Pragai, *Faith and Fulfilment,* p. 45.
9. Epstein, *Zion's Call, Christian Contributions to the Origins and Development of Israel,* p. 56.
10. Epstein, *Zion's Call, Christian Contributions to the Origins and Development of Israel,* p. 56.
11. Pragai, *Faith and Fulfilment,* p. 49.

12. Claude Duvernoy, *The Prince and the Prophet* (Jerusalem: Christian Action For Israel, Francis Naber Publishers, 1979) p. 64.

13. Epstein, *Zion's Call, Christian Contributions to the Origins and Development of Israel,* p. 86.

14. Pragai, *Faith and Fulfilment,* p. 87.

15. Quoted in Pragai, *Faith and Fulfilment,* p. 86.

16. Pragai, *Faith and Fulfilment,* p. 97.

17. Pragai, *Faith and Fulfilment,* p. 135.

18. Goeffrey Wigoder, ed., *Encyclopedia Judaica, Vol 15* (Jerusalem: Keter Publishing House Jerusalem, Ltd., Israel, 1971-1972) 1409.

19. Quoted in Pragai, *Faith and Fulfilment,* p. 7.

20. Pragai, *Faith and Fulfilment,* p. 23.

21. Epstein, *Zion's Call, Christian Contributions to the Origins and Development of Israel,* p. 50.

22. Pragai, *Faith and Fulfilment,* p. 77.

23. Goeffrey Wigoder, ed., *Encyclopedia Judaica, Vol 7* (Jerusalem: Keter Publishing House Jerusalem, Ltd., Israel, 1971-1972) p. 339.

24. Goeffrey Wigoder, ed., *Encyclopedia Judaica, Vol 6* (Jerusalem: Keter Publishing House Jerusalem, Ltd., Israel, 1971-1972) p.1300

25. Goeffrey Wigoder, ed., *Encyclopedia Judaica, Vol 12* (Jerusalem: Keter Publishing House Jerusalem, Ltd., Israel, 1971-1972) p. 1362.

26. Lydia Prince, *Appointment in Jerusalem* (Grand Rapids, MI: Chosen Books, 1975) p. 163.

27. Pragai, *Faith and Fulfilment,* p. 81.

28. See *The Jerusalem Post,* 24 March, 1995

29. William L. Hull, *The Fall and Rise of Israel* (Grand Rapids, MI: Zondervan Publishing Company, 1954) p. 9.

30. Calvin B. Hanson, *A Gentile... With the Heart of a Jew, G. Douglas Young* (Nyack, NY: Parson Publishing, Nyack, NY, 1979) p. 380.

-14-

LESSONS FOR GENTILE CHRISTIANS AND CHURCHES

The Word of God is alive (Heb. 4:12). It cannot pass away. God's promises cannot fail. Whether it be ten years, a hundred years, or a thousand years, it makes no difference. God's Word will still stand, and his promises will certainly come to pass. As Isaiah 40:8 states: *"The grass withers and the flowers fall, but the word of our God stands forever."*

Today there are many Christians who apparently feel that God's word in the Hebrew Scriptures (Old Testament) is no longer applicable to their lives, or even valid. We can assume this because so little attention is paid to the Old Testament by many. Some today even consider themselves "New Testament Christians."

These Christians do not stop to realize that the Hebrew Bible is the foundation of our faith. It was the only scripture the earliest Church had, and they clung to its every word. It was the Hebrew Bible that Paul spoke of when he said to Timothy: *"All Scripture is God-breathed and is useful for teaching, rebuking, correcting and training in righteousness..."* (2 Tim. 3:16). It was the same Hebrew Bible that Jesus spoke of in saying that *"...the Scripture cannot be broken..."* (John 10:35).

A NEW LOOK AT THE OLD TESTAMENT

The rise of Israel is forcing us to take a new look at the Old Testament or the Hebrew Bible. Why is this? Simply because in Israel today the Hebrew Bible is being fulfilled. The very presence of Israel in the Holy Land is a fulfillment of numerous scriptures like Isaiah 43:5-6 and Jeremiah 31:10-14. Like a seed that has lain dormant for centuries and suddenly sprouts, the Old Testament is coming alive today.

Now we are being forced to look at the part of the Bible that we previously overlooked. Why did we overlook it? Many times we overlooked it because we simply didn't understand it. Now that Israel has returned to the land, many things are becoming clearer to our understanding.

Since Israel is back in the land, it is possible for the first time in almost two thousand years to celebrate biblical festivals in their proper seasons. The sabbatical year, or *shmitah,* is observed once more by many devout Jews in the land. It sheds light on the *Jubilee,* which we see in the Old Testament, and even has significance for the New Testament.

There are numerous other things that have come to light since Israel has returned to the land. The discovery of the Dead Sea Scrolls is one example of this. These scrolls now shed great light not only on the Old Testament but the New Testament as well. The scrolls were discovered about the time that the nation of Israel was reborn. In fact, on the exact day the UN was voting on the Partition Plan, paving the way for a nation of Israel to be created, the first of these newly discovered scrolls was being acquired. Israeli Professor Sukenik acquired them after a perilous trip to Bethlehem. They had been hidden for the whole time Israel was dispersed among the nations, and only revealed as she was becoming a nation once again.

As Sukenik deciphered the first of these scrolls on November 29, 1947, he was getting simultaneous reports on the voting at the UN. This voting was to determine whether or not Israel could once more become a nation. It is interesting that the scroll he was working on at the time came to be known as the *Thanksgiving Hymns.* The passage on which he was working as the voting was taking place had been written long before Israel's dispersion, yet it had an incredibly prophetic bearing upon the events happening. The passage reads, "I was driven from my home like a bird from its nest... I was cast down, but raised up again."[1]

Had it not been for the keen interest and understanding of devoted Israeli academics at this point, the scrolls could have possibly been lost or destroyed.

It is now an indisputable fact that the Dead Sea Scrolls have revolutionized our understanding of the Bible. The scrolls now provide us with manuscripts many centuries older than those that were relied upon before their revelation. The scrolls provide us with a complete book of Isaiah, now on display at the Shrine of the Book in Jerusalem. They provide us with portions and fragments of all the other Old Testament books, with the exception of Esther. Numerous other commentaries and works were also found that shed new light on the Old Testament.

NEW LIGHT ON THE NEW TESTAMENT

Other archaeological discoveries in Israel have greatly helped us with our understanding of the New Testament. Consider the "Jesus boat" that was discovered almost intact on the shores of the receded Sea of Galilee in 1986. This boat literally brings the biblical story of Jesus to life, since it is dated generally in the period of 100 BC to AD 70.[2] Consider the discovery of what many scholars believe is St. Peter's House at Capernaum on the Sea of Galilee. According to archaeologists, this house was occupied in Jesus' time and soon became a Christian gathering place. On the site, archaeologists found crosses etched on the wall, Herodian coins, lamps and fishhooks from Jesus' era.[3] Consider the recent discovery of the tomb of Caiaphas the High Priest. His name is even etched on the outside of his ossuary.[4] These biblical accounts have now become more alive and are not just stories.

Many of these archaeological discoveries are being made because of current Israeli building and re-settlement activity. This was the case with the discovery of Caiphas' tomb. Numerous times when a new road is cut or the foundation for a house is excavated, a new discovery is made that increases our biblical understanding.

There are many other discoveries shedding light on our New Testament. A few years ago in the northern section of Jerusalem the remains of a crucified man were found. Interestingly, the rusty nail was still in place in the man's heel.[5] This find brings up the clear possibility that Jesus was not crucified as he has been often pictured, but that his legs were folded up underneath him and his heels nailed together.

A few years ago in Caesarea Maratima, an inscription was uncovered with the mention of Pontius Pilate. It was the first mention of Pilate in any archaeological record.[6] The find authenticates the New Testament story.

Also in a recent inscription the word "Nazareth" was uncovered. It was the first mention of the city in Jewish epigraphy. This third or fourth century inscription may shed some light on an old controversy. From the Greek language of the New Testament it is impossible to determine whether or not Nazareth was spelled with a "z" or with a "tz." The Hebrew inscription solves the problem in favor of the "tz."

This revelation may clear up an even greater controversy, because it clearly links Nazareth with the Hebrew word *"netzer,"* meaning "branch."[7] In Matthew 2:23 it is said, *"and he went and lived in a town called Nazareth. So was fulfilled what was said through the prophets: 'He will be called a Nazarene.' "* Scholars have been baffled by this statement for centuries, since there is no prophecy in the Bible stating this. Now through archeology we can understand how the prophecy is fulfilled, since the Messiah was called "the Branch" (Isa. 11:1).

Also, there are a great number of excellent Israeli archaeologists on the scene today to immediately interpret any new discovery. All these discoveries help with our understanding as they bring long-hidden truth to light.

A Christian tries her hand at the olive press.

THE WHOLE BIBLE COMES TO LIFE

Today in modern Israel it is possible to see, hear, taste, smell and feel the Bible. It is possible to observe weather patterns as they were in the Bible. One can experience the early and latter rains (Deut. 11:14); the hot desert wind and the fierce winter storm *(Sharkia)* that sweeps down without warning on the Sea of Galilee (Matt. 8:24).

One can observe the plants, animals and birds of Bible days. Lessons can be learned from trees like the palm with its straightness and fruitfulness (Psa. 92:12). At Ein Gedi the little coney or hyrax can be seen playing on its fortress of rocks (Deut. 14:7). The stork can be observed in its bi-annual migration (Jer. 8:7).

We can see with our own eyes the contrast between the wilderness and the inhabited land (Psa. 107:35). After a hard rain in the high country we can understand about streams in the low-lying desert (Psa. 126:4). We can smell the flowers of a restored and beautified Israel (Isa. 35:1). We can taste its luscious and abundant fruits (Isa. 27:6).

Two Christian tourists try grinding at the flour mill.

There are a thousand things we can learn about life in ancient times. We can see an old olive press; see an old flour mill and lift its mill stone (Matt. 18:6); climb up into the remnants of biblical watchtowers (Isa. 21:5-6); see an ancient stone sheep pen with its door (John 10:7). We can see shepherds leading their sheep and talking to them in much the same way our Hebrew fathers must have done and in the way Jesus would like to lead his followers (John 10:27).

We can drink from Jacob's well (John 4:6), wade through Hezekiah's water tunnel (2 Chron. 32:1-4), walk on Jerusalem's wall (Neh. 12:31-39). We can understand about city gates by walking through them ourselves (Psa. 87:2). We can try to roll back the massive stones on ancient tombs (Mark 16:3).

In the peaceful Galilee we can see fishermen working in small boats as they must have done in biblical times. At night we can hear them beating the water in an attempt to frighten fish into their nets. All these experiences in the land help us to better understand both the Old and New Testaments.

It is for these reasons that the land of Israel is often referred to by Christians as the "fifth gospel," the gospel that can be personally experienced.[8] We understand now that there is a history of salvation as well as a geography of salvation. There is a place on earth where God has revealed himself to man.

HELP IN UNDERSTANDING BIBLE PROPHECY

Today there is a great interest in Bible prophecy. Unfortunately, much of this prophecy seems off-center, because there is lack of understanding about Israel – about its land and its people. There are many prophecy conferences today, but often these conferences do not take into account the knowledge of Israel, nor do they express any real interest in or concern for Israel. They simply use Israel as some kind of time clock to suit their own purposes and fancies.

We see in the Bible that true prophets always talk about Israel and are always interested in the welfare of Israel. In the New Testament we see a prophet by the name of Agabus. Even Agabus was concerned with Israel and prophesied about a famine that would afflict the land (Acts 11:28).

Let us illustrate how this present lack of focus upon Israel may have caused us to err seriously in our prophetic interpretation. For the last century and a half, there has been a great prophetic emphasis upon the saints escaping or being rescued from this earth in the rapture. This teaching began with the Brethren movement in England and Ireland in 1830.[9] It was picked up by the Schofield Bible and publicized all over the world. Today it has probably become one of the most popular and fervently held eschatological beliefs of Western evangelical Christians.

This whole emphasis, however, may be contrary to the Hebraic and biblical idea of the righteous remaining on the earth. We see this clearly in many scriptures like Psalm 37:9,11, where we read that those who hope in the Lord and those who are meek will inherit the land. The Lord even repeats this promise in Matthew 5:5. In Psalm 37:29, it is affirmed with the words, *"the righteous will inherit the land and dwell in it forever."* In Proverbs 10:30, it is stated bluntly: *"The righteous will never be uprooted, but the wicked will not remain in the land."* These facts are underscored in the parables of Jesus, which again tell us that it is the wicked who will be removed from the earth.

Many fanciful schemes of interpretation have developed around the idea of an escape from the earth. One of these schemes deals with the Marriage Supper of the Lamb. This supper with Jesus and his raptured Church supposedly takes place during the time of the Great Tribulation. At that very time, the Jews who are left behind will be experiencing a terrible holocaust under the Antichrist.

This scenario not only seems non-biblical and non-Hebraic, but also appears anti-biblical and anti-Semitic. How could the Messiah of Israel rejoice at a festival supper at the exact time when his own chosen people were burning in the flames, and even while his beloved Jerusalem was being threatened? The Bible says of Israel, *"In all their distress he too was distressed..."* (Isa. 63:9).

Although it may be extremely painful for us, we need to carefully examine and judge these current prophecies. In the future we need to relate prophecies to Israel and to Hebraic and biblical understandings.

LEARNING FROM THE JEWISH PEOPLE

There are numerous things we can learn from the Jewish people. They have been around a long time and have had a lengthy relationship with the Living God. Let us consider just a few areas of Jewish/Hebrew understanding that would greatly benefit us today. Some of these areas are discussed at length in Marvin Wilson's classic and ground-breaking work, *Our Father Abraham.*

Family values

Today western families, including many Christian families are under great pressure. For instance, US Christians were recently shocked to learn that their divorce rate now exceeds the rate among the pagans.[10]   In many cases, the Church's troubled families have not received much help from their ministers. Charles Colson writes concerning this:

> The divorce rate among clergy is increasing faster than in any other profession. Statistics show that one in ten have had an affair with a member of their congregation, and 25 percent have had some illicit sexual contact.[11]

Many families are fragmented and dysfunctional, spending little time together. There is teenage rebellion, sexual promiscuity, and drugs even in the Church. Something is dreadfully wrong. How can it be repaired?

Concerning the area of family relationships and family values, the Church has a great deal to learn from its Hebrew heritage.

In the Hebrew culture, marriage between man and woman is expected and the relationship is honored. After all, the Bible does tell us that it is not good for man to be alone (Gen. 2:18). Wilson points out that in biblical Hebrew there is no word for "bachelor." He mentions that of the 613 commandments of the Law, the first is the command to be fruitful and multiply, or have children.[12]

Marriage was looked upon as a covenant (Mal. 2:14) or sacred agreement, patterned after God's own covenant with Israel. Fortunately, marriage in earlier times was not based upon our Hollywood concepts of "love." People who "fall in love" can also fall out of love. It is not so easy to fall out of covenant, however. The marriage covenant is to be a lasting agreement, as long as both husband and wife shall live. This is still reflected today in some of the older marriage vows that promise, "till death do us part."

In the Hebrew heritage, love was something expected to grow in a marriage relationship. It was not necessarily an original ingredient. Until the last century or two, many marriages were arranged in the Jewish culture. We also see this in the Bible, as Isaac never met his wife, Rebecca, until the wedding day (Gen. 24:62-67).   Love was expected to develop as time progressed.

The psychologist and pastor, Walter Trobisch, sums up the difference in our modern and in the biblical approach with these words: "We put cold soup on the fire, and it becomes slowly warm.   You put hot soup into a cold plate, and it becomes slowly cold."[13]

Also, in the Jewish culture, things like one's family, faith, social position, profession, learning, etc., were considered much more than "love."

Wilson also points out that the Jewish home has traditionally been a place of refuge, a little sanctuary *(miqdash me'at)* from the storms and pressures of life.   The lovely *Shabbat* (Sabbath) table with its loaves of *hallah,* cheerful candles, full cup of wine *(kiddush)* were all pictures of the Temple and Tabernacle of old and of the Lord's presence in the midst of his people.

The Jewish family, and even the extended family may gather around the *Shabbat* table and reinforce their family ties.   The father is head of the house and spiritual leader of the family.   At the *Shabbat* table he blesses each child, then he turns and publicly blesses the wife.   In many families the world over, children and wives receive cursings.   However, in Jewish families there are at least weekly blessings.

There are many other Jewish concepts related to the home that would be of great help to us in our modern Christian world today.   In Jewish teaching, the family is more important than the synagogue.[14]   The family is therefore the center of Jewish life and teaching.   This is a lesson from which we could well profit.   In this day, some families are rushing to church meetings two or three nights each week as well as all day on Sunday.   Small wonder that many families are feeling stressed out.

There is the concept of *shalom bayit* or a peaceful home.   The *Talmud* gives instruction that conversation be gentle (Yoma 86a).   Coupled with this, are the blessings that make up so much a part of Jewish life. The Jews not only bless the bread, the wine, the children and the wife, they bless almost everything else. There are blessings for washing the hands, seeing a rainbow, hearing it thunder, hearing good news or even bad news.[15]

Israel also has the concept of *hakhnasat orhim,* or of inviting guests into the home. This is to be done graciously and cheerfully. We Christians have a similar concept in Romans 12:13, but often we do not take time to practice it. The rabbis considered hospitality one of the most important functions of the home, even greater than attending the house of study or receiving the *Shekinah* (the glory of God).[16] Hospitality properly practiced, would be a sterling example of love and unselfishness set before youngsters in today's Christian family.

Learning, physical labor and respect for elders

In the Hebrew language, the word for parents is *horim.* It is taken from the verb "to teach, direct or shoot as an arrow." One of the primary functions of the parents was that of teaching and directing the children. This is not left to others. The Jewish Sages declare that when a parent teaches a child the Torah it is like teaching all the child's unborn children as well (Talmud -Kidushin 30a).

Today on the buses in Israel, it is common to hear parents continually teaching and instructing small children even as they ride along. During the season of Tabernacles, one can hear the father teaching the children as they sit outside in their makeshift tabernacles or booths.

The Jewish people have placed great emphasis upon learning. This learning is often first expressed in the religious field, but also it is expressed in secular areas. Jewish parents have traditionally pushed their children to excel. There is an old humorous story of the Jewish mother who introduced her small children by saying: "The doctor is three and the lawyer is two."

In Hebrew tradition the father had the sacred responsibility of not only teaching the child spiritual things, but even teaching him a trade. It is stated in the *Talmud,* "He who does not teach his son a trade is considered as having taught him thievery" (Kiddushin 29a). Wilson points out that Jewish law forbids one earning a living through religion, and that the excellent thing was to combine the study of Torah with a secular occupation.[17] We see this concept reflected in the New Testament. The Apostle Paul was a tentmaker as well as a preacher and teacher (Acts 18:3).

The Jewish historian, Paul Johnson, remarks that even the rabbis in earlier times were often some of the most efficient traders in the community. Johnson states, "...Rabbinical Judaism was a gospel of work, because it demanded that Jews make the fullest possible use of God's gifts..."[18]

In the Jewish tradition there has always been a respect for elders and for parents. In ancient times the elders sat in the gate of the city and made the daily decisions concerning the welfare of the people inside (Ruth 4:1-12). In New Testament times, the elder was the one in charge of the welfare of the Church. In biblical times, it was customary for one to rise in the presence of his elders (Lev. 19:32).

We see in Judaism, that the family is the refuge, the place of peace, of teaching, or worship. In its early centuries, the Church took an unfortunate turn away from the biblical norms of marriage and family. From the Greek philosophers, the Church seems to have gotten the idea of asceticism (askesis). In the Greek culture, those philosophers who retired from the world were called "solitaries," or monachoi, from which we get the word "monastic." They were also called anachoretai, from which the Christian usage of "anchorite" has evolved.[19]

These Greek ideas contained a dim view not only of marriage and sex but even of the human body. Soon, asceticism, with its denial of marriage began to be in vogue. The Church has never fully recovered from this influence.

Halakhah

Jewish life is determined by what is called halakhah, a word taken from the Hebrew "walk," (ha-lakh). Since Hebrew is a very poetic and expressive language, the word for walk has come to symbolize a person's manner of life, what he does and how he lives. In Judaism, the body of commandments and traditions governing the religion has come to be known as the *Halakhah.*

As we seek to return to our Hebrew heritage, it might surprise us to learn that there is also a long neglected Christian *halakhah.*[20] We see this in 1 John. 2:6, where it is said, *"Whoever claims to live in him (Jesus) must walk as Jesus did."* John tells us that the Christian walk involves loving one another with a deep and abiding love (1 John 3:11). We learn more about the Christian walk in other places in the New Testament, such as Romans 6:4, Romans 8:4, Philippians 3:18, and in the last chapters of Ephesians, starting with Ephesians 4:1. These passages all deal with practical instructions on how a Christian should live and conduct himself.

For instance, a Christian should be humble, gentle, patient, long-suffering, and ever striving for the unity of the Church (Eph. 4:1-3). He should live in righteousness, holiness, truthfulness, and productivity (4:23, 25, 28). He must get rid of unwholesome talk, bitterness, rage, anger, brawling, slander and malice (4:29-31). In their place he must be kind, compassionate and forgiving (4:32). The remainder of Ephesians is simply practical instruction on how a Christian is to live or walk. In many of Paul's epistles there is a theological section, and at the end a practical section, just like there is in Ephesians.

In our Christian tradition, we have placed a great deal of emphasis upon theology, being doctrinally correct, or being orthodox in our views. We hold firmly to a body of dogmas. We probably even developed the concept of dogma from the Greek philosophers, for they were the originators of it.[21] Unfortunately, we do not often get this dogma or doctrine translated into everyday life.

We often "talk the talk" without "walking the walk." In this area we can learn much from our Hebrew heritage, for the Jews place the emphasis upon the practical. When we look at our New Testament, we realize that the early Christians did the same, and their theology was constantly expressed in obedience and in works of righteousness. This outward expression of faith was the thing that separated true religion from the false religion of confession only, spoken of in James 1:22 and in 2 Peter 3:17.

We might talk about the theological correctness of visiting the sick, and even preach about it, without doing much to accomplish it. However, the Jews consider such visits *(bikkur holim)* as sacred obligations, and they are faithful to do them. We shun death and funerals while the Jews consider involvement in the funeral a *mitzvah* (good deed). For ages, the Jews have maintained a *Hevra Kadisha* (burial society), and consider it a great honor to serve on it. The work of preparing the body for burial, and the actual burial itself is done without recompense,[22] as a good deed on behalf of the dead.

Jesus asks us a stern question in Luke 6:46, *"Why do you call me, 'Lord, Lord,' and do not do what I say?"* There is a whole area of obedience and practical working out of our faith that needs great improvement. We can learn much from the Jews and from their understandings of *halakhah.* When we learn how to get our faith into our walk, we will be in for great blessings as John 13:17 tells us, *"Now that you know these things, you will be blessed if you do them."*

AN UNDISCOVERED SOURCE OF BLESSING

God makes Abraham an incredible promise: *"I will bless those who bless you, and whoever curses you I will curse; and all peoples on earth will be blessed through you"* (Gen. 12:3). This promise assures us that there is a blessing in Israel. There is a blessing for the individual and the nation that blesses Israel. There is also a blessing for the church that does so and that learns of its Hebrew heritage.

Some pastors and churches have already experienced this truth. They have blessed Israel and have become blessed in many ways. We do not mean to present this truth as some sort of magic charm or amulet that can be worked for our own selfish purposes. God forbid! However, it is a biblical truth, and if pursued it will have results. The blessings may not be measured in money or even in multitudes flocking to church, although these things may happen. The blessings may rather be measured in depth and soundness of teaching and spirituality. We need to mention that there may also be some tribulation for taking a biblical stand concerning this.

Long ago, Lot left the shadow of Father Abraham's tent. In the shadow of that tent he was greatly blessed.[23]   Even heavenly beings came on occasion to visit that tent and to speak with Abraham. Abraham's flocks and herds dramatically increased. Lot also increased and was blessed along with Abraham.

However, the day came when Lot turned from the heritage of Abraham. He pitched his tent in the luscious valley of the Jordan in the direction of Sodom. With this move, it seems that blessing permanently forsook Lot and his family. Soon he was carried away captive by the Babylonians and had to be rescued by Abraham (Gen. 14:1-16). Later he was smothered by the perverted life styles of his new home in Sodom.

Although Lot miraculously escaped the destruction of the city, he lost everything he had, except his two daughters (Gen. 19:30).   These daughters then proceeded to bring forth children by their own father. The resulting nations of Ammon and Moab, later became avowed and eternal enemies of Israel.

Lot forsook his heritage in Israel and dwelt in Moab, but what a contrast with the beautiful story of Ruth. She forsook her heritage in Moab and dwelt in Israel. Because of the ensuing blessings, this poor young widow became married to an outstanding man in Bethlehem. and even became a part of the Messianic line in Israel.

A REVELATION OF NEW TEACHING TOOLS

Today the modern church is usually in a frantic search for teaching tools. So often, these are brought in from the world around us and therefore do not produce the spiritual fruit we desire.

When we turn to our Hebrew heritage, we discover an abundance of teaching tools that are both biblical and spiritual in their nature. Many of these tools are found in the

A sukkah built by US Christians.

land of Israel. Israel might be called the biggest show-and-tell in the world. It is one designed by God to teach his people about their heritage. There are, however, many other tools that can be used by anyone regardless of what land they dwell in.

Today many Gentile churches are celebrating biblical festivals. In the spring they celebrate Passover. It is no longer unusual for churches, both large and small, to have regular Passover *seders*. The Passover *(Pesach)* is a great learning experience. In actuality, it is a celebration of our salvation. Young people can learn much about dabbling in sin by the lessons of the bitter herbs. As they taste the horse-radish, tears come to their eyes. They remember that Egypt (the flesh) was a bitter place of tears and sorrow of heart and not of enjoyment. They can re-live the biblical drama of salvation and visualize the slain lamb, the blood upon the doorpost, the death of the firstborn.

In the fall, some churches now erect tabernacles and celebrate the biblical Feast of Tabernacles *(Sukkot)*. Many of the holidays of Israel are child-oriented and *Sukkot* is one of these. The erection of booths; their decoration; and even eating or sleeping out in these booths is sure to delight children. Often children can help in the construction, and cer-tainly in the decoration of these tabernacles. It is a great opportunity to teach about the biblical heritage.

Many of the holidays we celebrate in the traditional church are influenced by paganism. We need to hold to the biblical truths concerning these and expunge the pagan influences. It might also prove to be a blessing for us to celebrate biblical holidays along with the traditional Christian ones, and thus have our knowledge of the Bible increased.

Today, many churches have been enlivened by the festivals, Israeli music and even the Israeli dance. This is evidence of a growing Hebrew influence in the Church. In a real sense, it is evidence of a return to Zion.

A BIBLICAL PROGRAM OF EVANGELISM

The modern Church is constantly struggling, and without much success, to reach the un-churched world. Could it be that we have evangelism all backwards? The Lord plainly commanded the Church to go first to Jerusalem, then to Judea, then to Samaria and afterwards to the whole world (Acts 1:8). Everywhere Paul went, he presented the gospel first to the Jews and only later to the Gentiles (Acts 13:14:

14:1;17:2). In Romans, Paul says, *"I am not ashamed of the gospel, because it is the power of God for the salvation of everyone who believes: first for the Jew, then for the Gentile"* (Rom. 1:16).

After the apostolic era, the gospel never went to the Jew first as the Bible instructs. Once the early leaders had passed on, the Church hardly gave the Jews a chance to hear the gospel. Even in early times, the gospel was presented along with the sword. The Jews often had the unpleasant choice of accepting it or being murdered. Obviously it didn't sound much like gospel or "good news" to them. Because we never approached Israel with our gospel, and because we even persecuted her with it, what we now consider good news is "bad news" to Israel. Our crosses and Christian crusades bring back horrible memories of Jews being burned to death in their synagogues by Crusaders, who also held and wore crosses.

We have a terrible past to live down. Indeed we owe it to the Jews to show them a different Christianity and a different "gospel" than they have seen in the last two thousand years. It will necessarily need to be a gospel of repentance on our part, of compassion and good deeds and not just another triumphalistic and anti-Semitic version like they have seen so many times in the past.

Had we done things God's way, the outcome would have certainly been different. Israel is the base of God's redemptive activity on earth. We need to understand this fact. We cannot neglect that base and have our programs succeed in the world.

In John 10:16 we read: *"I have other sheep that are not of this sheep pen. I must bring them also. They too will listen to my voice, and there shall be one flock and one shepherd."* Jesus was speaking from the perspective of Israel. The other sheep were obviously the Gentile believers.

The disciples and early followers of Jesus were all Jewish. Yet Jesus says in John 17:21, that he is praying not only for these followers, but for all those who would later believe (Gentiles): *"that all of them may be one, Father, just as you are in me and I am in you. May they also be in us so that the world may believe that you have sent me."*

This passage raises an interesting question with its statement *"that the world may believe."* Could it be that Jews and Christians coming together in unity will finally be the impetus for the whole world turning to God?

LIFE FROM THE DEAD

The Apostle Paul in speaking of Israel has these interesting words to say: *"For if their rejection is the reconciliation of the world, what will their acceptance be but life from the dead?"* (Rom. 11:15).

This promise first concerns the actual resurrection of the dead. However, it would seem that it is also a promise to "dead" churches and to half-dead Christians. The reconciling of Israel will bring life from the dead. It will bring the resurrection and renewal of faith and of life.

With this in mind we should pray for this reconciliation, and do all within our power to make it a reality.

WHAT CAN I DO?

Those reading this may ask, "Will my family and my church follow the old patterns of anti-Semitism? Will we ever find a biblical pattern in our lives and worship? Will there be blessing for me and my family? What can I do?"

Here are a few simple and practical things we can do to make a difference in the future of Israel, of ourselves, our families and our churches: [24]

- Become well informed about Israel and the Jewish people. The study of Israel can be a formidable task for many. The Jews have lived in almost every nation and in virtually every time frame in history. The study of Israel will keep us busy the rest of our lives. It will also help us to better understand that part of the Bible most of us skipped over – the Old Testament, or *Tanakh*. Some would probably rather dismiss Israel and the arduous task of finding out the truth concerning God's heritage, but let us persevere. Let us become informed.

- Become a source of information for others. We not only owe it to ourselves to become informed, we owe it to others. We need to help them – our families, our friends, and sometimes our teachers, or even our pastors. Many Christian organizations based in Israel and elsewhere would love to have Christians distributing their information to our family, friends, churches and other religious organizations. Many times, free or cut-rate bulk shipments of materials can be arranged for those interested in this work by simply contacting one of these organizations.

- Pray for Israel, Jerusalem and the Jewish people. There are several scriptures that will help us in this endeavor, such as Psalm 122:6-9 and Isaiah 62:7.

- Form a prayer group for Israel. This is an easy way to begin doing something constructive, in order that God's prophetic plans may unfold in the nations. Prayer groups can range from two or three people to twenty or thirty or even more. If one is shy about this there is practical help available that can be requested from most of the organizations mentioned.

- Link up with those who love Israel: One person alone faces severe handicaps, as well as the concentrated opposition of the enemy. We need each other for mutual assistance and encouragement. Hebrews 10:25 instructs us: *"Let us not give up meeting together, as some are in the habit of doing, but let us encourage one another – and all the more as you see the Day approaching."*

- Utilize God-given gifts and abilities. In I Corinthians 12:1-11, it is made clear that there are numerous gifts in the Body of Christ. All of us are not pastors or teachers. God has given other gifts for use in the Body that it may be edified. We need to ask God about our special gifts and make sure they are being used. Perhaps we have the latent gift of writing, speaking, singing, doing Israeli dance, or

*Volunteers from Bridges For Peace repair homes
for new immigrants, the poor and Holocaust survivors.*

playing an instrument. When we faithfully try to serve God in our area of gifts, God will increase and perfect the gifts given.

- Make a pilgrimage to Israel. Join one of the many scheduled Christian tours to the land. Some tours, like those provided by Bridges For Peace, are educational tours and have a period of preparation and study prior to arriving, with more study after entering the land.

- Volunteer in Israel. The founding of Israel in modern times has been made possible by volunteerism. Thousands of Jewish and Christian volunteers have labored in every conceivable position, from old age homes to support groups for the Israeli Army. Many Christian Zionist organizations now have volunteer programs where one can work for three, six, twelve months or longer in the land. Many of these opportunities are with the elderly, the poor and with new immigrants.

• Put some of your money to work in Israel, and thus strengthen the nation: The Apostle Paul taught Christians to try and repay their debt to Israel and the Jewish people. He says in Romans 15:27, *"...For if the Gentiles have shared in the Jews' spiritual blessings, they owe it to the Jews to share with them their material blessings."* It may surprise us that the bulk of stewardship teaching, as well as the offerings taken in the New Testament concerned a collection for Israel. This is a good and biblical pattern so lets keep it up. Share your Christian love with God's chosen, covenant people. Become a part of Bible prophecy.

• For those who absolutely cannot go to Israel, there is an alternative. It is possible to make *aliyah* (immigration) in your heart. The scripture says, *"Blessed are those whose strength is in you, who have set their hearts on pilgrimage"* (Psa. 84:5). One can dearly love Israel and pray for the peace of Jerusalem, yet never arrive in the land. Some of the greatest Zionists in history never actually reached the land of Israel.

SOME PITFALLS TO AVOID

There are obviously some dangers and pitfalls to avoid as we seek out our Hebrew heritage. One can be overzealous and become offensive both to Christians and Jews alike.

The Bible speaks of Gentiles clinging to the skirts (or perhaps prayer shawls) of the Jews in Zechariah 8:23. Although this is true, we should learn to do this in as dignified and mature manner as possible.

We spoke earlier of celebrating Jewish or biblical feasts. One word of caution needs to be mentioned here. Although we may certainly celebrate and enjoy Jewish festivals, we Christians should exercise caution in attempting to appropriate these festivals and make them our own. Often our attitude in this can be offensive to the Jewish community. They consider it just another form of triumphalism and anti-Semitism.

There are also a few real danger areas we should mention in regard to our Hebrew heritage. Here they are:

Making an idol of Israel

Anything can become an idol. Even religious things can become idols, or perhaps we should say that especially religious things can become idols.

Otherwise well-meaning Christians can make an idol of Israel and even of the Hebrew heritage. Christian teaching must be kept in balance. In the past, many heresies have arisen simply because one teaching was carried to an extreme while other important teachings of Christianity were ignored. Just because we rediscover the Old Testament is no excuse to ignore the New Testament.

Teaching about Israel has definitely been out of balance in the past history of the Church. It has been out of balance in the sense that it has been almost non-existent. Now we have an opportunity to balance this important teaching with the rest of the Bible. Let's not overdo it and turn the teaching into a heresy.

We must remember that Christ is central to our faith. He is the head. He must be first place in our hearts at all times (Col. 1:18). When we have Israel or anything else in that position, we become idol worshippers and the curses of idol worship will surely come upon us.

The bondage of legalism

The Apostle Paul warns us in Galatians 5:1, *"It is for freedom that Christ has set us free. Stand firm, then, and do not let yourselves be burdened again by a yoke of slavery."*

It is one thing to study our Hebrew heritage, however, it is quite another thing for us Gentiles to become compulsive about this heritage and especially about the requirements of the Old Testament Law. In the first century, the Judaizers were approaching the heritage in this manner and Paul sternly rebuked them in the book of Galatians.

Today there are Gentile Christians who feel compelled to keep the Sabbath and who expect that others do so. It is one thing to enjoy the Sabbath, but it is quite another thing to feel compelled and under bondage about it. The same applies to a host of things like wearing prayer shawls, refusing certain meats, etc. When we feel compelled, it is time to back off a bit, because we are getting into bondage.

The matter of circumcision for Gentile Christians is another problem area. The Bible is very plain in its teaching here. Listen to the stern words of Galatians 5:2: *"Mark my words! I, Paul, tell you that if you let yourselves be circumcised, Christ will be of no value to you at all."*

The scripture makes it crystal clear that we Christians are saved totally by grace and through faith. It is such a gift, that not even the faith to believe springs from ourselves. Even our faith is a gift of God (Eph. 2:8).

Let us not make the mistake of the Judaizers in the New Testament. However, let us not make the mistake the early Church did in reacting to the Judaizers. They turned totally away from the Hebrew heritage and ultimately cursed the Jews.

The Jerusalem Syndrome

For those Christians who visit Israel, and especially for those who live in Israel, there is another hazard. It is known as the Jerusalem Syndrome. This is a mysterious but well documented illness that affects visitors to the land. Dr. Yair Bar-El, psychiatrist for the Ministry of Health, has made a study of this illness. Between the years 1979 and 1993, Bar-El studied 470 cases of visitors from all over the world who were afflicted with it. Bar-El determined that about 66% of the afflicted were Jews and 33% were Christians. Another 1% had no religions affiliation.[25]

It seems that perfectly healthy and normal visitors can come to the land and within a few hours suffer a drastic change in personality. Perhaps it is due to the stresses in Jerusalem or the spiritual pressure felt in the land. Some feel it is due to the unrealistic expectations many have in coming to the land, and the resulting disappointment at seeing real people, and not saints with golden harps. It is thought that with this, some people loose their senses and decide that they alone are holy.

Those afflicted by the Jerusalem Syndrome sometimes imagine that they are some biblical character from the past, like Elijah, or perhaps someone from the future, like one of the Two Witnesses. There is only one cure for this affliction. It seems that when these pilgrims are taken back to their homes they become perfectly normal again, and that in a short time.

So when we visit Jerusalem, we must be careful not to get a sunburn from our own halo. We must not alarm our Christian brothers and sisters in Israel, as well as the Israeli police, by our strange behavior. We should try not to come out for the day's touring in a white robe or one made of camel's hair.

STUDY QUESTIONS:

Give one example of how the restoration of Israel as a nation has brought the Old Testament to life.

List two archaeological discoveries that have shed new light on the New Testament.

What is meant by the term "fifth gospel?"

How might the study of our Jewish heritage help stabilize Christian homes in the present day?

Briefly discuss how "Christian *halakhah*" might transform the application of our faith to present day situations and challenges.

Based on Hebrew understandings, how could we possibly alter our evangelism program to make it more biblical and effective?

What book in the New Testament will help us most in guarding ourselves against the heresy of legalism?

NOTES

1. Hirsh M. Goldberg, *The Jewish Connection* (New York: Bantam Books, Inc., 1976) p. 11.
2. John J. Rousseau, & Rami Arav, *Jesus and His World, An Archaeological and Cultural Dictionary* (Minneapolis MN: Fortress Press, 1995) p. 28.
3. Rousseau, & Arav, *Jesus and His World, An Archaeological and Cultural Dictionary,* p. 40.
4. Rousseau, & Arav, *Jesus and His World, An Archaeological and Cultural Dictionary,* p. 140.
5. Rousseau, & Arav, *Jesus and His World, An Archaeological and Cultural Dictionary,* pp. 74-78.
6. Rousseau, & Arav, *Jesus and His World, An Archaeological and Cultural Dictionary,* pp. 225-227.
7. Bargil Pixner, *With Jesus through Galilee According to the Fifth Gospel* (Rosh Pina, Israel: Corazin Publishing, 1992) p. 15.
8. Pixner, *With Jesus through Galilee According to the Fifth Gospel,* p. 7.
9. Oswald T. Allis, *Prophecy and the Church* (Philadelphia: The Presbyterian and Reformed Publishing Company, 1964) p. 9.
10. George Barna, *The Barna Report, Vol 1, Issue 1* (Ventura, CA: Regal Books, 1990) p. 6.
11. Charles Colson with Ellen Santilli Vaughn, *The Body: being a light in the darkness,* (Dallas, London, Vancouver, Melbourne: Word Publishing, 1992) p. 304.
12. Marvin R.Wilson, *Our Father Abraham, Jewish Roots of the Christian Faith* (Grand Rapids, MI: William B. Eerdmans Publishing Company and Center for Judaic-Christian Studies, Dayton, OH, 1989) pp. 199-200.
13. Quoted in Wilson, *Our Father Abraham, Jewish Roots of the Christian Faith,* p. 202.
14. Wilson, *Our Father Abraham, Jewish Roots of the Christian Faith,* p. 216.
15. Richard Siegel, Michael Strassfield and Sharon Strassfield, editors, *The Jewish Catalog* (Philadelphia: The Jewish Publication Society of America, 1973) p. 152.
16. Wilson, *Our Father Abraham, Jewish Roots of the Christian Faith,* p. 219.

17. Wilson, *Our Father Abraham, Jewish Roots of the Christian Faith,* p. 222.
18. Paul Johnson, *A History of the Jews* (New York: Harper & Row, New York, 1987) p. 172.
19. Edwin Hatch, *The Influence of Greek Ideas and Usages Upon the Christian Church* (Peabody, MS: Hendrickson Publishers, Inc., 1995) pp. 165-168.
20. See *Jerusalem Prayer Letter,* Bridges For Peace, Aug. 1992
21. Hatch, *The Influence of Greek Ideas and Usages Upon the Christian Church,* p. 119.
22. Siegel, Strassfield and Strassfield, editors, *The Jewish Catalog,* pp. 172-173.
23. See *Jerusalem Prayer Letter,* Bridges For Peace, Feb. 1993.
24. See *Jerusalem Prayer Letter,* Bridges For Peace, Dec. 1996.
25. See Leah Abramowitz, *The Jerusalem Post,* 6 Sep., 1995, p7.

- 15 -

IS GOD A ZIONIST?

In this highly politicized world, many are reluctant even to state their opinions. They are afraid of not being "politically correct" in their beliefs. Lovers of Jerusalem or Zion are sometimes a bit fearful and intimidated to declare themselves "Christian Zionists," lest they be ridiculed. Yet, when we read the scriptures, we see an astounding thing – God openly and unreservedly declares himself a Zionist. Let us examine this relationship that God has to Zion or the city of Jerusalem.

Now we seldom think of God as needing a place to sit and rest, or as needing a footstool for his feet. God is the God of the universe. He merely speaks, and millions of stars and planets come into existence. He is the Lord of the heavens and of the vast reaches of space. Why would he need anything from lowly earth, which is indeed one of the smallest of his planets?

Yet, it appears from scripture that God has a special relationship with earth. The scripture says that *"...The earth is the Lord's, and everything in it, the world, and all who live in it"* (Psa. 24:1). Furthermore, we are told that the Lord has chosen a tiny spot on earth, a small city. To be more specific, he has chosen a 35 acre plot within that small city. We are told that on this tiny plot, known as the Temple Mount, God plans to establish his throne forever.

It would seem that if the Creator were actually intent upon establishing such a headquarters upon earth, he would at least have chosen one of earth's illustrious cities, such as New York, London, or perhaps Paris. Yet, the Bible assures us that God desires Zion more than all of these. This choice makes Zion or Jerusalem unique among all the earth's cities. The choice also makes God a Zionist.

Let us look at God's dealings with this city over the long ages of history.

JERUSALEM – CENTER OF THE WORLD

Jerusalem is one of earth's oldest cities. But God's choice of Jerusalem was undoubtedly made even before time began. The scriptures tell us that God chose us believers before time (Eph. 1:4). In order for God's eternal plan to have completeness and continuity, he must have also chosen Zion before time, since Zion, the heavenly Jerusalem, is a central focus of our faith pilgrimage (Heb. 12:22).

Indeed, to understand the beginnings of Jerusalem, we must probe into the dim beginnings of history. Several Jewish and Christian traditions shed some light on Jerusalem's ancient beginnings. The great Jewish philosopher and physician, Maimonides, had this to say about the city:

> By a universal tradition, we know that the Temple which David and Solomon built stood on the site of Araunah's threshing floor; and that is the place where Abraham had built an altar to sacrifice his son Isaac; and that is where Noah built an altar when he emerged from his ark; and that Cain and Abel offered sacrifices on the altar there, and that Adam offered a sacrifice there when he was created, and that indeed, it was from that spot that he was created...[1]

Early Christians accepted Jerusalem as the physical and spiritual center of the earth. Even early maps of the world show Jerusalem as the center.[2] At Jerusalem's Church of the Holy Sepulchre there is actually a place that marks the center of the world. Early Christians also assumed that Jerusalem was the place where Adam was both created and buried.

Moslem tradition, which builds upon earlier Jewish and Christian traditions, also accepted Jerusalem as the center of the world and the place of creation. Moslems still believe that underneath the Dome of the Rock on the Temple Mount, one can hear the roar of the five rivers of Eden.[3]

ITS HISTORICAL SIGNIFICANCE

Let us look very briefly at the history of Jerusalem in biblical times. In the early chapters of Genesis we encounter Jerusalem, although we yet do not know her by that name. In the fourteenth chapter of Genesis we are introduced to the city of Salem and to the mysterious king of this city. We know from the Bible, that Salem was the name given to Jerusalem in ancient times.

Melchizedek, the king of Salem, went out to meet Abraham as the latter returned from his miraculous defeat of the Babylonian armies. Salem was at that time the name of the ancient city just below Mt. Moriah. It was that ancient city which would later become David's Jerusalem.

Melchizedek was the king of this small city. It is interesting that in the Hebrew language, Melchizedek means "king of righteousness." He was also king of Salem, which means "king of peace." In a day when everyone was cognizant of his genealogy, it is strange indeed that this man is said not to have one (Heb. 7:2-3). Abraham must have thought it strange too, for he gave Melchizedek a tithe of all his spoils of war.

In Psalm 110, David develops this interesting encounter between Abraham and Melchezidek. Under God's inspiration, he relates the story to God's coming Messiah. He states that the Messiah would be both king and priest; that he would be King of Righteousness and King of Peace; without beginning of days or end of years. The coming Messiah would therefore be *"in the order of Melchezedek"* (Psa. 110:4).

Many years after Melcheizedek's appearance, a young lad by the name of Jacob stumbled wearily along his journey. He stopped a few miles north of the present Temple Mount (but easily within the sacred portion described in Ezekiel 48:9-10). As he laid his head upon a rock and went to sleep, he had a vision of a staircase that reached to heaven. The lad awoke in fear and trembling and exclaimed, "...*How awesome is this place! This is none other than the house of God; this is the gate of heaven*" (Gen. 28:17).

Finally, centuries later, as Moses led the children of Israel out of Egyptian bondage, and as they miraculously crossed the Red Sea, Moses and the Israelites sang these words:

> *You will bring them in and plant them on the mountain of your inheritance – the place, O LORD, you made for your dwelling, the sanctuary, O Lord, your hands established* (Ex. 15:17).

Moses was speaking here of Jerusalem, but it was Jerusalem before it was actually named in scripture.

As the Israelites entered the land of Canaan they were soon attacked by Adoni-Zedek the king of Jerusalem (Josh. 10:1-4). This is the first mention of Jerusalem by name in the Bible. The name seems to be a compound word utilizing the earlier "Salem." Jerusalem may mean "possession of peace, or vision of peace." Joshua and the Israelites were victorious over the Jebusites of Jerusalem, however it seems that they did not conquer the walled portion of the city, or Jebus as it was then called.

Centuries later, young David must have realized the great redemptive importance of Jerusalem. Perhaps he often gazed at the city as he herded sheep in nearby Bethlehem. Many of his Psalms speak of Jerusalem or Zion and her significance to mankind.

The final conquest of the city would be left to David and his men some years later. After his conquest it was named "the City of David" (2 Sam. 5:9), not to be confused with Bethehem which is called this in Luke 2:11. Still today the most ancient portion of Jerusalem is called by this name.

Jews praying at the Western Wall.

JERUSALEM'S UNIQUENESS

Jerusalem is unique among all the world's cities for several reasons. Naturally speaking, it is constantly in the limelight of world attention. Jerusalem is probably on the lips of the world's newscasters more than any other place on earth.

Jerusalem is the center of literary attention with an estimated 50,000 to 60,000 books already written about it.[4] Jerusalem's famous sights have probably also been photographed more than most other sites.

The real uniqueness of Jerusalem lies in the fact that it is the city of God. It is indeed the only city on earth specifically chosen by God. God did not choose New York or London or Paris. He chose the tiny mountain town of Jerusalem. The scriptures tell us some amazing things about this choice. In Psalm 132:14, God says of Jerusalem, *"This is my resting place for ever and ever; here I will sit enthroned, for I have desired it –"* The scripture makes it very plain that God dwells in Jerusalem or Zion (Psa. 9:11; 135:21).

The choice of Jerusalem is highlighted several other places in scripture, such as 1 Kings 11:32, 1 Kings 14:21, and 2 Chronicles 7:12. In Psalm 68:16, the Psalmist speaks of the mountains of present day Jordan as looking with envy upon Mt. Zion because of its unique relationship with the Creator. We are told further in scripture that God's rule will someday be fully established in Jerusalem:

> *At that time they will call Jerusalem The Throne of the LORD, and all nations will gather in Jerusalem to honor the name of the LORD. No longer will they follow the stubbornness of their evil hearts...* (Jer. 3:17).

In Ezekiel 43:7, God says of Jerusalem:

> *...this is the place of my throne and the place for the soles of my feet. This is where I will live among the Israelites forever...*

Now back to the matter we mentioned earlier of God needing a place of rest and a place for his footstool. It is clear in scripture that Jerusalem is that place of rest and that footstool. It is given this title several places in scripture. For instance, in Psalm 99:5, the Bible says, *"Exalt the LORD our God and worship at his footstool; he is holy."*

In 1 Chronicles 28:2, it is clear that David felt he was building a place for God's footstool when he planned the building of the Temple. He says:

> *...Listen to me, my brothers and my people. I had it in my heart to build a house as a place of rest for the ark of the covenant of the LORD, for the footstool of our God, and I made plans to build it.*

As we see from these scriptures, Jerusalem and her Temple are considered as the very house of God. This is not only reflected in the Old Testament in places like 1 Chronicles 22:7, and Daniel 5:3, but it is also reflected in the New Testament. In Luke 2:49, Jesus refers to the Temple built by Herod as his "Father's house."

Jerusalem from the Mount of Olives.

In his holy Word, God shares other things with us – things that make Jerusalem unique on earth. We learn that God is very jealous over Jerusalem. He says in Zechariah 1:14, *"...I am very jealous for Jerusalem and Zion,"*

Imagine that! The God of the whole universe is actually burning with jealousy over one tiny city on earth – over Jerusalem. Woe to those people and nations who carelessly touch this city.

In Isaiah 49:16, God himself speaks through the prophet saying, *"See, I have engraved you on the palms of my hands; your walls are ever before me."* What a unique relationship this tiny city has with the Creator! We read further in scripture that God has put his name in Jerusalem (1 Kings 9:3); and that his presence is there. In fact, there will be a day coming in the future when Jerusalem will have a new name – *"...And the name of the city from that time on will be: THE LORD IS THERE."* (Ezek. 48:35).

Jerusalem is like an umbilical cord between heaven and earth. It is God's base of operations, his earthly headquarters.

However, perhaps the most unique thing about Jerusalem is its eternal quality. Jerusalem has been called, and not un-rightly so, "the eternal city." In Joel 3:20 the prophet says, *"Judah will be inhabited forever and Jerusalem through all generations."* In Jeremiah 17:25 the prophet is more specific when he says, *"...and this city will be inhabited forever."*

The Bible says that God dwells in Jerusalem forever (Psa.132:14). God has seen fit to put his name in Jerusalem. We see in 1 Kings 14:21 that Jerusalem is *"...the city the LORD had chosen out of all the tribes of Israel in which to put his Name..."* Jerusalem is God's holy mountain (Zech. 8:3).

GOD'S BASE OF WORLD REDEMPTION

Neither the Jewish people nor Jerusalem were chosen simply because God likes to play favorites. They were both chosen for God's world-wide redemptive purposes; that the revelation of God could be delivered and kept intact. They were chosen that the final plan of redemption would be completed, and that the good news of God could go out to all earth's distant lands.

In Psalm 87:1, we are told that God has set his foundation in Jerusalem. This city is the eternal foundation for all of God's redemptive work on earth. Compare this verse with Psalm 11:3, in which the Bible says, *"When the foundations are being destroyed, what can the righteous do?"*

To put it in modern terms, God had to build an infrastructure of salvation. The building of this infrastructure has taken thousands of years. Think how necessary this infrastructure is. What if God had simply gone out into the pagan world and said, "Hello, I am the Savior!" After their initial shock, the savages would have probably responded, "OK, but what is a Savior?" God had to draw us many pictures and give us the types and patterns so that we could grasp these invisible truths and concepts.

God established Israel so that we could understand the concept of Holy Nation. He established Jerusalem and Zion so that we could visualize the Holy City and New Jerusalem.

For centuries the Temple stood and rivers of blood flowed into the Kidron Valley. All this pictures for us what sin is about and what sacrifice means. From the Temple we can understand what it means to be a priest of God, or temples of God, and what it means to be holy and separate. There are a thousand other things that God had to picture for us in his infrastructure of salvation.

Now obviously, pagan lands were desperate for God's redemption. In every place altars were being built as man searched vainly for the true God. Man in his ignorance and his lost condition was attempting to provide the necessary sacrifice. That could never do. However, once God's salvation infrastructure was fully in place, emissaries from Zion could go to the whole world with the good news that there is a God, that the sacrifice has been made and that his great salvation is available to all.

A PLACE OF OFFERING

It is often necessary to remind Christians living in Jerusalem about one important facet of her existence and purpose. Jerusalem is a place of sacrifice. Many people living in Jerusalem even in modern times have realized this uncomfortable fact as they have offered up various aspects of their lives to God.

Long ago, father Abraham was called of God to take his precious, only son and offer him to God as a burnt offering. Abraham obeyed, taking his son and journeying many miles as God had instructed him to Mount Moriah (pronounced Mor-ee-ah). As Abraham was about to make that awful sacrifice, even as the knife was drawn, God's angel called out for him to stop. There in the thicket, Abraham saw that a ram was caught by its horns. Abraham then offered the ram instead of his son. He must certainly have realized that the lamb would someday be the substitutionary atonement in the place of mankind.

Surely father Abraham had a great vision of redemption that day. He must have realized the connection between beloved son and lamb. Later God would give His only beloved Son as the true Lamb for the sins of the world. It is interesting that Abraham gave a name to that place. It was called *Adonai Yireh,* and it means that the Lord will provide. He will provide the Lamb. This incredible fact stands at the center of world history, that almost two thousand years ago God sacrificed his beloved Son as the Lamb for the sins of humankind.

Is it possible that Abraham really saw the Messiah at this time. In John 8:56, we read these words of Christ himself, *"Your father Abraham rejoiced at the thought of seeing my day; he saw it and was glad."* As we have mentioned before, the place of that sacrifice, according to long-standing Jewish tradition, was none other than Mount Moriah, or the present Temple Mount in Jerusalem. It was the same area where Messiah would later be sacrificed on a cross for the sins of all humankind.

Many years after David and his men had conquered the city, he sinned against God by numbering Israel. Because of his sin, a great plague engulfed the city (2 Sam. 24:18-25). The angel of the Lord was standing near what later came to be known as the Temple Mount. He had already drawn his sword and was ready to bring disaster upon Jerusalem. In order to stay the plague, David was instructed to go to the site and make an offering to God. When he approached the place, he immediately purchased the area from Arunah the Jebusite and there he built an altar and made sacrifice. The plague was stayed and Jerusalem was spared. The plague of sin upon all humankind would later be stayed by the offering up of Jesus in this same area.

After David's death, his son Solomon built the Temple on Mount Moriah. God made this promise to Solomon: *"...I have consecrated this temple, which you have built, by putting my Name there forever. My eyes and my heart will always be there."* (1 Ki. 9:3). To emphasize God's acceptance of his Holy Hill as a place in which he would meet all nations, we read in 2 Chronicles 5:14 that *"...the glory of the LORD filled the temple of God."*

In Israel's long history there was not serious question as to where offerings were to be made. They had to be made in Jerusalem as the scripture commanded. In Deuteronomy 12:13-14 we read,

> *Be careful not to sacrifice your burnt offerings any-where you please. Offer them only at the place the LORD will choose in one of your tribes, and there observe everything I command you.*

According to God's word it was necessary for Israelite males to appear before the Lord three times each year in Jerusalem to bring their offerings. These appearances had to coincide with the pilgrimage festivals of Passover, Pentecost, and Tabernacles (Exo. 23:14-17).

Now as we look back over the hundreds and thousands of years of God's redemptive program we can readily see why offerings could not be made outside of Jerusalem. It was in God's plan all the time that the Messiah would offer himself as a Lamb without blemish for the sins of the whole world in that very place.

During the great festival times there were thousands and thousands of animals sacrificed in Jerusalem. In addition there were thousands of gallons of wine poured forth as a libation to the true God.

All these things were but pictures of the real sacrifice that would take away sins forever. The blood of bulls and goats could not take away sin (Heb. 10:4). The very fact that these sacrifices had to be repeated year after year testified to their inability to deal adequately with the sin problem (Heb. 10:2). The author of Hebrews tells us that they were merely shadows of the redemption that was to come.

When time had reached its fullness, the Messiah came to earth as predicted by Israel's prophets and began his short earthly ministry (Gal 4:4). At the end of his spectacular ministry, he knew that he must go to Jerusalem, although his disciples tried hard to dissuade him. Jesus proclaimed in Luke 13:33, *"...surely no prophet can die outside Jerusalem!"*

He was the fulfillment of all God's promises as to the redemption of humankind. Jesus came as a talking Lamb. It was spoken of him in the Old Testament in Psalms 40:6-8 (cf. Heb. 10:5-10):

> *Sacrifice and offering you did not desire, but my ears you have pierced ; burnt offerings and sin offerings you did not require. Then I said, "Here I am, I have come – it is written about me in the scroll. I desire to do your will, O my God; your law is within my heart."*

Isaiah spoke even more graphically of Him in these words:

> *He was oppressed and afflicted, yet he did not open his mouth; he was led like a lamb to the slaughter, and as a sheep before her shearers is silent, so he did not open his mouth. By oppression and judgment he was taken away. And who can speak of his descendants? For he was cut off from the land of the living; for the transgression of my people he was stricken* (Isa. 53:7-8).

THE HUB OF EARLY CHRISTIANITY

After the death, resurrection and ascension of Jesus, Jerusalem became the hub of the early Church. Indeed this was assumed in the last command Jesus made to his disciples before his ascension. He said in Acts 1:8:

> *But you will receive power when the Holy Spirit comes on you; and you will be my witnesses in Jerusalem, and in all Judea and Samaria, and to the ends of the earth.*

It is clear from these words that Jerusalem was to be the starting point for the expansion of the early church.

This concept was certainly in line with Old Testament prophecies. In Psalm 14:7 we read, *"Oh, that salvation for Israel would come out of Zion!..."* In Isaiah 46:13 we read, *"...I will grant salvation to Zion, my splendor to Israel."*

Mount of Olives

Our Christian faith has the words "Made in Jerusalem" stamped all over it. The Church has often tried to disguise this fact however. Everything we hold dear came from Jerusalem. In Psalm 87:7 the Bible writer says of Jerusalem, sing, *"...All my fountains are in you."* From Jerusalem we have our Bible, our Messiah and our redemption. That redemption was purchased for us on a tiny hill within the present walls of Jerusalem's Old City.

Once our redemption was completed, the early Church was then formed in Jerusalem. The Upper Room where the disciples gathered was there. The setting for Pentecost was there. It is likely that the thousands of new converts were baptized in some of the many *mikvaot* that have been found in the southern wall area of the Temple. Stephen, the first martyr died in Jerusalem, and even today one of the eastern gates is named for him.

No doubt the most important thing about Jerusalem is that the Messiah will return to her. Today many gentile nations claim the Messiah as their own. However, he will not return to any one of these nations. He will return only to Jerusalem as Zechariah 14:4 declares: *"On that day his feet will stand on the Mount of Olives, east of Jerusalem…"*

The scripture makes it very clear that the Messiah will then rule from Jerusalem and his rule will extend throughout the whole world. Psalms 2:6-9 declares:

> *I have installed my King on Zion, my holy hill. I will proclaim the decree of the LORD: He said to me, "You are my Son ; today I have become your Father. Ask of me, and I will make the nations your inheritance, the ends of the earth your possession. You will rule them with an iron scepter; you will dash them to pieces like pottery."*

Today we may think Jerusalem is the center of world attention. However, we have not seen anything yet. When the Messiah returns to Jerusalem we are assured that *"…every eye will see him, even those who pierced him; and all the peoples of the earth will mourn because of him. So shall it be! Amen."* (Rev. 1:7).

PRAYER FOR ZION

Now that we glimpse something of the importance and critical nature of Jerusalem in God's plan, we can understand why Jerusalem needs our prayer. This fact applies both to the Jewish people and to Christians.

In Psalm 122:6, we are instructed with these words: *"Pray for the peace of Jerusalem:'May those who love you be secure.'"* Praying for Jerusalem means praying for her well-being, her unity, her completeness, her physical peace, her defense, along with numerous other things. In the following verses we see that we are to pray for her walls and palaces (v.7). Of course we should pray for her Temple, that in God's good time it should be rebuilt (v.9).

We are to pray for the Jewish people who have returned to Jerusalem. They are a part of God's great plan of redemption that will ultimately reach the whole earth. We are to pray for our brethren and companions (v.8). This may well include those hundreds of Christian brothers and sisters who now make Jerusalem their home. Sometimes the spiritual pressure upon these lives becomes almost unbearable. Pray for their peace and well-being.

The Devil has long realized the importance of Jerusalem in God's plan. Remember, he also reads the Bible. For this reason he has attacked Jerusalem with all his might, and especially in this day when God's people are returning back home. We need to pray against all the current plans to divide Jerusalem or to turn the city over to unbelievers.

We should learn to take Psalm 137:5-6 seriously. It says:

> *If I forget you, O Jerusalem, may my right hand forget its skill. May my tongue cling to the roof of my mouth if I do not remember you, if I do not consider Jerusalem my highest joy.*

Then there is that amazing verse found in Isaiah 62:6-7. It reads:

> *I have posted watchmen on your walls, O Jerusalem; they will never be silent day or night. You who call on the LORD, give yourselves no rest, and give him no rest till he establishes Jerusalem and makes her the praise of the earth.*

This seems to be the only verse in the Bible where we are authorized and encouraged to "bug God" about something. Here we are literally told to give God no rest until he establishes Jerusalem and makes it a praise in the earth. It is something close to God's heart.

Yes, God is a Zionist. Zion is critically important to his program. He loves Zion. He loves Jerusalem, and he wants his people to do the same. Pray for the peace of Jerusalem!

STUDY QUESTIONS:

Give one reason why the expressions "Zion" or "Zionism" may not sound "politically correct" today.

Why does it seem odd that God would choose Zion as his eternal resting place?

Why would God need a base for his program of world redemption?

Give two reasons why we should pray for Jerusalem.

NOTES

1. Quoted in Eliyahu Tal, *Whose Jerusalem?* (Jerusalem & Tel Aviv: The International Forum For A United Jerusalem, 1994) p. 17.
2. Tal, *Whose Jerusalem?* p. 16.
3. Israel Tour Guide (Englewood, NJ: SBS Publishing) p. 256.
4. Tal, *Whose Jerusalem?* p. 11.

- 16 -

IS THE DEVIL ANGRY
OVER JERUSALEM?

If Israel is God's country; if Jerusalem is God's city; if the Temple Mount is the place of God's throne; then we can understand that the devil must be very angry today. Of course, when we speak of the devil, we are speaking of the ancient spiritual being who is very much alive, and whose existence is fully documented in the Bible. Some additional proofs of his existence can be seen in the numerous and unexplainable persecutions of the Jews through the ages as well as the continuing insane hatred against Israel in the Middle East.

The devil must be angry because he had all of what is now the land of Israel in his clutches and under his total control for hundreds of years, but in the last few generations the control has been snatched away. This has resulted as the people of Israel have returned to their native land and to the city of Jerusalem, and with their miraculous wars to defend themselves and their land.

The devil may not only be angry, but we can assume that he is also very nervous about this situation. We particularly sense this nervousness in regard to the City of Jerusalem, and most especially in regard to the Temple Mount. The Temple Mount is the most important 35 acres on the face of this earth, and the devil, being the strategist he is, certainly realizes this fact.

It is noticeable that even small events in Jerusalem quickly take on world-wide significance. Many times, even when a stone is thrown in Jerusalem, the event attracts world-wide media attention. In the fall of 1996, there was an event that clearly illustrated the devil's nervousness and rage over the Temple Mount.

The Israelis decided to open the end of an ancient tunnel that ran alongside the Western Wall. The tunnel itself had already been open to tourists for several years, but it was crowded and inconvenient. The problem was that the tunnel had an entryway but no exit. The simple routine of opening a tunnel exit near the Temple Mount set off a small-scale war in Israel and sent shock waves all over the world.

Contrary to most media reports, this tunnel had nothing to do with endangering a Muslim mosque. The closest mosque was over 1/2 kilometer away.[1] The area in which the tunnel was located, the area of the Western Wall, was an area controlled by the Jews. The real problem was not with the tunnel at all, but it was the fact that Jews were too close to the Temple Mount. It was a threat to the devil who himself desires to be enthroned on the Temple Mount rather than the God of Israel (Isa. 14:13).

If Israel, Jerusalem and the Temple Mount all indeed figure in God's plan for the end days, then the devil cannot allow this plan to succeed. He must do everything possible to stop it. Its success means his demise.

MADNESS OF THE MIDDLE EAST

The continual madness and insanity in the Middle East attests to the apparent rage of the devil concerning Israel. We see clearly in Daniel 10:12-14, that the devil manipulates nations in his hatred of Israel. Probably because of this hatred, the Middle East has been called "the world's deadliest neighborhood."[2] This satanic rage has made the Middle East probably the most politically and militarily unstable area of the world today.

The madness touches most all the Muslim nations in the Middle East. Indeed, Islam is a very convenient tool for the devil in his purposes. Even nations like Iran, which is over 600 miles away from Israel, is almost insane with Israel hatred. Each year, on their "Jerusalem Day," screaming mobs march through their streets, vowing the total destruction of Israel. This nation, which has no common borders with Israel, and is certainly not threatened by Israel in any way, has spent millions to maintain its *Hizbollah* terrorists on Israel's northern border.

Likewise Iraq, which also has no common border with Israel, has the same insane Israel hatred. While Iraq was fighting for her very life against the coalition forces in the Gulf War of 1991, she was spending her precious missiles, not to destroy the coalition forces, but to senselessly strike out at Israel. Why would Iraq, who was fighting for her life, launch a missile attack on Israel, who was not even fighting in the war? The whole episode hints of an other-worldly spiritual source behind these attacks.

One wonders if these attacks were not launched to try and discourage or even stop the massive flow of new immigrants. At precisely that time thousands were arriving in Israel from the former USSR.

POLITICS AS A TOOL

No doubt, Satan has found politics a very successful tool in his age-old effort to deprive the children of Israel of their heritage. Because of politics, world statesmen and even religious leaders have to take great care today to sound "politically correct" when they speak of Israel.

The UN and its resolutions

Satan has likely found the United Nations a cooperative tool for his purposes. Although it was the UN vote that made

Israel possible in 1947, since that time the organization has become extremely anti-Israel.

UN resolutions over the years have been heavily weighted against Israel. From 1947 until 1989, there were 321 General Assembly resolutions in condemnation of Israel. During this same period there were no resolutions condemning any Arab state or the PLO. During this period there were also 49 Security Council resolutions condemning Israel and none condemning Arab states or the PLO.[3] On the average, the UN still passes 30 anti-Israel resolutions each year.[4]

On June 9,1991, a Jerusalem Post editorial marveled that although Israel was only one-thousandth of the world's population, she had managed to occupy 30 percent of the UN Security Council meetings, and to be the subject of a third of its resolutions. The editorial went on to say that since the establishment of the UN, that organization has spent more time and energy seeking to condemn and de-legitimize Israel than it has spent on any other agenda item.[5]

The UN has no scruples at meddling in Israel's internal affairs. After Israel declared Jerusalem its capital in 1980, the Security Council adopted Resolutions 476 and 478. These resolutions called for all member states maintaining their diplomatic missions in Jerusalem to withdraw them.[6] The nations responded and virtually all missions were transferred to Tel Aviv.

On November 10, 1975, the anniversary of the infamous *Kristallnacht* in Germany, the UN chose to pass its General Assembly resolution number 3379 against Israel. This resolution which was drafted ostensibly to combat racism, declared that "Zionism is a form of racism and racial discrimination." This resolution, basically declaring Zionism illegal, was not rescinded until December 16, 1991.

Although Israel is one of the older members of the UN, she has remained as the only member state excluded from serving on the Security Council. One European diplomat quipped that Israel is "the only permanent non-member of the council."[7]

The hypocrisy of the UN is clearly seen in its failure to censure radical Muslim nations such as Syria, when 20,000 of its citizens were slaughtered at Hama in 1982, or when, contrary to the first Geneva Convention, Egypt in 1966, and Iraq in 1988, both used poison gas.[8] Yet when Israel destroyed the Iraqi nuclear capability in 1981 she was roundly condemned. Had Israel not done so, the Gulf War a decade later may have had a far different outcome for the nations. It would surely have taken on nuclear proportions.

There has been much discussion in the UN and among the nations of the world in regard to UN resolutions 242 and 338. These resolutions were passed by the UN immediately after Israel's wars of 1967 and 1973. They both have to do with establishing secure borders.

There is hardly a border on earth that has not been established in some way by war. Traditionally, the loser aggressor nations have to pay a big price in territory lost for their aggression. That is true in every place on earth except in Israel. In Israel, due to UN and world pressures, the aggressors are usually rewarded and Israel is forced to surrender territory won in order that aggressors may live to fight another day.

Resolution 242 calls for Arab nations to end their state of belligerency in regard to Israel. It calls for Israel to withdraw from territories, without specifying what territories or how much territory. The wording "territories" and not "all territories" or "the territories" was deliberate.[9] Israel was not expected to withdraw to its indefensible positions before the 1967 war.

Resolution 338, which was drafted after the 1973 war, was simply a call for the implementation of resolution 242. The Arab nations have refused to understand these resolutions according to their careful wordings, but have insisted that Israel withdraw from all territory conquered in these wars. It may be added that many of the Arab nations have made little effort to cease from their belligerency as also required in these resolutions. These resolutions have been the basis for virtually all modern peace negotiations in the Middle East.

After the Camp David Accord between Israel and Egypt in 1978, Israel withdrew from the Sinai. This amounted to over 90 percent of all land she had conquered in the wars.[10] Israel paid a dear price for peace by surrendering her newly developed oil reserves, airfields, settlements and strategic depth.

UN observers

As Israel has traditionally surrendered territory, UN observers or UN forces are moved in. This was the case in previous surrenders of the Sinai by Israel. The problem with "impartial" UN forces is that they are never impartial. From 1948 to 1967, the UN Truce Supervision Organization utterly failed to prevent the infiltration of Palestinian terrorists into Israel.[11] When Egypt's President Nasser ordered the UN out of the Sinai as he prepared for the invasion of Israel in 1967, they promptly complied.

The UN in Lebanon has done similarly. When the Israeli forces routed the PLO out of Lebanon in 1982 they were horrified at what they found. They learned that the PLO had established its central training facility for young terrorists in a vocational school run by the UN Relief and Works Agency. Some 600 boys and girls ages 18-19 were being trained there to become PLO officers.[12] The UNRWA staff was unable to give an explanation of the PLO's presence there.

The Peace Process

The peace negotiations of the last decade were kicked off at an international meeting in Madrid in 1991. The process was largely as an aftermath of the Gulf War, but somewhat as a result of the *Intifada* (Arab Uprising) that began in 1987. The peace momentum greatly increased over the next few years, and secret direct negotiations began to be conducted between members of Israel's Labor government and the PLO. Many of these negotiations were under the sponsorship of Norway and in time the new peace initiative resulted in the Olso Accords.

The Oslo Accords were hastily put together by Israel's Labor government. The accords were then put into action

PLO ravages in Lebanon. *(Courtesy Embassy of Israel, Washington D.C.)*

without proper study and without approval of the public. In the accords, Israel agreed to pull her forces out of Jericho and Gaza first of all (Oslo I - 1993). Later Israel pulled out of the major cities of the West Bank, including Bethlehem, Shechem and most of Hebron (Oslo II - 1995). Israel is scheduled to make additional withdrawals of her forces until almost half of the West Bank (Judea and Samaria) is surrendered to the newly created Palestinian Authority (PA).

Only after she was deeply involved did Israel learn that the PA was not keeping its end of the agreement. The hateful

Palestinian Covenant which called for the eradication of Israel had not been amended as agreed. In numerous instances, the PA had violated its agreement.[13]

Israel then learned that the Norwegian leaders who framed the agreement were, in their student days, passionate advocates of the PLO, and the establishment of a Palestinian secular state replacing Israel. This group included even the Foreign Minister Bjorn Tore Godal.[14]

Israel began to pay a heavy price for its supposed "peace." Israel was surprised to learn that more of her citizens had been killed by terror during the peace process than before it started. Immediately the PLO began to increase the size of its police force until it swelled to a small army of almost 50,000. The Gaza-Jericho Accords of May 1994 had stipulated a police force of no more than 9000.

Arafat then began to illegally import and stockpile weapons of all kinds. The PLO began to use its newly acquired areas as safe bases for its terror attacks.

The Arabs in these areas began to steal everything possible from the Israelis. In 1996 they stole Israeli vehicles at the rate of about 100 each day. This rate amounted to about one out of every six vehicles in Israel stolen each year.[15] These vehicles were immediately transported to the safety of the Palestinian Authority. Some were even used later by the Palestinian policemen.

In the spring of 1996, Israel was devastated by massive attacks on buses in Jerusalem, at other bus stations, and in the commercial area of Tel Aviv. After the attacks, 69 Israelis were dead and scores were wounded.

Through the Oslo Accords, Israel was committed to her own self-destruction. She was committed to import into her area some of the most deadly terrorists in the world. In fact, upon their arrival these deadly terrorists are routinely made officers in the PA police force. For all future wars, Israel would now have a well armed "fifth-column" within her own borders, and this group would be devoted to her complete destruction.

The prestige of the world's great nations has been placed squarely behind "solving" the Israel problem. Even the White House has been the scene for the signings of these agreements. In October, 1998, Israel and Palestinian leaders were summoned there and kept there for nine days until an agreement for withdrawal by Israel could be hammered out. The so-called Wye Plantation Agreement that resulted seems destined to worsen the security situation in Israel as more precious land is surrendered.

At the turn of the second millennium, a new initiative was begun by the US at Shepherdstown, West Virginia. This initiative was aimed at forcing the Israelis to withdraw from Golan Heights. The Golan is a small strip of land some 25 kilometers wide and 75 kilometers long that was gained by Israel in the defensive war of 1967. However this small strip is of great strategic worth to Israel. Israeli soldiers perched on Mt. Hermon can see deep into Syria, thus virtually eliminating a Syrian surprise attack. The Golan also controls many of the water sources for the Sea of Galilee, which provides about a third of Israel's water. Other considerations are that the Golan, which now has some 18,000 Jewish residents, was an area of ancient Israelite settlement from the time of Moses.

Those who are anxious to cede the Golan for a piece of paper forget that the Golan has been Israel's quietest border, even without a peace agreement.

THE REFUGEE PROBLEM

Israel has been consistently bashed by the media, the UN and the world's leaders. A convenient area of bashing is the resettlement of Arab refugees from all her wars, particularly the war of 1948.

The Palestinian refugee problem is a problem that cannot be solved. It cannot be solved precisely because Arab governments and the PLO will not allow it to be solved. It is too convenient to use as a political weapon against Israel.

Our world has seen millions of refugees. After World War II there were some 3,000,000 Sudeten German refugees. West Germany alone since World War II is said to have rehabilitated over nine million refugees.   There were also vast population shifts in other parts of the world. It is estimated that since World War II there have been over 40 million refugees in the world.[16] Most of these refugees have been quickly resettled in other countries. Not so the Palestinians.

The Arab countries quickly perceived the propaganda potential of these helpless people and they have been exploited for a half century for this purpose.

The Arab refugee problem was originally much the fault of Arab countries.   During Israel's war of Independence, Arab leaders advised Palestinians to flee the land until their invasion was complete. Great numbers complied, even over the objections of Jewish authorities.

It has been calculated that the total number of Arab refugees was 650,000, with some estimates as low as 472,000.[17] Soon, however, UNRWA, the UN affiliate in charge of the refugees began to speak of numbers exceeding one million. Later it was disclosed that the lists had been greatly padded by unreported deaths and forged ration cards. The figures continued to be inflated until they were speaking of two million and even three million refugees. All this served the Arab propaganda machine very well.

Now as a part of the peace process, the PLO is demanding that these refugees be returned to the land. Of course, such a move would spell the end of the sovereign state of Israel.

What has been cleverly obscured in all the clamor concerning refugees, is that an almost parallel expulsion of Jews from Arab lands occurred in 1948 at the time Israel was becoming a state. Some 820,000 Jewish refugees fled or were forced out of Arab countries, in most cases leaving all their wealth behind. About 586,000[18] of these refugees fled to Israel and they were quickly absorbed by the newly formed nation.

With each passing year the Palestinian refugee problem grows larger and larger. It is an unfortunate act of manipulation by the Arabs of their own people as it continues to be used as a powerful media tool to bash Israel.

THE MEDIA

Being a member of the media in the Middle East can be a very hazardous job. Islam does not tolerate opinions contrary to its own beliefs and goals. This was vividly illustrated to the world recently by the author Salmon Rushdie. He wrote a book critical of Islam and because of it he now has a permanent death threat on his head. Several years after the book's publication, Rushdie still remains in hiding.

During Israel's war with the PLO in Lebanon, a completely biased job of reporting was done by the media there. Should we even wonder why? The answer is easy.

Edouard George, former editor of the French language daily, *L'Orient le Jour* in West Beirut, has related a detailed story of intimidation of the media by the PLO, as well as a list of foreign journalists murdered by the organization. The list includes, Larry Buchman of ABC Television; Mark Tryon of Free Belgium radio; Robert Pfeffer, correspondent for the weeklies *Der Spiegel* of West Germany and *Unita* of Italy; Italian journalist Tony Italo and Greciella Difaco; ABC correspondent Sean Toolan; and Jean Lougeau, correspondent for French TF-1.[19]

George relates how Lebanese papers had their offices bombed and destroyed by the PLO. He relates how editors and owners of newspapers were intimidated and murdered. For instance, there was Salim Lawzi, owner of the prestigious weekly *Al-Hawadit*. Lawzi "was apprehended at a PLO check-post in July 1978 and taken to Aramoun village, where he was tortured. His eyes were gouged out and his body cut to pieces. Photos of his body were distributed among the press community of Beirut as a warning."[20] It is no wonder that the reports we heard out of Lebanon were biased against Israel and in favor of the PLO. The reporters and publishers simply wanted to live.

The same tactics are presently being used by Yasser Arafat and the PLO in the new Palestinian Authority. The international organization "Reporters Without Borders," stated that in the first year and one half of the Palestinian Authority's operation, 29 reporters were arrested and 10 newspapers were closed down. The group stated that the PLO has no scruples at using threats and violence to control the media.[21]

During the Christmas season in 1995, Maher Alami, editor of the *Al-Quds* newspaper in Jerusalem was kidnapped by the PLO. His crime was that he failed to put a favorable article of Arafat on the front page of his paper. It seemed not to matter that *Al-Quds* was the most pro-Arafat paper in print at the time.[22]

In addition to all this, the Muslim world is spending millions of petrodollars to buy up newspapers and radio networks worldwide.[23] Obviously, these media outlets will play the PLO tune.

The media characteristically uses politically loaded terminology in speaking of Israel. We constantly hear of "occupied territories." This term immediately paints a picture of cruel occupiers rather than Israeli settlers on their own God-given land. At the same time we never hear Jordan called an occupied territory, and yet it is. We never hear of Syria occupying all of Lebanon, yet that is exactly what she has been doing for the last several years. We hear of "West Bank" instead of Judea and Samaria or biblical Israel. We never hear of the "East Bank." That one was stolen away from Israel long ago by the British and given to create Transjordan.

Slanted versions of stories and Palestinian attempts at historical revisionism are rampant today. One can check on Internet with the PLO's "historian," Wallid M. Awad, and will be amazed to learn that "almost 30 years of [massive] excavations [in Jerusalem] did not reveal anything Jewish, no tangible evidence of theirs was unearthed... Jerusalem is not a Jewish city, despite the biblical myth implanted in some minds..."[24]

What is much more frightening is the PLO attempt to distort history for all future generations by tampering with encyclopedias. Encyclopedias have an extremely long shelf life. They remain in homes and schools for decades and are generally considered as factual by those who use them. Now with the advent of electronic encyclopedias the information in these volumes is dispersed to people all over the globe.

In recent years the Muslims have made great strides at revising the history of the Holy Land in these volumes, almost to the point of eliminating the Jews altogether. *Colliers Encyclopedia* has joined with *The Encyclopedia Britanica* and *Webster's New World Encyclopedia* in re-writing the history of Israel.

In *Colliers,* Rashid Khalidi and Zachary Lochman join together to contribute to the modern Palestine and Israel sections. Khalidi speaks of a sovereign Palestinian state, although such an entity has never existed in history. Lochman finds Israel guilty at every turn and is an unblinking apologist for the PLO.[25] One wonders what school children will believe about Israel in the next generation.

SURROUNDING NATIONS, PAWNS OF THE DEVIL

It seems that the devil has cleverly used the surrounding Arab nations in his age-old plot to destroy Israel. This is sad indeed when we consider that many of these surrounding nations are also children of Abraham through Ishmael, Esau, and other of his descendants. Yet, they were lured into this plot thousands of years ago and are still victims of it.

We read in scripture that Jerusalem will ultimately drive these surrounding Arab nations mad. We see this brought out clearly in Zechariah 12:2, as the Lord says: *"I am going to make Jerusalem a cup that sends all the surrounding peoples reeling..."*

The Arab nations have been duped to fight against Israel. The Arab people have been drawn into this struggle, believing it simply to be a struggle for Palestinian rights. In truth, it is a spiritual struggle destined to become more and more intense with time.

Why did the Olso Accords seek to strip Jericho from the Israelis first of all? Could it be because Jericho was the first city conquered by the Israelis almost 3500 years ago? How interesting! The devil would certainly like to undo that conquest forever. The valley of Achor which is near Jericho is called in the scripture *"a door of hope"* (Hos. 2:15). Somehow, in ways we cannot understand, Israel's door of hope was stolen away by the devil when the Oslo Accords gave Jericho to the Palestinians.

What one thing did all these cities have in common that are now given over to the Palestinians? These cities were Jenin, Kalkilya, Tulkarem, Nablus (Shechem), Ramalla, Bethlehem and most of Hebron. These cities are all situated on the mountain ridge that runs north and south through the land of Israel. That mountain ridge comprises what we can assuredly call biblical Israel. God speaks specifically that this mountainous area is the place to which the children of Israel shall return after their dispersion (Ezek. 36:10).

It was at Shechem (Nablus) that God first promised Abraham the land, while the latter was actually standing upon it (Gen. 12:6-7). At Shechem the covenant was first written down and affirmed in the land (Josh. 8:30-35). It is the place of Joseph's Tomb and Jacob's Well. Now due to the Olso Accords, it is lost to Israel and is now a part of Palestine Authority.

Bethlehem, on the outskirts of Jerusalem, was the scene of the drama of Ruth and Boaz. It was the home of David, but most important of all it was the birthplace of Jesus. Just a few decades ago it was a predominantly Christian city. Today it is largely Muslim and now given over to the Palestinian Authority. The tomb of Rachel still stands forlornly just outside Bethlehem. We might wonder if Rachel is once more weeping for her children, who have had this precious and meaningful heritage stolen from them once again (Jer. 31:15).

Hebron, like Shechem was a city of refuge in biblical times. It was the burial place of Israel's patriarchs and matriarchs, including Abraham and Sarah. It was the first capital of King David before he moved to Jerusalem. It was the southern gateway city into the mountains of Biblical Israel. Today it is largely given over to the Palestinian Authority.

There is an apparent other-worldly plan in all this. The plan is to undo Joshua's ancient conquests of the mountains, and to insure that Israel will not resettle her ancient homeland. In biblical times Israel lived in the mountains. It was the Philistines who lived in the coastal plains. Today, something of the reverse is the case. The Palestinians, who erroneously call themselves Philistines, control the mountains and the Israelis are squeezed into the coastal plains.

This is not satisfactory for the devil. His ultimate intent is to drown Israel in the sea. This intent has been spoken many times by Arafat and other Muslim radicals. Even this is not satisfactory as we see in a 1995 quote from *Babel,* a leading Iraqi newspaper: "The idea of throwing the Israelis into the sea is not good enough, since the Jews know how to swim and will survive."[26]

We can see now how the much touted "land for peace" will never bring peace in the Middle East. Today Israel could offer every inch of her land holdings to the Palestinians and keep only one tiny 35 acre plot known as the Temple Mount. If Israel only visited this plot by helicopter one day a year, the *jihad* against Israel would continue unabated.

The problems in the Middle East are therefore not political or geographical. They are spiritual and can only be dealt with from a spiritual frame of reference.

JERUSALEM, A GLOBAL CONSENSUS

In recent years, the division of Jerusalem has become a "global consensus." The UN, the US, and nations everywhere are eager to divide Jerusalem once more.

The nations of the earth are reluctant and even fearful to place their embassies in Jerusalem. To date only Costa Rica and El Salvador dare to have embassies in the city. Even a mighty nation like the US has vacillated and trembled about this decision for years and seems very reluctant to move its embassy from Tel Aviv. There is no other country on earth where the nations have boycotted the capital city as they have done to Jerusalem. The devil must love it.

This is only one of the numerous hypocritical acts of the nations regarding Israel. We can be sure that God will not put up with such hypocrisy much longer. In ancient times the area of the Temple Mount was an ancient threshing floor. David purchased this threshing floor and later Solomon's Temple was built on that spot (2 Sam. 24:18).

What happens on a threshing floor? There the grain is separated from the stalk by running it over with a threshing sledge. Then when the Mediterranean breezes blow in the late afternoon, the grain can be winnowed or separated from the chaff.

It is appropriate that the Temple was built on a threshing floor. God is about to "thresh" the nations and the devil on that very spot.

STUDY QUESTIONS:

Why might the devil be nervous over Jewish activity in Jerusalem?

Explain why UN fairness may be just a modern myth.

List three things that could cause many Israelis to look upon the Oslo Accords with suspicion.

What one fact would seemingly counterbalance the Arab refugee problem?

Why might news reports originating from the Middle East be unfactual or biased?

What is significant about the mountain cities of ancient Israel being handed over to the Palestinian Authority?

NOTES

1. See Clarence H. Wagner, Jr., "Israel Accused by the Nations," *Dispatch From Jerusalem,* January/February, 1997, p.1.
2. Ramon Bennett, *The Great Deception Philistine* (Jerusalem: Arm of Salvation, Jerusalem, 1995) p. 19.
3. See *The Jerusalem Post,* 27 October, 1995.
4. See Editorial, "No Golden Anniversary," *The Jerusalem Post,* 28 June, 1995.
5. See Editorial, "The UN Impediment," *The Jerusalem Post,* 9 June, 1991.
6. See Shlomo Slonim, "Why Israel Had To Say No," *The Jerusalem Post,* 6 November, 1990.
7. See *The Jerusalem Post,* 28 June, 1995.
8. See Yosef Ben-Aharon, "Why Not Just Talk To Us," *The Jerusalem Post,* 17 June, 1991.
9. Dr. Mitchell G. Bard, Ed., *Near East Report* (Washington, DC: Near East Research, Inc., 1991) p. 62.
10. See Eugene V. Rostow, "The Truth About 242," *The Jerusalem Post,* 5 November, 1990.
11. See Aharon Levran, "UN Observers Recipe For Disaster," *The Jerusalem Post,* 29 May, 1990.
12. Eliyahu Tal, *PLO* (Jerusalem: Department of Information, WZO, 1982) p. 33.
13. See *Dispatch From Jerusalem,* September/October, 1996, p. 8.
14. See Steve Rodan, "Norwegian Leaders Supported Termination of Jewish State," *The Jerusalem Post,* 5 May, 1996.
15. See *Jerusalem Prayer Letter,* March, 1997.
16. See *Dispatch From Jerusalem,* 1st. qtr., 1992.
17. Mitchell G. Bard and Joel Himelfarb, *Myths and Facts, A Concise Record of the Arab-Israeli Conflict* (Washington, DC: Near East Report, 1992) p. 120
18. Bard and Himelfarb, *Myths and Facts, A Concise Record of the Arab-Israeli Conflict,* p. 121.
19. Tal, *PLO,* p. 78.
20. Quoted in Tal, *PLO,* p. 78.
21. See *Dispatch From Jerusalem,* March/April, 1996, p. 8.
22. See *Dispatch From Jerusalem,* January/February, 1996 p. 2.

23. Tal, *PLO,* p. 78.
24. See Moshe Kohn, "What 'New Middle East,'?" *The Jerusalem Post,* 3 January, 1997.
25. See *Dispatch From Jerusalem,* March/April, 1994 p. 2.
26. Quoted in *Dispatch From Jerusalem,* July/August, 1995 p. 8.

- 17 -

GOD'S FINAL CHAPTER

One thing is for sure. God is going to wind up his program and bring this present evil age to a swift conclusion.

There are many things concerning the end of the age and the coming of the Lord that our finite minds cannot grasp. For one thing, many of the hints the Lord gives us concerning this time are in a sort of veiled language. We see only dim reflections in the mirror (1 Cor. 13:12). God has simply not revealed the whole to mankind.

We must therefore always be careful in our interpretations to avoid naming names and setting dates. We cannot be too specific, but we can talk quite confidently in general terms. God has given enough hints about the end of the age, that if we are careful to read and weigh his word, we can recognize the time when it comes. Long ago, the aged Simeon and Anna recognized Jesus as the Messiah. They had waited long for him in the Temple area; they had savored the promises of the prophets. When he was brought to the Temple, even as a small baby, they were quick to proclaim him as the Messiah of Israel.

In this respect we would be wise to steer clear of the fanciful schemes of interpretation we hear today. Many of these schemes could possibly be advanced by the false prophet himself. We should simply read and weigh all scripture and allow the scriptures themselves to form our conclusions concerning the end day.

It is good to treat the weight of scripture much like we would treat a set of balances. When the weight of Bible opinion tilts in a direction, that should help us make up our minds in that direction. We must believe what the Bible says even if it should make no sense from our present perspective. This is far better than imposing a system of end-day interpretation upon the Bible.

With this in mind, there are some basic end-time events we should consider.

GATHERING OF THE NATIONS

The continued existence of Israel over the last three thousand years is a marvelous proof that there is a God. Likewise, the persistent and well-orchestrated attempts to destroy Israel over that same period are excellent proofs that there is a devil. The persecution of Israel has been far too consistent, too well planned, too diabolical, and too universal to have simply sprung from the mind of man.

For this reason, we would be very foolish to believe that the nations, who have been led to persecute Israel for these thousands of years, will not ultimately follow her home. They will in fact surround and invade this tiny nation.

Indeed the prophets of Israel are uniform in their opinion that the nations will come together and invade the land of Israel. We cannot be certain, but perhaps this will occur through the auspices of the UN, since the UN now has the authority to mobilize the nations as at no other time in history. All this seems even more likely since the UN has consistently been a tool in allowing Muslim hatred toward Israel.

There is another aspect in regard to the nations coming against Israel. The scripture assures us that God will

---

Psa 33:10 *The LORD foils the plans of the nations; he thwarts the purposes of the peoples.*

actually draw the nations to this end. He will do so in order to bring his fierce judgment upon them. So the coming together of the nations of earth will not be accidental, or even the work of the devil in the final analysis. It will be the hand of the Most High who works through history to achieve his ends. In Joel 3:2, the Lord says:

> *I will gather all nations and bring them down to the Valley of Jehoshaphat. There I will enter into judgment against them concerning my inheritance, my people Israel, for they scattered my people among the nations and divided up my land.*

In Zechariah 14:2, we read a similar promise, that God will gather all nations to battle against Jerusalem. Zechariah speaks of a difficult time in which most of the city of Jerusalem will be taken. There will be rape and pillage and some of the people will be taken into captivity. This invasion has all the hallmarks of Muslim *jihads* over the past centuries and even up to the present era. Perhaps those spoken of as beheaded in Revelation 20:4, are also victims of Muslim rage, since people are still regularly beheaded in Muslim lands.

Zechariah assures us that at this point in history, the Lord will arise to avenge his people and his city. At this juncture, Zechariah tells us that the Messiah will stand once more on the Mount of Olives at Jerusalem (Zech. 14:4). Have we Christians ever wondered why Jesus would return specifically to the Mount of Olives? Zechariah's context makes plain that he is coming to defend the people of Israel against a worldwide attack.

THE STORM BEFORE THE CALM

Thus we see clearly in scripture that before Israel can have peace, there must be a terrible war involving all the nations of earth drawn together against her. Although it is true that Ezekiel speaks of Israel living in peace before she is attacked (Ezek. 38:11, 14), we do not live in such a period of peace today, nor is one likely. His reference to this attack seems to be far off in the distant future, at the very end of time when Gog and Magog will invade the land (Ezek. 38:7 ff.). It is definitely pictured as being after the millennium, or the thousand year reign of peace, mentioned in Revelation 20:7-8:

> *When the thousand years are over, Satan will be released from his prison and will go out to deceive the nations in the four corners of the earth – Gog and Magog – to gather them for battle. In number they are like the sand on the seashore.*

This is not the attack that concerns us today, although many modern interpreters talk as if Gog and Magog were at our doorstep. It must be admitted, however, that prophecy is a strange thing, in that it may have partial fulfillments before the final one.

In the meantime, as this evil age plays out, we will probably see more strife, more lawlessness, more tension, more distress of nations, and more attacks with dreadful and widespread terrorism. For sure, we will see Jerusalem coming clearly into focus as the real problem in the Middle East, and in the world for that matter.

Again, in respect to Jerusalem, God warns the nations. He promises to make Jerusalem an extremely difficult problem, one that will injure nations who become involved with it:

> *On that day, when all the nations of the earth are gathered against her, I will make Jerusalem an immovable rock for all the nations. All who try to move it will injure themselves.* (Zec. 12:3).

We can imagine that all political means and maneuvers will be exhausted in the futile attempt of the nations to move the rock, that is to snatch Jerusalem from the Jews. However we are promised in scripture that the rock of Mount Zion will not be moved (Psa. 125:1). We can believe that the surrounding Muslim nations will be in a fuming rage over their inability to move the rock. These surrounding nations will be sent reeling (Zech. 12:2). So we can watch for Muslim nations to become more and more emotionally involved with the status of Jerusalem.

THE GREAT WAR AND ARMAGEDDON

The scripture makes it plain that the beast and the kings of the earth will be gathered together (Rev. 19:19). In other places, this beast is called the Antichrist and the lawless one. Paul speaks of him and his activity in these words:

> And then the lawless one will be revealed, whom the Lord Jesus will overthrow with the breath of his mouth and destroy by the splendor of his coming (2 Thess. 2:8).

God's word speaks of perplexity among the nations at this time in history (Lk. 21:25). As the spiritual fiber of nations is lost through lawlessness there will be no reason to stand up for Israel. After all, support of Israel makes no sense politically, or economically, but only spiritually.

As lawlessness increases, the lawless one or Antichrist will finally arise. As we have said, God will then draw all nations to Jerusalem to battle. In Zephaniah 3:8, we see that God is determined to gather all nations and kingdoms to pour out his wrath upon them. We need to notice that all nations of earth will be involved here.

Why is God so angry with the nations? We read in Isaiah 34:8: *"For the LORD has a day of vengeance, a year of retribution, to uphold Zion's cause."* The nations will suffer God's fierce judgment for mistreating the Jews these thousands of years. Surrounding Muslim nations will suffer God's fierce wrath for their virulent hatred of Israel over the many centuries. They have dared repeatedly to touch *"the apple of His eye"* (Zech. 2:8).

Nations will suffer God's fierce wrath for the horrors they have inflicted upon the land of Israel over the centuries. They will suffer God's wrath for their hypocrisy in regard to the Jews and in regard to Israel and Jerusalem. The Bible in Zechariah 1:14-15, tells us that God is very jealous for Zion, and sore displeased with the nations.

Psa 92:9 *For surely your enemies, O LORD, surely your enemies will perish; all evildoers will be scattered.*

This great battle with Antichrist and the nations of the earth against tiny Israel may be fought at several locales. It may be fought on the mountains of Israel, in Jerusalem and at Megiddo. We might ask, how can the battle be on Israel's mountains, at Jerusalem and at Megiddo (Armageddon) all at the same time. Can this be reconciled?

Remember that Israel, excluding her desert area, is a very small land. An international attack on the land would certainly affect every part of it. Thus we can understand how Jerusalem could be surrounded, how the battle could be waged on the mountains around Jerusalem, and how nations might attempt to cut the nation in two at the ancient mountain pass of Megiddo (Armageddon) on the edge of the beautiful Jezreel Valley (Rev. 16:16).

THE INFLUENCE OF BABYLON

We see that a great part of the deception leading up to this end-day battle will be brought about due to the influence of ancient Babylon (modern Iraq). Evil spirits from this area will go out from the devil to lure all nations into the battle of this great day of God (Rev. 16:12-14). In ancient times the angel who came to the prophet Daniel had to fight for days with a mighty spirit ruling in this area of the world (Dan. 10:13,20). It appears certain that spirits will rise up from this area once more to draw all nations to battle at Armageddon (Rev. 16:16). In recent years we have seen a great deal of activity from the area of Babylon and this should be cause for concern.

The area of ancient Babylon is a spiritually dangerous area. We need to keep our eyes on it and to be alert. Radical Muslim nations like Iraq and Iran who inhabit this general

View of the Jezreel Valley from Har-Megiddo (Armageddon).
(Courtesy Israel Information Office)

area could have a big role to play in events leading up to this last day battle. Already these nations are highly advanced in the production of nuclear and biological weaponry. These radical Muslims could also lead their nearby Muslim brethren to war with Israel. They could also bring with them multiplied millions of Muslims from the former USSR, Pakistan and even China into a frenzied *jihad* against Israel.

The attempt of the nations to solve the Israel problem once for all – that last "final solution" for this age will apparently create immense pressures in Israel. It will also likely create immense pressures among God's people far and wide. Prior to the end of this period there will be much suffering for God's Church. Before his defeat the Antichrist will gain a partial victory over God's people (Dan.7:21). We are told in Daniel 7:25, that he shall "wear out the saints" with his persecution.

GOD POURS OUT HIS SPIRIT ON ISRAEL

It seems clear that preceding this great battle, as incredible pressures are mounting in Israel, there will be a long promised spiritual awakening in Jerusalem.   Under the specter of what will surely look like total annihilation, Jews will turn to God *en masse*.   On this day, God will put his New Covenant fully into effect with Israel (Jer. 31:31).

In this time frame, when all nations gather against Jerusalem (Zech. 12:3), God will pour out a spirit of grace upon the people. They will begin to mourn for the one they have pierced (Zech. 12:10).   Zechariah says, *"On that day a fountain will be opened to the house of David and the inhabitants of Jerusalem, to cleanse them from sin and impurity"* (Zec. 13:1).   Israel will cry out: *"Blessed is he who comes in the name of the Lord"* (Mat. 23:39). The Messiah of Israel will be longed for, and at last welcomed with open arms.

As Christians, we believe fervently that this Messiah is none other than Jesus Christ or *Yeshua*.   There is growing evidence that many Jews the world over are also coming to this conclusion. The rise of Messianic synagogues and assemblies in virtually all places attest to this growing and vigorous movement.   Even in Israel during the last twenty years, the Messianic movement has blossomed into thousands of people with the establishment of scores of assemblies.

Messianic Jews, of course, are those who believe that Jesus *(Yeshua)* is the Messiah of Israel.   Messianic Jews often hold tenaciously to their Judaism while espousing *Yeshua* as Messiah.   Many often hold to various traditions and teachings of Judaism as well as to those of Christianity.   They appear at this point very much akin to the earliest believers in the church and thus have much to offer to the Church and to Israel.   Jesus said in Matthew 13:52 *"...Therefore every teacher of the law who has been instructed about the kingdom of heaven is like the owner of a house who brings out of his storeroom new treasures as well as old."*

Messianic Jews, though often misunderstood by their brothers in the flesh and by the Church, appear in an excellent position to bridge the gap between Gentile Christians and Jews in the last days.

THE MESSIAH COMES

When Israel turns to her Messiah and cries for his coming and assistance, he will appear. In 2 Thessalonians 1:7-10 we read:

> ...*This will happen when the Lord Jesus is revealed from heaven in blazing fire with his powerful angels. He will punish those who do not know God and do not obey the gospel of our Lord Jesus. They will be punished with everlasting destruction and shut out from the presence of the Lord and from the majesty of his power on the day he comes to be glorified in his holy people and to be marveled at among all those who have believed...*

The cleansing of Israel makes possible the Messiah's appearance to his nation and to the world. It also finally clears the way for God to defend his people and his nation wholeheartedly. Thus we see the Messiah fighting for Israel against all the nations of earth.

He is clearly the one on the white horse in Revelation 19:19. In Revelation 19:17-18, 21, we see that the birds of prey will be called together to gorge themselves upon the slain of the nations.

In the past we have often sought to interpret last-day events from the New Testament only. This can be misleading. We must try to reconcile New Testament passages with the numerous Old Testament ones which speak of the same events. This is not easy and at times appears almost impossible. We must remember that the writers of the New Testament had these Old Testament passages in mind as they wrote. In the Old Testament, the great emphasis is upon Israel and Jerusalem. That emphasis will also necessarily carry through in the New Testament.

We see God defending Israel as the prophets have long fore-told. God has kindled his fire in Zion and his furnace in Jerusalem. He will refine the nations there (Isa. 31:9). Zechariah says of that day:

> *On that day the LORD will shield those who live in Jerusalem, so that the feeblest among them will be like David, and the house of David will be like God, like the Angel of the LORD going before them. On that day I will set out to destroy all the nations that attack Jerusalem* (Zech. 12:8-9).

Isaiah speaks of that day in this wise:

> *... so the LORD Almighty will come down to do battle on Mount Zion and on its heights. Like birds hovering overhead, the LORD Almighty will shield Jerusalem; he will shield it and deliver it, he will 'pass over' it and will rescue it."* (Isa. 31:4-5).

And again,

> *"I will defend this city and save it, for my sake and for the sake of David my servant!"* (Isa 37:35).

God is jealous for Jerusalem with a great jealousy (Zech. 1:14). Through the ages, God has been hindered in his plans by the rebellion and unbelief of his own people. When his people turn to him he will defend them mightily. The enemies will vanish away as at many times in past history.

We may not have too many details of this particular battle in scripture. Perhaps the results of it are pictured in Revelation 14:20, where we see the blood flowing as high as the horses' bridles and for a distance of 180 miles. The Lamb will have an immediate and decisive victory over the beast and his armies.

There is one thing for sure, when this battle is over, every-one will know that the Lord is God. Everyone will also know the identity of his Messiah, whom we Christians know as Jesus or *Yeshua*. In Isaiah 25:9 Israel cries out, *"Surely this is*

our God; we trusted in him, and he saved us. This is the LORD,
we trusted in him; let us rejoice and be glad in his salvation."

When we realize that all the nations of earth will gather to
fight against Jerusalem, and when we realize that these
nations will also be fighting against the Messiah, it is cause
for concern. How many so-called "Christians" and "Christian
nations" will be caught up in this battle against Israel and
against the Messiah himself? We need to pray that we can
have clear understanding as the end-day events unfold, lest
we be found fighting against God.

THE MILLENNIAL ADVENT

When the international war against Israel is over and
Armageddon is history, we will see some tremendous changes
in our world. As we enter the millennial age, we will see God's
plan for Israel go into effect as it has not done since ancient
times.

The millennial age is passed over today by many Bible
teachers. This trend began with Origen and Eusebius long
ago. An age of peace for natural Israel simply did not fit into
their allegorical scheme of interpretation and therefore it was
shunned. Many modern teachers apparently feel the same
way today.

Although we do not fully understand the peculiarities of
the millennial age and it leaves us with many questions, we
had best believe in its existence until we understand it better.

We can perceive some things about this age. Shortly before
it begins, the beast and the false prophet will be thrown into
hell (Rev. 19:20). Never again will men be deceived by the
false prophet. Satan himself will then be bound for a
thousand years, and will not be able to tempt men and
nations (Rev. 20:2-3). The world will enter an age of peace
and tranquility unknown since the Garden of Eden. The
Messianic government will be fully established in the earth.
In Micah 4:3-4 we read of this period:

He will judge between many peoples and will settle
disputes for strong nations far and wide. They will

> *beat their swords into plowshares and their spears*
> *into pruning hooks. Nation will not take up sword*
> *against nation, nor will they train for war anymore.*
> *Every man will sit under his own vine and under his*
> *own fig tree, and no one will make them afraid, for*
> *the LORD Almighty has spoken.*

The law of God will begin to regulate all affairs on earth. The prophet pictures this law of God as going out from Jerusalem:

> *Many peoples will come and say, "Come, let us go up*
> *to the mountain of the LORD, to the house of the God*
> *of Jacob. He will teach us his ways, so that we may*
> *walk in his paths." The law will go out from Zion,*
> *the word of the LORD from Jerusalem* (Isa. 2:3).

In reflecting on the millennial age, we can perhaps see it as a prototype kingdom of God on earth, probably designed to display God's righteousness before angels, principalities, powers and men. It is also designed to display the glory of the Messianic government before all nations. The unleashing of the devil after this age may be for a similar purpose. It may be designed to illustrate to all his hopelessly evil intent, and the righteousness of God's final judgment against him.

The millennial age may also be looked upon as a transition period between heaven and earth. While it has heavenly qualities, it also still has earthly ones. For instance the Lord will reign with his victorious saints for this thousand years (Rev. 20:6). Yet, some people will apparently still grow old. They will also still build houses and plant vineyards (Isa. 65:20-21). In this period the wolf and the lamb will feed together (Isa. 65:25).

GOG AND MAGOG

The peaceful days of the millennium will be briefly shattered by the sudden and incredible invasion of Gog and Magog. It will probably be one of history's shortest wars. God will end this one and in doing so, he will end all wars forever.

This war will result because Satan, that ancient enemy, has again been loosed for a span. God's act of loosing Satan is incomprehensible to us at this time, but it certainly must be necessary in God's great plan. We must remember that this is a different age – one carefully hidden from our understanding. Because of the binding of Satan, many people in this age may never have experienced temptation. Once loosed, Satan will go about his work. He will do the same thing he has always done, that is to gather men and nations against Israel (Rev. 20:7-10). This time he will bring Gog and Magog.

These distant peoples in the north will bring their hordes to fight on the mountains of Israel. They will have some ready allies in Persia (Iran), Cush, Put and many other nations with them (Ezek. 38:5-6). This attack, however great, does not seem to be as international in scope as the first great battle or Armageddon.

At this last-day invasion, God's hot anger in battle will be aroused one last time (Ezek. 38:18). Strange things will begin to happen as in battles of ancient biblical times. There will be earthquakes and mountains will be overturned (vs. 19-20), plagues, torrents of rain, hailstones, and burning sulfur will fall (v. 22). These armies will be destroyed as fire comes down upon them from God. It will be such an incredible defeat from the hand of God, that Israel will spend the next seven months just burying the dead (39:12).

Soon after this last battle of the ages, the book of Revelation informs us that the world as we have known it will officially end. It will end with the great judgment of God over men and nations. The devil will be thrown into hell and his temptations forever ended. The New Jerusalem will come down and heaven and earth will be one (Rev. 20:11 - 21:27).

It is interesting though in Revelation 22:2, we see that even after Satan's final destruction, there is still a need for the healing of the nations. This pictures for us that the problem of evil is surely much deeper and more complex than we have understood it to be. It will apparently take a great amount of time for earth to be completely delivered, healed and cleansed.

BE WISE AND ALERT

Until the end of this age we must be alert to events and movements that affect Israel. We must remember that Israel will always be the center of divine activity on earth.

The events of the first massive and international war against Israel could be much closer than we imagine. The world is becoming more and more lawless. It is likely that lawlessness must precede the coming of the lawless one, for law is indeed a restraining force. We see this portrayed for us in graphic detail in 1 Timothy 4:1-8 and 2 Timothy 3:1-5. The situation Paul describes in both these passages is one of gross lawlessness before the end of the age. Paul also speaks in 2 Thessalonians 2:3 of the falling away before the end:

> *Don't let anyone deceive you in any way, for that day will not come until the rebellion occurs and the man of lawlessness is revealed, the man doomed to destruction.*

One of the biggest and most dangerous problems the Church faces as this time draws near is deception. Many in the Church may already be deceived to some degree by fanciful schemes of the last days painted for them by soothsayers. Many are already deceived in regards to Israel and are unable to assess the critical role this nation will play in the end-day events. It is certainly interesting that much of the "prophecy" we see today appears patently anti-Semitic in its goals. This is evident in the separation of Jew and Christian in the last days according to some of their schemes. The Jews receive dreadful punishment by the Antichrist while Christians fly away to glory. This whole scenario certainly goes against the grain of the two becoming one as scripture indicates.

The Antichrist, whoever he is, could already be on the scene today and waiting for the exact timing of his great war with Israel. We would certainly not say that Yasser Arafat is the Antichrist or the lawless one, but can say for certain that he is a lawless one. He is certainly well known for his atrocities against God's people in modern times, yet he is absolutely adored by the nations and the media. Although he is an outright bandit and warmongerer, he has nevertheless won the prestigious Nobel Peace Prize. What is especially troubling, is that some Christian leaders have been deceived about Arafat and are also now adoring this antichrist type.

Arafat has shown us one thing. He has made it clear how easily people and nations will be deceived and made into followers of the lawless one when he is revealed.

We need to keep our eye on the Lord and on Israel, while at the same time being alert to the evil currents in this world. We must not believe the slanders we hear on the radio and TV. We must search our Bible and see what God says about Israel. We must always guard against deception. Jesus warns us in Matthew 24:10-13:

> *At that time many will turn away from the faith and will betray and hate each other, and many false prophets will appear and deceive many people. Because of the increase of wickedness, the love of most will grow cold, but he who stands firm to the end will be saved.*

WHEN ALL THE SMOKE CLEARS

When all the smoke of last day battle clears, we will see some developments in our world which scripture describes for us. Many of these developments will have already begun in the millennial period and they will continue on through the end of the age and into eternity:

God to establish his throne in Jerusalem

We read in Jeremiah 3:17:

> *At that time they will call Jerusalem The Throne of the LORD, and all nations will gather in Jerusalem to honor the name of the LORD. No longer will they follow the stubbornness of their evil hearts.*

Ezekiel speaks of this time in these words:

...Son of man, this is the place of my throne and the place for the soles of my feet. This is where I will live among the Israelites forever. The house of Israel will never again defile my holy name – neither they nor their kings – by their prostitution and the lifeless idols of their kings at their high places (Ezek. 43:7).

Jerusalem is God's dwelling place and he has established it forever (Psa. 48:8). The city can rejoice for God is coming to live in her midst (Zech 2:10). Jerusalem, that has been long lied about, will become the city of truth. Jerusalem that has been claimed by numerous conquerors will at last be the Lord's Holy Mountain (Zech.8:3). God's King, the Messiah himself will rule from this city. God speaks of this plainly in Psalm 2:6-8.

In that day the earth will no more be divided over religion. Jerusalem will be the center of religion for the whole world. There will at last be unity among mankind:

The LORD will be king over the whole earth. On that day there will be one LORD, and his name the only name (Zec. 14:9).

God to deal with warring nations

The Bible makes it clear that God will deal sternly with the warring nations of this world. In Zion, God will break their bows, their arrows their swords and shields (Psa. 76:2-3). God's Messiah will deal with the nations as God instructs him:

You will rule them with an iron scepter; you will dash them to pieces like pottery." Therefore, you kings, be wise; be warned, you rulers of the earth. Serve the LORD with fear and rejoice with trembling. Kiss the Son, lest he be angry and you be destroyed in your way, for his wrath can flare up in a moment. Blessed are all who take refuge in him (Psa. 2:9-12).

In that day the Law will go forth from Jerusalem to the ends of the earth. People and nations will beat their swords into plowshares and their spears into pruning hooks. They will no longer learn war. Many peoples will come to Jerusalem begging to be taught about God's way (Isa. 2:2-4).

Those surrounding hateful nations will no longer be prickling briars to harm the people of Israel (Ezek. 28:34). Those who are left after the great battles will go up to Jerusalem to keep the feasts (Zech. 14:16). For the descendants of those who have fought Israel relentlessly over the centuries, God has this promise in Isaiah 60:14:

> *The sons of your oppressors will come bowing before you; all who despise you will bow down at your feet and will call you the City of the LORD, Zion of the Holy One of Israel.*

Blindness of nations to be healed

From Jerusalem God's saving light and revelation will shine forth. In Isaiah 25:7, the Lord says to us:

> *On this mountain he will destroy the shroud that enfolds all peoples, the sheet that covers all nations;*

We are assured in this verse, that the gross blindness that has afflicted the nations will be lifted on this mountain. Yes, there is something about Jerusalem that will ultimately destroy the darkness of the human mind throughout the whole world. As it is said in Psalm 50:2, *"From Zion, perfect in beauty, God shines forth."*

Glory of Jerusalem to be revealed

Jerusalem will be a place of glory for all the nations to behold. It will become a show place of God's grace. The Bible assures us that the Lord will shine from Mt. Zion:

> *The moon will be abashed, the sun ashamed; for the LORD Almighty will reign on Mount Zion and in Jerusalem, and before its elders, gloriously* (Isa. 24:23).

Or as Isaiah 4:5 states:

Then the LORD will create over all of Mount Zion and over those who assemble there a cloud of smoke by day and a glow of flaming fire by night; over all the glory will be a canopy.

We can be assured that Jerusalem will have the world's lowest light bill, because the Lord will be her everlasting light (Isa. 60:19-20), and her days of mourning will be ended forever. Beautiful Jerusalem will have a new name given to her by God. She will be a crown of glory, a royal diadem in God's hand. She will never again be called a forsaken city (Isa. 62:2-4).

In Ezekiel 48:35, the prophet tells us that Jerusalem will be known by this title: *"THE LORD IS THERE."*

All nations will come to worship

God will gather the nations once more, but this time not for battle. Jerusalem will become the world center of religious pilgrimage. Nations will flock there to worship the Lord (Isa. 2:3). The Psalmist assures us that all the earth will come (Psa. 22:27: 65:2). Isaiah tells us that the Gentiles will come to Israel's light (Isa. 60:3). Gentile kings will come bowing and bringing presents to the true God (Psa. 68:29). Even the strong nations of earth will come to Jerusalem to seek the Lord (Zech. 8:22). They will come confessing the worthlessness of their idols and their religions (Jer. 16:19).

Jerusalem will no longer be a place forsaken, but a place sought out by many (Isa. 62:4). People the world over will ask the way to Zion so that they can make a covenant with God (Jer. 50:5). Gentile people will cling to the skirts, or perhaps the *tallits* of Jews and ask the way to Zion because they know that God is with the Jews (Zec. 8:23).

The Bible tells us then that *"...the earth will be full of the knowledge of the LORD as the waters cover the sea"* (Isa. 11:9).

Jerusalem to be a place of holiness

In this day, we will see the redeemed of the Lord returning to Zion. However, it will be a different kind of return than we have experienced previously. It will be a return in holiness as seen in Isaiah 35:8-10. The unclean will no more travel to Jerusalem.

Those who walk uprightly and work righteousness will live in Jerusalem (Psa. 15:1). Those who have clean hands and pure hearts will worship there (Psa. 24:3). The prophet Zechariah tells us:

On that day HOLY TO THE LORD will be inscribed on the bells of the horses, and the cooking pots in the Lord's house will be like the sacred bowls in front of the altar. Every pot in Jerusalem and Judah will be holy to the LORD Almighty, and all who come to sacrifice will take some of the pots and cook in them. And on that day there will no longer be a Canaanite in the house of the LORD Almighty (Zech. 14:20-21).

Jerusalem, a place of beauty, joy, peace, blessing, and salvation

In that day Jerusalem will be a place of beauty (Psa. 50:2). The days of her shame will be ended.

Jerusalem will not only be beautiful, but the *"joy of the whole earth."* (Psa. 48:2). The earth certainly does not realize that fact at present, but it will in time. The ransomed will come to this hill and everlasting joy will be theirs. Their sorrow and sighing will be gone forever (Isa. 51:11). Not only will the people of God rejoice, but God will rejoice over his people. The sounds of crying will no longer be heard (Isa. 65:19).

The so-called city of peace will know real peace at last. It will not be a peace devised by men or nations, with their evil and selfish plans, but a peace devised by God in his goodness. In that day the streets of the city will be filled with boys and girls playing safely (Zech. 8:5).

The prophet Isaiah tells us about this day:

The wolf and the lamb will feed together, and the lion
will eat straw like the ox, but dust will be the ser-
pent's food. They will neither harm nor destroy on all
my holy mountain," says the LORD (Isa. 65:25).

God will make Zion a blessing as he has commanded long
ago (Psa. 133:3; Ezek. 34:26). Living waters will flow out of
Zion to refresh a parched and dreary world (Zech. 14:8). Her
people will call upon the name of the Lord and will be saved
and delivered. The gift of eternal life will be given in
Jerusalem (Psa. 133:3). God will hear their prayers.

AFTER ALL – THERE IS JERUSALEM

After all is said and done, Jerusalem will still be there as
Zechariah 12:6 says: *"...but Jerusalem will remain intact in*
her place." Jerusalem will be the connection between heaven
and earth. The New Jerusalem will come down from heaven
to cover the old city in brilliance and glory. The city will bathe
in that glory undisturbed forever.

Those saints who have loved her and fought for her
throughout her agonized history will at last be blessed in her.

We are assured of this in the sweet words of Isaiah 66:10-14:

Rejoice with Jerusalem and be glad for her, all you
who love her; rejoice greatly with her, all you who
mourn over her. For you will nurse and be satisfied
at her comforting breasts; you will drink deeply and
delight in her overflowing abundance. For this is
what the LORD says: "I will extend peace to her like
a river, and the wealth of nations like a flooding
stream; you will nurse and be carried on her arm
and dandled on her knees. As a mother comforts her
child, so will I comfort you; and you will be
comforted over Jerusalem." When you see this, your
heart will rejoice and you will flourish like grass; the
hand of the LORD will be made known to his
servants, but his fury will be shown to his foes.

HISTORICAL TIME LINE

BC (BCE)

3150-2200	Early Bronze Age Civilizations in Egypt & Mesopotamia
2200-1550	Middle Bronze Age
2000 c.	Abram called
1550-1200	Late Bronze Age
	Israel conquers Canaan
1125	Victory of Deborah and Barak
1100	Gideon defeats Midian
1050	Fall of Shilo
1020	Saul becomes king
1004	Saul killed on Mt. Gilboa
1004	David becomes king in Hebron
998	David conquers Jerusalem
965	Solomon's Temple begun
928	Israel and Judah divided
877	King Omri establishes Samaria
871	King Ahab marries Jezebel
722	Fall of Samaria
701	Jerusalem delivered from Assyrians
627	Jeremiah begins his work
605	First deportation to Babylon
597	Second deportation
586	Nebuchadnezzar destroys Jerusalem
538	Jews return from Babylon
535	Work on Temple begun and halted
520	Work renewed by Haggai and Zechariah
516	Second Temple finished
486-480	Events of Book of Esther
458	1st Decree of Artaxerxes
458	Ezra's arrival in Jerusalem
450-400	Approximate dates of Malachi
445	Walls of Jerusalem built by Nehemiah
444	Walls completed
336	Alexander the Great invades Asia

332	Legendary visit of Alexander to Jerusalem
167	Antiochus (Epiphanes) defiles Temple
164	Temple rededicated by Maccabees
63	Roman Emperor Pompey enters Jerusalem
37	Herod conquers Jerusalem with Roman backing
19	Herod begins Temple enlargement
4 (6?)	Birth of Jesus (*Yeshua*)

AD (CE)

30	Jesus crucified
66-73	Jewish revolt against Rome
70	Jerusalem destroyed
73	Fall of Masada
80-120	Sages of the Mishna
132-135	Second Jewish revolt
200c	Mishnah completed
312	Emperor Constantine accepts Christianity
325	Council of Nicea
570	Muhammed is born
614	Persians conquer Jerusalem
629?	Byzantine rule is restored
636	Muslims enter Israel
638	Jerusalem falls to Muslims
661	Omayyad rule from Damascus
691	Dome of the Rock built
701	El-Aksa Mosque completed
750-877	Abbasid rule from Baghdad
878	Tulun, Governor of Egypt conquers Palestine
904	Jerusalem returns to Abbasid rule
934	Egyptian Ikhshidi princes conquer Palestine
969	Fatamid Caliphs conquer Palestine
1010	Caliph al-Hakim destroys synagogues and churches in Jerusalem
1070-80	The Seljuks Turks pillage and rule
1099	Crusaders conquer Jerusalem
1187	Saladin captures Jerusalem
1215	Fourth Lateran Council

1219	Jerusalem's walls raised
1242	Burning of Talmud in Paris
1244	Khawarezmian Turks pillage Holy Land
1260	Mamluk rule in Holy Land
1291	End of Latin (Crusader) Kingdom
1299-1303	Mongol invasion
1480	Inquisition established in Spain
1492	Jews expelled from Spain
1496-97	Jews expelled from Portugal
1516	Ottoman rule begins in Palestine
1531	Inquisition established in Portugal
1541	Golden Gate is sealed to prevent entry of Messiah
1648-49	Chmielnicki massacres
1799	Napoleon proclaims the restoration of Holy Land to the Jews
1831	Mohammed Ali of Egypt gains control of Holy Land
1838	Edward Robinson begins archaeological work in Jerusalem
1840	English writers and statesmen begin to consider Jewish restoration
1854	Crimea War begins over disputes regarding Jerusalem
1864	Sir Charles Wilson begins archaeological work
1867	Captain Charles Warren begins excavations
1871-82	First agricultural settlements
1881-84	Pogroms sweep Russia
1882	First *Aliya* begins
1894	Dreyfus trial in Paris
1897	First Zionist Congress
1904	Second *Aliya* begins
1909	Tel Aviv founded
1917	Jerusalem surrenders to Allenby
1919-23	Third *Aliya*
1920	British pre Mandate begins
1920	Massive anti-Jewish riots in land
1922	Mandate confirmed by League of Nations

1923	Palestine Mandate begins operation
1923	British give away 75% of the Mandate
1924	Fourth *Aliya*
1925	Hebrew University opened
1929	Arabs riot in Jerusalem, Hebron and Safed
1933	Hitler becomes chancellor of Germany
1933-39	Fifth *Aliya*
1937	Peel Commission proposes partition of land
1938	Kristallnacht
1938	Wingate organizes special Jewish units to fight Arabs
1939	Outbreak of World War II
1940	Nazi Germany introduces gassing of Jews – six million perish
1947	UN General Assembly decides to partition Palestine
1948	Proclamation of independence and War of Independence
1948	Transjordan occupies Judea and Samaria
1953	Beginning of Arab Fedayeen attacks
1956	Sinai Campaign
1957	Israel evacuates Sinai
1967	Six Day War
1973	Yom Kippur War
1982	Lebanon War
1987	First Intifada Arab uprising begins
1989	Massive *aliya* from former USSR begins
1991	Gulf War and missile attacks on Israel
1991	Madrid Peace Conference
1993	Oslo Accords
1998	Israel's 50th anniversary (Jubilee)
2000	Israel withdraws from Lebanon (security zone)
2000	Second Intifada Arab uprising begins

BIBLIOGRAPHY

Allis, Oswald T. *Prophecy and the Church.* Philadelphia PA: The Presbyterian and Reformed Publishing Company, 1964.

Alon, Azzaria. *Flowers and Trees of the Holy Land, Israel.* Palpot Ltd.

Bahat, Dan, ed. *Twenty Centuries of Jewish Life in the Holy Land, The Forgotten Generations.* Jerusalem, Israel: The Israel Economist, 1976.

Bard, Mitchell G. and Joel Himelfarb. *Myths and Facts, A Concise Record of the Arab-Israeli Conflict.* Washington, D.C., Near East Report, 1992.

Barna, George. *The Barna Report,* Vol. 1, Issue 1. Ventura, CA: Regal Books, 1990.

Bennett, Ramon. *The Great Deception Philistine.* Jerusalem, Israel: Arm of Salvation, 1995.

Boyle, Isaac, trans. *The Ecclesiastical History of Eusebius Pamphilus.* Grand Rapids, MI: Baker Book House, 1976.

Brown, Michael L. *Our Hands are Stained With Blood, The Tragic Story of the "Church" and the Jewish People.* Shippenburg, PA: Destiny Image Publishers, 1992.

Budge, E.A. Wallis. *Babylonian Life and History.* New York: Dorset Press, 1992.

Buttrick, George Arthur, ed. *Interpreter's Bible,* Vol. 5. New York: Abingdon Press, 1956.

Charlesworth, James H. *Jesus Within Judaism, New Light from Exciting Archaeological Discoveries.* New York: Doubleday, 1988.

Colson, Charles with Ellen Santilli Vaughn. *The Body: Being A Light In The Darkness.* Dallas, TX: Word Publishing, 1992. Comptons Interactive Encyclopedia, CD-ROM, 1992, 1993, 1994.

Danby, Herbert. *The Mishna.* New York: Oxford University Press, 1933.

Davis, Leonard. *Myths and Facts, A Concise Record of the Arab-Israeli Conflict.* Washington, DC: Near East Report, 1984.

Denny, Frederick M. *Islam.* San Francisco, CA: Harper & Row, 1987.

DeLange, Nicholas. *Origen and the Jews, Studies in Jewish-Christian Relations in Third-Century Palestine.* London: Cambridge University Press, 1976.

Deloach, Charles F. *Seeds of Conflict.* Plainfield, NY: Logos International, 1974.

Dowley, Dr. Tim, ed. *A Lion Handbook: The History of Christianity.* Tring, Herts, England: Lion Publishing, 1977.

Duvernoy, Claude. *The Prince and the Prophet.* Jerusalem: Christian Action For Israel, Francis Naber Publishers, 1979.

Epstein, Lawrence J. *Zion's Call, Christian Contributions to the Origins and Development of Israel.* Lanham, MD: University Press of America, Inc., 1984.

Facts About Israel, Ministry of Foreign Affairs, Information Division. Jerusalem, 1985

Finkelstein, Louis, ed. *The Jews: Their History, Culture, and Religion,* Vol. III. Philadelphia: The Jewish Publication Society of America, 1949.

Flannery, Edward H. *The Anguish of the Jews, Twenty-Three Centuries of Antisemitism.* Mahwah, NY, 1985.

Flusser, David. *Jewish Sources in Early Christianity.* New York: Adama Books, 1987.

_____. *Jesus.* Jerusalem: The Magnes Press, The Hebrew University, 1997.

Gerrish, Jim, "Islam, Religion of the Other Brother," *Dispatch From Jerusalem,* 2nd qtr. 1990.

_____. "The Dhimmi People: Jews and Christians Under Islam," *Dispatch From Jerusalem,* 1st qtr. 1993.

_____. "The Sickness of Anti-Semitism," *Jerusalem Prayer Letter,* July 1991.

_____. "Blessing or Cursing," *Jerusalem Prayer Letter,* Nov. 1990.

Gilbert, Martin. *The Arab-Israeli Conflict, Its History in Maps.* London: Widenfeld and Nicholson, 1974.

_____. *Jewish History Atlas,* 4th Edition. Jerusalem: Steimatzky Ltd., 1992.

Goldbergh, M. Hirsh. *The Jewish Connection.* New York: Bantam Books, Inc., 1976.

Grazel, Solomon. *A History of the Jews.* Philadelphia: The Jewish Publication Society of America, 1947.

Gruber, Daniel. *The Church and the Jews: The Biblical Relationship.* Springfield, MO: General Council of the Assemblies of God, 1991.

Hanson, Calvin B. *A Gentile... With the Heart of a Jew. G. Douglas Young.* Nyack, NY: Parson Publishing, 1979.

Hatch, Edwin. *The Influence of Greek Ideas and Usages Upon the Christian Church.* Peabody, MS: Hendrickson Publishers, Inc., 1995.

Hull, William L. *The Fall and Rise of Israel.* Grand Rapids, MI: Zondervan Publishing Company, 1954.

Hulley, John. *Comets, Jews & Christians.* New York & Jerusalem: The Root and Branch Association, Ltd., 1996.

Hurnard, Hannah. *Watchmen on the Walls.* Nashville, TN: Broadman & Holman Publishers, 1997.

Israel Tour Guide SBS Publishing, 14 West Forest Ave., Englewood, NJ

Johnson, Paul. *A History of the Jews.* New York: Harper & Row, 1987.

Katz, Samuel. Battleground, *Fact and Fancy in Palestine.* New York: Bantam Books, 1973.

Kiernan, Thomas. *Yasir Arafat.* London: Sphere Books, Ltd., 1975.

Lambert, Lance. *The Uniqueness of Israel.* Eastbourne, England: Kingsway Publications Ltd., 1980.

Larsson, Goran. *"The Jews! Your Majesty."* San Diego, CA & Jerusalem, Israel: Jerusalem Center for Biblical Studies and Research, San Diego, CA, Jerusalem, Israel, 1989.

Lewis, Bernard. *The Middle East, 2000 Years of History From the Rise of Christianity to the Present Day.* London: Phoenix Books Ltd., a division of Orion Books, Ltd., London 1995.

Lewis, David Allen. *Israel and the USA, Restoring the Lost Pages of American History.* Springfield, MO: Menorah Press, 1993.

Lippman, Thomas. *Understanding Islam, An Introduction to the Muslim World.* Penguin Books USA Inc., revised edition 1982.

Loftus, John and Mark Aarons. *The Secret War Against the Jews, How Western Espionage Betrayed the Jewish People.* New York: St. Martin Press, 1994.

Lowdermilk, Walter Clay. *Palestine Land of Promise*. London: Victor Gollancz Ltd., 1944.

Morey, Robert. *The Islamic Invasion, Confronting the World's Fastest Growing Religion*. Eugene, OR: Harvest House Publishers, 1992.

Murray, Iain H. *The Puritan Hope.*, Edinburg, Scotland and Carlisle, Pennsylvania: The Banner of Truth Trust 1971.

Negev, Avraham. Ed. *The Archaeological Encyclopedia of the Holy Land, Third Edition*. New York: Prentice Hall Press, 1986.

Netanyahu, Benjamin. *A Place Among the Nations, Israel and the World*. New York: Bantam Books, 1993.

Patai, Raphael. *The Messiah Texts, Jewish Legends of Three Thousand Years*. Detroit, MI: Wayne State University Press, 1979.

Payne, Robert, *The History of Islam*. New York: Dorsett Press, 1959.

Peters, Joan. *From Time Immemorial, The Origins of the Arab-Jewish Conflict Over Palestine*. New York: Harper & Row, Publishers, 1984.

Pixner, Bargil. *With Jesus through Galilee According to the Fifth Gospel*. Rosh Pina, Israel: Corazin Publishing, 1992.

Plitman, Uzi, Clara Heyn, Avinoam Danin and Avishai Shmidah. *Plants in Israel*. (Hebrew edition), Israel: Masada, 1983.

Pragai, Michael J. *Faith and Fulfilment, Christians and the Return to the Promised Land*. London: Valentine, Mitchell and Company, Ltd., 1985.

Prince, Lydia. *Appointment in Jerusalem*. Grand Rapids, MI: Chosen Books, 1975.

Rausch, David A. *A Legacy of Hatred: Why Christians Must Not Forget the Holocaust*. Chicago: Moody Press, 1984.

Roth, Cecil. *The Spanish Inquisition*. New York: L W.W. Norton & Company, 1964.

_____. *A History of the Jews*. New York: Schocken Books, 1954.

Rousseau, John J., & Rami Arav. *Jesus and His World, An Archaeological and Cultural Dictionary*. Minneapolis, MN: Fortress Press, 1995.

St. John, Robert. *Tongue of the Prophets*. No. Hollywood, CA: Wilshire Book Company, 1952.

Schaff, Philip. *History of the Christian Church, Vol 2, Anti-Nicene Christianity.* Grand Rapids, MI: Wm. B. Eerdmans Publishing Company, 1910.

Siegel, Richard and Carl Rheins, ed. *The Jewish Almanac.* New York: Bantam Books, Inc., 1980.

Siegel, Richard, Michael Strassfield and Sharon Strassfield, ed. *The Jewish Catalog.* Philadelphia: The Jewish Publication Society of America, 1973.

Tal, Eliyahu, ed. *PLO.* Jerusalem: Department of Information, WZO, 1982.

_____. *Whose Jerusalem.* Jerusalem: International Forum for a United Jerusalem, 1994.

The Macmillan Dictionary of Quotations. Macmillan Pub. Co. NY, 1987.

Twain, Mark. *The Innocents Abroad.* New York: Hippocrene Books Inc., originally published by American Publishing Co., Hartford, CT, 1869.

Wagner, Clarence H., Jr. Lessons From The Olive Tree, *Israel Teaching Letter.* Bridges For Peace, July 1995.

_____. "Israel Accused by the Nations," *Dispatch From Jerusalem.* January/February 1997.

Walker, Williston. *A History of the Christian Church.* New York: Charles Scribner's Sons, 1959.

Walsh, Michael. Roots of Christianity. London: Grafton Books, 1986.

Westermann, Claus. *Isaiah 40-66.* London: SCM Press Ltd., 1969.

Whiston, William, trans. *The Works of Josephus, Complete and Unabridged.* Peabody, MA: Hendrickson Publishers, 1987.

Whybray, R.N. *The Second Isaiah.* Sheffield, England: JSOT Press, Department of Biblical Studies, The University of Sheffield, 1983.

Wigoder, Geoffrey, ed. *Encyclopedia Judaica* 16 vols. Jerusalem: Keter Publishing House, 1971-72.

_____. *Israel Pocket Library, Geography.* Jerusalem: Keter Publishing House Jerusalem Ltd., 1973.

_____. *Israel Pocket Library, History From 1880.* Jerusalem: Keter Publishing House Ltd., Jerusalem, 1973.

_____. *Israel Pocket Library, Holocaust.* Jerusalem: Keter Publishing House Jerusalem Ltd., 1974.

_____. *Israel Pocket Library, Immigration and Settlement.* Jerusalem: Keter Publishing House Ltd., 1973.

Wilson, Marvin R. *Our Father Abraham, Jewish Roots of the Christian Faith.* Grand Rapids, MI: William B. Eerdmans Publishing Company and Center for Judaic-Christian Studies, Dayton, OH, 1989.

The World Book Encyclopedia, Vol. 2, World Book-Childcraft International, Inc.,Chicago, Frankfurt, London, Paris, Rome, Syndey, Tokyo Toronto, 1978

Yamauchi, Edwin M. *Persia and the Bible.* Grand Rapids, MI: Baker Book House, 1990.

Yassen, Leonard C. *The Jesus Connection.* New York: The Crossroads Publishing Co., 1985.

Ye'or, Bat. *The Dhimmi, Jews and Christians Under Islam.* Cranbury, NJ: Associated University Presses, Cranbury, N.J., English edition, 1985.

Young, Brad H. *Jesus The Jewish Theologian.* Peabody, MS: Hendrickson Publishers, Inc., 1995.

FROM PERIODICALS

"The UN Impediment," Editorial, *The Jerusalem Post,* 6/9/91.

Quoted from "Birds of Passage Pass Over," *Dispatch From Jerusalem,* Sept.-Oct. 1995, p. 9.

Dispatch From Jerusalem, Jan./Feb. 1994.

The Jerusalem Post, 9/13/98.

Jim Gerrish, "Exploring Our Jewish Roots," *Jerusalem Prayer Letter.* Bridges For Peace, August, 1990.

Israel Teaching Letter. Bridges For Peace, January, 1995.

Reported in *Dispatch From Jerusalem,* July/Aug. 1994 Vol. 19, No. 4.

The Jerusalem Post, 12/6/96.

The Jerusalem Post, 11/24/98.

Dispatch From Jerusalem, 2nd qtr. 1991, Bridges For Peace.

Dispatch From Jerusalem, 1st qtr. 1992. p. 10, Bridges For Peace.

The Jerusalem Post, 3/24/95.

Jerusalem Prayer Letter. Bridges For Peace, Aug. 1992.

Jerusalem Prayer Letter. Bridges For Peace, Feb. 1993.

Jerusalem Prayer Letter. Bridges For Peace, Dec. 1996.

Leah Abramowitz, *The Jerusalem Post,* Sep 6, 1995, p. 7.

Reported in *The Jerusalem Post,* 10/27/95.

"No Golden Anniversary," Editorial, *The Jerusalem Post,* 6/28/95.

"The UN Impediment," Editorial, *The Jerusalem Post,* 6/9/91.

Shlomo Slonim, "Why Israel Had To Say No," *The Jerusalem Post,* 11/6/90.

Yosef Ben-Aharon, "Why Not Just Talk To Us," *The Jerusalem Post,* 6/17/91.

Eugene V. Rostow, "The Truth About 242," *The Jerusalem Post,* 11/5/90.

Aharon Levran, "UN Observers Recipe For Disaster," *The Jerusalem Post,* 5/29/90.

Reported in *Dispatch From Jerusalem,* Sep./Oct. 1996, p. 8.

Steve Rodan, "Norwegian Leaders Supported Termination of Jewish State," *The Jerusalem Post,* May 5, 1996.

Reported in *Jerusalem Prayer Letter,* March 1997.

Reported in *Dispatch From Jerusalem,* 1st qtr. 92.

Reported in *Dispatch From Jerusalem,* Mar./Apr. 1996, p. 8.

Reported in *Dispatch From Jerusalem,* Jan./Feb. 1996, p. 2.

Moshe Kohn, "What 'New Middle East,'?" *The Jerusalem Post,* 1/3/97.

Reported in *Dispatch From Jerusalem,* Mar./Apr. 1994, p. 2.

Reported in *Dispatch From Jerusalem,* Jul./Aug. 1995, p. 8.